Edward Jenks

An Outline of English Local Government

Edward Jenks

**An Outline of English Local Government**

ISBN/EAN: 9783337312145

Printed in Europe, USA, Canada, Australia, Japan

Cover: Foto ©Suzi / pixelio.de

More available books at **www.hansebooks.com**

# AN OUTLINE

OF

# ENGLISH LOCAL GOVERNMENT

BY

EDWARD JENKS, M.A,

FELLOW OF KING'S COLLEGE, CAMBRIDGE; BARRISTER-AT-LAW; PROFESSOR OF
LAW IN UNIVERSITY COLLEGE, LIVERPOOL.

Methuen & Co.
36 ESSEX STREET, LONDON, W.C.
1894

# PREFACE

THIS little book is the outcome of a course of lay lectures delivered in University College, Liverpool, a few months ago, under the joint auspices of the Corporation of the city and the Liverpool Board of Legal Studies. Its aim is at once modest and ambitious. On the one hand, it professes to give nothing more than the bare skeleton of the English system of Local Government. On the other, it does attempt to state, in Christian English and in concise form, the outlines of a subject usually relegated to the fathomless abysses of those professional treatises which Charles Lamb (had he been required to pronounce judgment upon them) would assuredly have classed as *biblia abiblia*—books which are no books. I say "usually," for it would ill become me to ignore the debt which the English citizen of ten years ago owed to the admirable little volume of Judge Chalmers, now, by reason of changes in the law, out of date, and, by reason of its own merits, out of print. And, though county and parish councils have brought upon us a shower of practical manuals, I think there is room for a book which shall aim at giving to the non-professional citizen some reasonably coherent ideas concerning that

## PREFACE

mass of governmental machinery which he is presumed himself to manage, and which, whether he manages it or not, does very substantially affect his daily life.

My great temptation has, of course, been to take the reader behind the existing machinery, and to show him the rudimentary forms from which it has developed, and which are of such intense interest to all genuine students of English institutions. But this temptation has, in most cases, been sternly resisted. Only in the matter of early municipal history have I ventured upon anything like historical speculation; and here it is a matter of great satisfaction to me that my tentative suggestions have, on the whole, been supported by the authority of Mrs J. R. Green's admirable work on *Town Life in the Fifteenth Century*, which has appeared since my book went to press. In the matter of authorities, I have refrained from loading my pages with that apparatus of statute and decision which is so painfully familiar to lawyers; but, in the hope that even a stray lawyer or two will not disdain to glance at my book, I have given such general references to Acts of Parliament and decisions, that any reader, who wishes to know more concerning any topic, will easily find guidance in his search. And, whether the exact authority is specified or not, I beg the reader to believe that I have never been guilty of the rashness of making a statement without verifying it at the fountain-head.

In giving illustrations from earlier history, I have purposely chosen examples from the readily accessible works of the

## PREFACE

Bishop of Oxford, and to him I tender (if he is not by this time weary of thanks) my best acknowledgments for this and much other help derived from his writings. To Mr William Rathbone, M.P., I am indebted for the valuable loan of current Parliamentary reports. To Professor Maitland, of Cambridge, I owe more than can be won from any books—the inspiring help and the wise counsel which it is the pleasure of great teachers to extend to those privileged to come into personal contact with them. In the hope that it is not altogether unworthy of his teaching, I send this little book into the world.

E. J.

UNIVERSITY COLLEGE, LIVERPOOL.
*July* 1894.

# CONTENTS

|  | PAGE |
|---|---|
| CHAPTER I. | |
| INTRODUCTORY . . . . . . . . . | 7 |
| CHAPTER II. | |
| THE PARISH . . . . . . . . . . | 19 |
| CHAPTER III. | |
| THE SCHOOL DISTRICT . . . . . . . | 54 |
| CHAPTER IV. | |
| THE HUNDRED . . . . . . . . . | 65 |
| CHAPTER V. | |
| THE PETTY SESSIONAL DIVISION . . . . . . | 68 |
| CHAPTER VI. | |
| THE COUNTY COURT DISTRICT . . . . . . | 76 |
| CHAPTER VII. | |
| THE POOR LAW UNION . . . . . . . | 87 |
| CHAPTER VIII. | |
| THE SANITARY DISTRICT . . . . . . . | 99 |

# AN OUTLINE
## OF
# ENGLISH LOCAL GOVERNMENT

## CHAPTER I.

### INTRODUCTORY

IN every civilised State of any importance the functions performed by the various governing bodies and individuals are capable of one great and useful classification. They are either **central**, that is, exercised by persons whose jurisdiction extends over the whole area ruled by the State, or **local**, that is, exercised by persons whose jurisdiction is limited to some special portion of the State's territory. It is not a question of the situation, nor of the method of appointment, but of the *jurisdiction* of the body or official in question. The magistrates for the county of Leicester might (conceivably) live and hold their meetings in London; but, so long as their jurisdiction was limited to the county of Leicester, they would be a local not a central authority.

Central and Local Government.

This distinction is always found in civilised States, but the relationship between the two classes of governing bodies varies greatly in different countries, and the nature of the difference is of vast importance. Too much attention has

Importance of distinction.

in the past been paid to the forms of government, and too little to its scope. Whether a State calls itself a Monarchy or a Republic may be of small consequence in practical affairs; few people would deny that there is more real liberty in monarchical England than in republican France. But the relationship between the central and the local institutions of a country must always be of great practical moment; for upon it will depend the real extent and value of the share open to the average citizen in the work of government.

To illustrate. Civilised States fall roughly into two great classes, in respect of the relationship between their organs of central and local government respectively. Centralised States. Either the local organs are a creation of and subordinate to the central government, or the central government is a Localised States. creature of and historically subordinate to the local organs. Of course very few States fall completely on either side of this line of demarcation, but it is generally easy to tell of a particular State to which side it inclines. The type of the former class is the new country, such as the western States of the American Union and the Australian colonies, or the country which has violently broken with its past, such as France. The type of the latter is the "old" country, such as England, Norway, and the Puritan Influence of colonies of America. Between the two classes of State distinction on political the differences of political character are immense; and character. they are partly the result, partly the cause, of the difference of organisation. It is the purpose of this book to deal with machinery, not with results; but it may be said, briefly, that, in countries where the organs of Local Government are under the thumb of the central authority, although the efficiency of administration may be great, the political character of the people will be unsatisfactory; it will be apathetic for long periods, and then dangerously excited, with the result of instability and corruption in the central government. On the other hand, a country of strong local government may be slow to move, and blundering in its methods, but it will be a country of steady progress, and of political stability and honesty.

England is pre-eminently the country of local government. True it is that the central legislature has in recent times created, perhaps somewhat arbitrarily, new units and organs of local government. But the great outlines of local government in England were drawn ages before central government (as we understand it) came into existence. Central *administration*, as distinct from mere political overlordship, dates from the twelfth century, and is the work of French officials. Local administration is at least five hundred years older, and was probably the unconscious adaptation of primeval Teutonic custom to the conditions of new settlement. Treasury, King's Bench, and Parliament come down to us from Angevin and Plantagenet kings. But Township and Hundred and Shire carry us back to the days before Alfred, to the dim beginnings of our story, and it was, in fact, only by an integration or union of these smaller groups that England became a nation at all. Consequently, central government, when it came, had to reckon with local government as an established fact, and has had to do so ever since. Even in its most drastic moods, even when creating sanitary districts and electoral divisions, Parliament has, in the great majority of cases, followed the old lines. Either it has given the old area a new name, or it has given a new area the old name. Nothing more clearly shows the profound conservatism of

*England the type of a localised State.*

INTRODUCTORY 11

will be of service to him all through his study. Then he can turn to examine the subject piece by piece. The rest of this chapter will be devoted to the statement of five points which will, it is hoped, serve as a kind of life-saving apparatus after the great plunge.

**Point I.**—Township, Hundred, and Shire, these names still give us the key to English local government. The township is now known by its ecclesiastical name of **parish**, and the shire by its Norman name of **county**; but the old identity is substantially preserved, and the institutions themselves are as much alive to-day as they were a thousand years ago. With the hundred the case is different. Its name survives,[1] but, as an institution, the thing is almost dead. Nevertheless its place has been taken by a number of organs which, though they differ widely from it in scope and function, still from the fact that they generally occupy an intermediate position between the parish and the county, it seems convenient to group as analogues of the hundred. {Township, Hundred, Shire.}

But there is one very important organ of local government which refuses to be classed under any one of our three heads. This is the **Borough**, an unit which formed no part of the original Teutonic scheme of settlement, but which very early began to insist on being treated as a distinct organ. The borough, in the course of its development, {The borough.}

[1] In the counties of York and Lincoln, the hundreds are generally replaced by the Danish *Wapontakes;* in Northumberland, Durham, Cumberland, and Westmoreland by *Wards*. In Kent the hundreds are grouped into *Lathes*, and in Sussex into *Rapes*, but these divisions have long ceased to have any political meaning. On the other hand, the *Ridings* of Yorkshire and the *Parts* of Lincolnshire are, as we shall see, almost equal to counties.

borrowed its organisation indiscriminately from township, hundred, and shire, but it never exactly resembled any one, and at last made good its claim to separate recognition by taking rank alongside the shire as a constituency, returning members of its own to serve in the national Parliament. Since that date its history has been entirely special, and it must be treated separately. For some reasons it would be convenient to take it first; for it has outrun its rivals in the race, it now presents the highest form of local government, and other institutions are rapidly tending to imitate its organisation. But the difficulties would be too great. The borough is really a development of simpler forms, and the simpler forms must be understood first. The borough, therefore, shall stand as our last item.

Here, then, is our scheme of the subject—

*Group A.*—The *parish* and its analogues.
 1. The Urban Parish.
 2. The Rural Parish.
 3. The School District.

*Group B.*—The *hundred* and its analogues.
 4. The Hundred.
 5. The Petty Sessional Division.
 6. The County Court District.
 7. The Poor Law Union.
 8. The Sanitary District.
 9. The Highway District.

*Group C.*—The *county* and its analogues.
 10. The Parliamentary County.
 11. The Military and Judicial County.
 12. The Administrative County.
 13. The Joint-Committee.

INTRODUCTORY 13

*Group D.*—The *borough.*
14. The Parliamentary Borough.
15. The Municipal Borough.

This is not quite chaos.

Point II.—We classify the functions of government into the four groups of *legislative, administrative, executive,* and *judicial.* Though not logically defensible, this classification is practically useful. By legislation we understand the business of laying down express general rules for the guidance of conduct. By administration we mean the discretionary use of powers conferred by legislation, more especially the important power of raising and expending money. By execution we understand the enforcement, through officials who are not allowed much discretion, of the provisions of imperative law; and by judicature we mean the business of deciding whether the general provisions of the law apply to particular cases.

Now, these functions are generally, though not always, in different hands, and the persons to whom the work of local government is entrusted can be classified accordingly. And, as a rule, we shall find that persons who do legislative or administrative work are **elected** to their positions by a suffrage more or less popular, and receive no remuneration for their labours, while the executive and judicial officials are usually **appointed** by some small body or by an individual without any popular vote, while they receive pecuniary return for their services. This rule is not, of course, universally true, but it tends to become more and more true as time goes on. The Justice of the Peace is an apparent exception to the rule, but in truth he is one of its most striking illustrations. When the Justice of the Peace

*Classification of functions of government.*

*Legislation and Administration.*

*Executive and Judicature.*

14 ENGLISH LOCAL GOVERNMENT

was created, he was first an executive and then a judicial person. He was fairly well paid, and, by strict law, he can still claim to receive wages. As most people know, he has long ceased to do so. But if we look back on his history we shall perhaps notice that the time at which he ceased to draw his wages corresponds pretty closely with the time at which administrative functions were first committed to him; while the fact that a person with so many administrative powers as the Justice of the Peace till recently possessed should never be subjected to the "baptism of popular election," has long been denounced as an anomaly in our system. It need hardly be pointed out that the separation between election and remuneration makes our politics vastly different from others which, at first sight, they appear to resemble—from American politics, for example.

The *legal* character of English local government.

Point III.—English local government is **legal,** not **prerogative.** No local body, no local official, can act without definite legal authority. If it be alleged that such a body or person has committed what in private hands would be a wrongful act, the accused must prove specific legal authority. No general plea of discretion or justification will suffice. And, moreover, the accused will be judged in precisely the same courts and in precisely the same way as a private individual. If the charge be proved, doubtless reprimand or dismissal will come from the official superior. But the ordinary legal punishment comes too. This rule, which extends even to the organs of the central government, and to which there are but very few exceptions, is justly regarded as one of the keynotes of the English political system. The acts of the sovereign body,

INTRODUCTORY 15

the Queen in Parliament, can, of course, never be legally questioned; the acts of every other official person or body can be questioned in the same way as those of a private citizen. A Secretary of State, with the highest motives, but without legal authority, breaks into X's house to search for papers. He can be sued in trespass precisely as if he were a coal-heaver. Contrast this with the state of things in some continental countries, where any dispute between an official and a private person is remitted to an administrative bureau.

Point IV.—English local government is **independent**, not **hierarchical**. Generally speaking, each organ is free to act as it pleases within its authority, provided that it acts *bona-fide*. Each organ is under the special care of some department of the central government, whose duty it is to see that local powers are not abused. Thus, if a Justice of the Peace should palpably misconduct himself, the Lord Chancellor will remove or otherwise censure him. If a Board of Guardians neglects its duty, it will be taken to task by the Local Government Board. But the control thus exercised is *critical* or *censorial* only, not absolute. So long as the local authority does its best, and keeps within the law, however mistaken that best may be, the central government has no right to interfere, even at the request of a person suffering from the consequences of the mistake. To this rule there are some exceptions, the most important being the power of the High Court of Justice to entertain appeals on questions of law from the County Court judges in all but very trifling cases. But the rule is generally followed, and it is of great political importance. Without it local government would be a mere shadow, a convenient

<small>Independent character of English local government.</small>

# ENGLISH LOCAL GOVERNMENT

... of the central authorities, not an
... expression of popular views.

Point V. Lastly, there is one warning which should
... the mind of the student of English
... As has been before hinted, English
... apt to call *different institutions by the*
... point of view of the layman this is
... but it leads with almost deadly certainty
... of the institutions thus similarly named.
... known as the "county" exists in at
... capacities ... as a military and judicial
... unit, and as an administrative unit.
... covered by the expression "the
... may be totally different for all these
... obvious that a student may fall into
... assumes the identity of all the three
... expression "the county of X——."
... example, that a man caught poaching
... necessarily be brought before the
... county ... that to which County
... Whereas the village
... the county of X——,
... the county of Z——.
... constantly on the alert
... a given institution is

... proceed to consider
... element

GROUP A

# THE PARISH AND ITS ANALOGUES

1. THE URBAN PARISH . . ⎫
2. THE RURAL PARISH . . ⎬ CHAPTER II.
3. THE SCHOOL DISTRICT . . CHAPTER III.

## CHAPTER II.

### THE PARISH

IT has been incidentally remarked that the Parish is the ecclesiastical name of the Township. This statement, though not strictly accurate, is true enough for general purposes. The original unit of settlement among the Saxons in England was the *tun* or *town*, which originally meant simply an enclosure surrounded by a wall or hedge; and the township (*tun-scipe*) was merely the area claimed by the town—its jurisdiction as we should say—just as the lordship is the jurisdiction of the lord, the stewardship of the steward, and so on. The township is the very kernel of English local government, and though most of its ancient history has perished, enough survives to show that it was once a real political organism, with a distinct life of its own. It consisted of a group of householders carrying on agriculture and industry on a co-operative plan, combining together also for purposes of defence and administration of justice. The discussions necessary to shape the policy of the township were carried on in the town moot, or meeting, which was at first probably held under some sacred tree or on a sacred hill. There the assembled townsmen appointed the officials of the township—the *reeve* or headman, the *pindar* or common-keeper, the *beadle* or messenger—by the mouths of their elders declared *folk-*

*The original "town."*

*Town meeting.*

*right*, *i.e.*, customary law, and, with uplifted hands, "held men to witness," *i.e.*, recorded certain transactions in their memories. Somewhat later, the township began to send its reeve and four best men to represent it in the courts of the hundred and shire, and the best men were probably chosen in the town meeting. As to the origin of this primitive organisation there is keen dispute, and we do not deal here with controversial matters. But the existence of the organisation seems indisputable. How did this secular organisation acquire the ecclesiastical name of "parish"?

Introduction of Christianity.

The ancient Britons had been more or less Christianised before the arrival of the Saxons, but the latter were pure heathens, and utterly refused to acknowledge the British Church, probably because it was organised on a tribal model unsuited to their ideas. So they remained heathens until, at the close of the sixth century, the Benedictine monk Augustine converted Ethelbert of Kent, and founded the see of Canterbury. From that time Christianity spread rapidly throughout the Saxon kingdoms, until, before the lapse of a century from the landing of Augustine, the Church was ripe for organisation on a national basis.

The parish and the township.

The work of organisation was undertaken by Archbishop Theodore, and he, in making his plans, wisely adopted existing institutions. The bishops' sees were already identical with the heptarchic kingdoms; though he subdivided them, he carefully followed the lines of the older sub-kingdoms, out of which the heptarchic kingdoms had been formed. Later on, the archdeaconries and rural deaneries corresponded with the shires and the hundreds. But in Theodore's time there was little between the bishop of the kingdom and the priest whose sphere was a township, and accordingly priest and township were by him treated as natural correlatives. And as the early missionaries were often at least as much Greek as Latin (Theodore himself came from Tarsus in Macedonia), it is no wonder that the township comes to be called, by ecclesiastics, a *parish*, that is, the dwelling-place (*paroikia*) of a priest. True that township and parish were in many cases not identical, even in ancient times. But the very differences show how the two were connected ɪ.ɪ men's minds. In the south of England, where population was comparatively thick, two parishes were often formed out of one township; in the north, where population was scanty, and the supply of priests apt to run short, two or three townships go to a parish, always, however, preserving their ancient identity. Very rarely did the boundaries of parishes and townships cut one another until recent changes took place. A township not included in a parish came to be stigmatised as "extra-parochial," and was looked upon with suspicion.

Then came the decay of the township as an institution. This process, due to the corresponding rise of the feudal institution known as the *manor*, need not be more than hinted at here, for the manor has practically ceased to be an organ of local government. Suffice it to say, that the rise of that peculiar social system which we call *feudalism*, the main idea of which is the dependence of the vassal upon the lord above him, as opposed to the *inter-dependence* of the members of a co-operative group like the township, gradually drew away the life from the town meeting on the hill to the Leet held in the hall of the lord who had his manor or dwelling in the township,[1] until at last

*Decay of the township.*
*The manor.*

*The Court Leet.*

[1] A section (the 7th) of the Vestries Act of 1818 raises a strong presumption that in extra-parochial places the town meeting survived the introduction of the vestry system elsewhere.

the town-meeting, as a separate institution, almost disappeared.

The Vestry.
Meanwhile the parish priest had not been idle. At first, no doubt, he took a prominent part in the town meeting, and ecclesiastical and secular matters were there discussed indiscriminately. But the Church did not in the least intend to allow her affairs to be settled in the manorial courts. On the contrary, in the later Middle Ages she began to draw more and more away from secular affairs, and to aim at isolated and purely ecclesiastical organisation. This is the meaning of the great struggle between the kings and the archbishops, which lasted from Henry I. to Edward I., and which was revived once more at the time of the Reformation. One result of this great movement was, that the parish priest now gathered his flock round him in the *vestry* or robing-room of the church, when he wished them to dispose of ecclesiastical business. Here he was secure from secular interference, for the lord and his steward would not venture to dispute his pre-eminence in the sacred building. Thus was the town meeting deserted on both sides.

But, in course of time, the feudal system itself decayed, and local government in England became almost extinct. The parish vestry came to be recognised as a regular meeting, and gradually acquired a few of the powers which had fallen away from the decaying courts of the manor. But its position with regard to them was purely traditional; the vestry had no legal powers. It was not till the general break up of medieval conditions brought to the front a question of appalling magnitude, requiring wholesale treatment, that the parish vestry secured a recognised position in secular matters.

This great question was the relief of the poor. The Great Plague of the fourteenth century, which had practically abolished serfdom, had given the bondsman a liberty which frequently meant liberty to starve. It was no lord's interest to feed the man whom he could not keep to labour. The Wars of the Roses had thrown a crowd of destitute and idle soldiers on the country. The dissolution of the monasteries added its quota to the general distress, by drying up a source of relief which had mitigated, while at the same time it had probably encouraged, the social evil. Something had to be done, and the Elizabethan statesmen, following up the tentative suggestions of their predecessors, laid down a comprehensive scheme which made each *parish* responsible for the maintenance of its own poor and for the administration of its own poor-relief. There was no other local machinery available, and it seemed natural to associate the work of relief, which had always been looked upon as one of the primary duties of the Church, with an ecclesiastical institution. So the parish became the Poor-Law unit; the Poor-Law official, the *overseer*, was to be chosen from, if not by, the parish vestry; and the funds necessary to enable him to carry out his duties were to be raised by a rate levied upon the householders of the parish. [Poor-relief]

From the date of the great Poor Law of 1601 we mark the revival of the parish or township as an organ of local government. One matter after another—highways, bridges, drainage, police, education—became parochial, until all, and more than all, the old powers of the town meeting were won back. But the township still retained its adopted name of parish, and its meeting was still the parish vestry. [The first great Poor Law.]

During the present century a counter-movement has set in, which tends again to draw a sharp line between the [Separation of parish and township.]

secular and ecclesiastical aspects of the township or parish. The great increase of population which followed upon the industrial revolution of the eighteenth century created a necessity for the sub-division of areas. New churches were required to meet the spiritual needs of the population, and new ecclesiastical districts (ultimately called parishes) were carved out of the old parishes for them. On the other hand, the poor-law unit needed sub-division, and new "poor-law parishes" (as they came to be called) were created. But the two movements did not follow the same lines. Whereas the new poor-law parishes virtually revived the older *townships*, of which two or three had gone to form the old northern parishes, the new ecclesiastical districts proceeded upon other methods. Again, the removal of the *administration* of the poor-relief from the parish to the poor-law *Union*, by the Act of 1834, tended to weaken the connection between civil and secular business in the parish. The introduction of "select vestries" and, still more, of the recent "parish councils," has done, and will do yet more to emphasise the distinction. So that, in a work on local government, we are entitled to leave the ecclesiastical parish altogether out of account, and proceed to consider what is still called the *parish* or the *civil parish*, but what is really the old township in disguise. And the connection of this unit with the subject of poor-relief may be best judged from the fact that, by virtue of a recent Act of Parliament, the official definition of a civil parish is now "a place for which a separate poor-rate is or can be made, or for which a separate overseer is or can be appointed." Recent legislation compels us to consider civil parishes as divided into two classes—urban and rural.

Gilbert's Act.

Civil and ecclesiastical parishes.

The parish a Poor-Law unit.

A.—*The Urban Parish.*

It follows by clear implication from the terms of the Local Government Act, 1894 (generally, but most misleadingly, called The "Parish Councils" Act) that an urban parish may now be defined as a parish situated within an urban sanitary district, or, as it will be called when the Act of 1894 comes into operation, an "urban district." Of the nature of urban sanitary districts we shall have to speak later on. Here it is sufficient to say that an urban sanitary district may be at present either a municipal borough, an Improvement Act area, or an area governed by a Local Board of Health.[1] Any parish falling within the limits of one of these areas is an urban parish; any parish not so situated will be a rural parish. Where a parish at present, or at the passing of the Act of 1894, lies or lay partly in a rural and partly in an urban sanitary district, it will have to be divided in accordance with the sanitary line, and will henceforth constitute two distinct parishes, rural and urban respectively.

The chief organ of an urban parish is still the

(1) **Vestry**, which, in the absence of special custom or provision, is not a representative, but a primary, body, consisting of all occupiers (male and female) of property within the parish who are rated or are liable to be rated to the relief of the poor in respect thereof, whether the rates are actually paid by them or by their landlords. But no one may vote in respect of property the rates of which are in arrear. Questions in the vestry are usually settled by a show of hands, *Members.*

*Voting.*

---

[1] After November next (1894) these will all be included in the term "urban district." *See* post, p. 104.

but if a poll is demanded the members vote on a cumulative scale, the first vote representing property rated at £50 a year or less, with an additional vote for each £25 till a maximum of six is reached, beyond which no voter can go.[1]

Select vestries.

Sometimes, however, a vestry is representative, or, as it is called, *select*. In a few cases a select vestry has sprung spontaneously into existence, and it is then said to be a select vestry *by custom*, and its constitution is governed by the traditions of the parish. But, more often, the select vestry has been deliberately created under the provisions of an Act of the year 1831, known as "Hobhouse's Act." This statute, which is only permissive, not compulsory, enables the ratepayers of any parish in a city or town, or of any other parish having not less than 800 ratepaying householders, to adopt its provisions for erecting a select vestry. If the ratepayers so resolve, there will be formed a select vestry of *resident* householders, each occupying property within the parish in respect of which he is rated upon a rental of at least £10. The number of the vestrymen will vary from 12 to 120, according to the number of rated householders in the parish,—12 for every thousand householders, —and the vestrymen will hold office for three years from the date of election, retiring annually by thirds. The electors are, of course, the ratepayers of the parish,—they vote by ballot if a poll

Hob-
house's
Act.

---

[1] The chief authority on the subject of vestries is still the Vestry Act of 1818, but it does not apply to parishes in London or Southwark. Speaking generally, the London parishes are regulated by the Metropolis Local Management Act of 1855 and its amendments.

is demanded,—and it is presumed that they, and likewise the vestrymen in meeting assembled, have each but one vote. In addition to the elected vestrymen, the minister and churchwardens of each ecclesiastical parish within the civil parish are *ex-officio* members of the select vestry.

The duties necessarily falling upon the vestry of an urban parish may be very light, being practically confined to an Easter meeting, at which officials are elected and parish affairs discussed. But by adopting the provisions of various statutes (hereafter to be noted), the parish may give its vestry a good deal of work. It will, however, be better to treat of these matters separately. The vestry can be summoned to meet at any time by the churchwardens. The minister has generally a prescriptive right to take the chair; if he is not present, the meeting elects a chairman.

(2) The **churchwardens** of the parish, two in number,[1] are its recognised officials. It is said that the minister and parishioners "ought to agree" in appointing them; but this is a counsel of perfection, and in practice the minister appoints one and the vestry elects the other. The churchwarden may be any ratepaying householder of the parish, man or woman, churchman or dissenter. His term of office is one year, but he may be re-appointed or re-elected. It is said that no parishioner can refuse to serve once without possessing one of the special qualifications[2] which

<small>Compulsory office.</small>

---

[1] It has been held that by custom a parish may have only one churchwarden. *Rex* v. *Inhabitants of Hinckley*, 12 East. 365.

[2] These are, principally, peerage, membership of Parliament, service of public office, and actual engagement in professional practice. No clergyman is bound to serve as a churchwarden.

exempt from the duty of serving parish offices. But a Catholic or a Dissenter may, if he pleases, execute the office by deputy, and it is difficult to see how a churchwardenship could be forced on a really unwilling parishioner.

The chief secular duties of a churchwarden (with his ecclesiastical duties we have here nothing to do) are to see that the nave of the church and the churchyard are kept in repair, to act as *ex-officio* overseer of the poor (as to whom see hereafter), to manage, in conjunction with the overseers, the secular property of the parish (such property being, in the absence of special provision, legally vested in the churchwardens and overseers), to return annual accounts of parochial expenditure to the Local Government Board, and to summon vestry meetings when necessary. By a very recent statute[1] the duty of burying bodies cast up by the sea or tidal rivers has been expressly re-imposed upon him. Under the various Church Building Acts he has financial duties of a more or less secular character to perform in connection with pew-rents and stipends.

Next in importance to the churchwardens come the

(3) **Overseers of the poor**, virtually the creation of the great Poor Law scheme of 1601, and for two centuries the actual administrators of that scheme. By the statute of 1601 they were to raise in each parish a stock "for setting the poor on work," to put poor children out as apprentices, and to furnish relief for the impotent poor. But their administrative functions were virtually abolished by the new Poor Law scheme

[1] 49 Vic., c. 20.

of 1834, and the overseers themselves reduced to the position of executive officials obeying the behests of Guardians and other authorities.[1] Their duties are, however, still, especially in populous parishes, onerous and difficult, and require the exercise of some discretion.

It was the scheme of 1601 that the churchwardens of every parish should be *ex-officio* overseers of the poor for the same, and that, in addition, there should be not less than two, nor more than four "substantial householders" specially appointed as overseers each year by the Justices of the Peace, "dwelling in or near the same Parish or division where the same Parish doth lie." A statute of the year 1662 provided that "by reason of the largeness of the Parishes" within the eight northern counties of England, overseers should in those counties be appointed for each township and village, and in many places overseers are still appointed by virtue of this statute. But the Poor Law Amendment Act of 1844 prohibited any extension of the practice to parishes which had not by that time adopted it, and the definition of the civil parish now adopted by statute (*see* page 24) will include the township which has its own overseers. *Ex-officio and nominated overseers.*

The policy of the statute of 1601 was, as we have seen, to place the appointment of overseers in the hands of the Justices of the Peace, and, so far as regards *urban* parishes, this policy is still in force. True that by the provisions of the Local Government *Overseers in urban parishes appointed by Justices.*

---

[1] A somewhat different view has been expressed by a high legal authority, but as a general statement the text may pass.

Act, 1894, it will be open to the Local Government Board, upon the application of any urban sanitary authority, to confer upon the authority, or any other representative body within its district, the power of appointing overseers, as well as any other of the powers which (as we shall see) are conferred upon rural parish councils; but it is quite impossible at present to say how far those provisions will be exercised. It is stated that, in practice, retiring overseers submit to the Justices lists of "substantial householders" to guide them in their selection.[1] And the vestry of a parish may, if it pleases, elect and pay out of the poor-rate, persons known as "assistant overseers," who virtually do the work of the overseer's office. But even these officials must be formally appointed by the Justices. By a modern statute,[2] where two fit overseers cannot be found in a parish, the Justices may be content with one, and may even, if need be, appoint a stranger to the parish. But in this case, contrary to the usual rule, the overseer cannot be compelled to serve, and he may be paid a salary out of the poor-rate of the parish which he serves, if he does consent to act.

Assistant overseers.

Like that of churchwarden, the office of the ordinary overseer is annual, compulsory (in the absence of special exemption), open to all ratepaying householders, male and female, and no remuneration attaches to it.[3] An appeal against the appointment

[1] Steer: *Parish Law*, 5th ed., p. 377.
[2] 29 and 30 Vic., c. 119.
[3] In addition to the usual exemptions, there are certain express *disqualifications* for service of the post of overseer. The chief are—

## THE PARISH

by the Justices lies at the suit of any party aggrieved to Quarter Sessions, and, indirectly, to the High Court of Justice. But, of course, in the latter case, only on a real question of law.

Now that the power of the overseer to give relief has been restricted to cases of urgent and temporary necessity, his most important function is the making and levying of *rates*. The position of the overseers is briefly this, that they must be prepared to supply money to any extent (within certain limits) upon the demand of authorities entitled to call upon them for funds. For this purpose they must know the exact rateable value not only of their parish as a whole, but of each occupant of land within it; and they must be able to distribute the liability to payment with absolute impartiality. The process by which they satisfy these requirements is briefly as follows.

In order to obtain a record of the rateable value of their parishes, the overseers draw up and sign a list of all the "rateable hereditaments," which, after being open to public inspection for fourteen days at the offices of the Guardians of the Poor for the Union (as to whom *see* post, p. 89), is transmitted to the special committee of the Guardians, known as the **Union Assessment Committee**. This committee, chosen annually by the Guardians for the express purpose of investigating and supervising the valuations made by the overseers, and consisting of not less than six and not more than twelve members, proceeds to hear any

*Rates.*

*Valuation List.*

---

holding a paid office in the poor-law administration of the parish or union in question, dealing with the authorities as a contractor, conviction for certain crimes.

objections which may be made to the *amount* of the rating of any particular hereditament, or to the *omission* of any hereditament. When the committee is satisfied of the correctness of the valuation it approves it, and, until altered or superseded by a new list, it remains in the custody of the overseers as the **valuation list**, or official basis of rating of the parish. A copy is also sent to the clerk of the peace for the county, for the county rate may also be framed upon it. But the overseers may, with the consent of their vestry, appeal to Quarter Sessions on the ground of over-valuation of their own parish, or under-valuation of any other parish in the same Union; and any occupier or owner may indirectly appeal to Petty, and ultimately to Quarter Sessions, from a decision of the committee upon an objection duly taken by him. If, in any of these cases, the appeal goes against the committee, the list must be altered accordingly.[1]

The list being now complete, it becomes the duty of the overseers to estimate the demands likely to be made upon them by various authorities.[2] They then proceed to "make" a rate—*i.e.*, to calculate how much in the pound, having regard to the total rateable value of the parish, will be sufficient to produce the sum required—and to assess it upon the different hereditaments in accordance with the valuation list. In theory, the overseers, although they must specify in

---

[1] For the general law on the subject of the valuation list the authority is the Union Assessment Committee Act, 1862 (25 and 26 Vic. c. 103).

[2] The chief of these are—the School Board, the parish council, the Guardians of the Poor, the rural district council, the county council, and (if the parish is situated in a borough) the borough council. The urban council collects its own rates.

# THE PARISH

each rate the period which it is estimated to cover, are not bound by this statement, but may make another at any time. In practice they make a rate once a year, supplementing deficiencies by increasing the next year's rate, and conversely. Before the rate can be enforced, it must be "allowed" by two or more Justices dwelling in or near the parish, but this duty of the Justices is ministerial only, and the allowance cannot be refused. The "making" of the rate is held to date from its allowance by the Justices, and immediately thereupon the overseers must give public notice of it. It is then open to any party aggrieved by the rate to appeal to Quarter Sessions against the rate as a whole or any item of it; but, subject to appeals, the overseers may proceed to collect the rate from the parties liable, and may "levy" or enforce their demands, if necessary, by summons, distress, and, ultimately, imprisonment. If the Justices perceive that a parish is not able to maintain its own poor, they may assess any other parishes in the same hundred, or, if the hundred is too poor, in the same county, *or any of the inhabitants of such parishes*, to a "rate in aid" of the poor parish. [*Allowance.*] [*Levy.*]

The person primarily responsible for the rates assessed upon a particular hereditament is the occupier thereof, *i.e.*, the person entitled to exclusive possession. But it is only an occupation which may possibly be pecuniarily beneficial in its character[1] that [*Occupant primarily liable for rates.*]

---

[1] The decisions as to what is pecuniary benefit appear to be somewhat conflicting. A place used exclusively for divine worship or for the "charitable" education of the poor is not rateable. On the other hand, a Board School and a hospital are.

renders the occupier liable to rates, although, of course, it is immaterial whether or not the occupier actually makes a profit out of it. And in the case of small tenements let for periods less than a year, the vestry may resolve, either with or without his consent, to hold the owner responsible, in which case the latter will be entitled to deduct a commission for collection if he pays his rates promptly. As a matter of fact, the owner in such cases simply raises the rent of the occupier, technically known as the "compound householder," to an extent sufficient to cover the estimated amount of the rates. But recent legislation has provided that the fact of payment (or non-payment) of rates by an owner shall not damage an occupier's claim to the parliamentary or municipal franchise. The importance of the machinery wielded by the overseers of the poor may be estimated from the fact that the total amount of poor rates raised during the year ending Lady Day, 1892, was between fifteen and sixteen millions sterling, of which upwards of thirteen millions were actually collected by the overseers. Of this sum, however, only about one-half was needed for the purposes of strict poor relief.[1]

**Other duties of overseer.**

It is only possible to touch very briefly upon the other duties of an overseer, though they are numerous and important. In conjunction with the churchwardens he manages the parish property, and with the trustees of allotments he carries out the provisions of the older Allotment Acts, in so far as they have not been superseded by later legislation.[2] He

[1] Local Government Board Report, 1892-3. Appendix F, p. 293.
[2] *e.g.*, The Allotments Act, 1887, which transfers much of the management of allotments to sanitary authorities and elective managers.

must keep a register of persons in receipt of poor relief from his parish, and an annual register, duly published, of persons residing in his parish who are liable to serve on juries. He has many important duties with respect to the preparation and publication of lists of voters for parliamentary, municipal, county, and poor-law elections; in fact, he may be said to be the official Registrar of the parish for electoral purposes. In all the duties of the overseer's office the acts of a majority are the acts of the whole body.

The remaining officials of the urban parish may be very briefly disposed of. They are—

(4) **The Clerk**, who, in the absence of special custom, is appointed by the minister and licensed by the bishop. He was originally, and has again very nearly become, a purely ecclesiastical official; but during the seventeenth and eighteenth centuries various civil duties, such as the custody of plans for various public works, were imposed upon him, and a few of these duties still survive. The office is one of great historical interest. The parish clerks of London appear to have formed themselves into a gild or brotherhood of St Nicholas as early as the thirteenth century, and in Stow's day they were an important and influential body, whose musical talents were greatly in demand at weddings and funerals. With the introduction of printing they immediately acquired an important position, being licensed by the Archbishop of Canterbury to keep a printing press in their common hall for the purpose of publishing the weekly record of births and deaths, or "Bills of Mortality," in the metropolis. Bills of Mortality.

This was perhaps the first scientific attempt to record vital statistics made in England. It is said that a parish clerk holds his office for life, unless expressly appointed for a shorter period. But he may be deprived by the archdeacon for misconduct. He is paid by fees, the amount of which is regulated by statute.

(5) **The Beadle**, an ancient official of humble character, is found attached to courts of justice and deliberative assemblies far back in Teutonic history. In origin he was probably the messenger or summoner of the township moot, and the subordinate of the leet constable. With the introduction of the Poor Law scheme in the sixteenth century, he acquired new importance as the agent of the overseers, but, with the transference of poor-law administration to the guardians, and the virtual abolition of the parochial system of police, he has dwindled to a shadow of his former self. Where appointed, he is appointed by the vestry, which also fixes the amount of his remuneration. His principal occupation is the service of notices and summons. The apotheosis of beadleship is to be found in the person of the *Esquire Bedell* of the older English Universities, who, on any Sunday, may be seen carrying the silver mace before the Vice-Chancellor as he proceeds in state to the University church.

### B.—*The Rural Parish.*

56 & 57
Vic., c. 73.
*Ante*, p. 25.

The Local Government Act, 1894, has created a new legal entity, the "rural parish." In defining an urban parish we described it as any parish which is contained within the area of an urban sanitary district, that is to say,

THE PARISH 37

of a municipal borough, an Improvement Act district, or a district governed by a Local Board of Health.[1] Negatively, then, we may define a rural parish as a parish which does not fall within any one of these areas; positively, as a parish which falls within a rural sanitary district. A rural sanitary district may be defined as a Poor Law Union or any part of a Poor Law Union which does not fall within an urban sanitary district as above defined; or, putting it in another way, an area in which the Guardians of the Poor have hitherto acted as the sanitary authority.[2]

From the day on which the first elections under the new Act take place, rural parishes will fall into two classes—(*a*) those which have parish meetings *and* parish councils; (*b*) those which have only parish meetings. The lines of separation are thus drawn by the Act. Every rural parish which, by the census of 1891, had a population of 300, falls into class (*a*); every other rural parish falls *primâ facie* into class (*b*). But the parish meeting of a parish having a population between 99 and 299 may compel its county council to provide for the establishment in it of a parish council, and even in the case of a parish with a still smaller population, the county council may (if it thinks fit), with the consent of the parish meeting, make a similar provision.[3] Small parishes[4] may

Two classes of rural parishes.

[1] After November next (1894) we shall have to say, "of a municipal borough, or of any other urban district." *See* post, p. 104.

[2] For practical purposes the easiest way to discover whether a parish is urban or rural is to look at one of Mr Edward Stanford's excellent sixpenny Diagrams of Sanitary Districts, which show also the civil parishes. If the parish is not coloured it is rural. Care must, however, be taken to ascertain that no changes have been made since the Diagram was drawn.

[3] The Act of 1894 expressly makes the census of 1891 the criterion; but it is presumed that this will be altered on the taking of the next census.

The section does not in express terms confine the power of grouping

also, but with their own consent, be grouped by the same authority under a common parish council; but *every* rural parish will have its distinct parish meeting.

*The Parish Meeting.* Obviously, then, we must first examine the **parish meeting**. This, like the old parish vestry, is a primary, not an elective body; but the terms of membership are very different from those of the vestry.

*Parochial electors.* All persons, male and female, who are on the roll of electors entitled to vote at elections to Parliament or County Council, will be entitled to attend and vote at the parish meeting of that parish in respect of which their names appear on the parliamentary or county registers. Practically speaking, this means that all male owners of landed property worth £5 a year,[1] all male occupiers of land to the value of £10 a year, all *resident* occupiers (male or female) of any house within the parish rated to the relief of the poor, and whose rates have been duly paid, and all male lodgers occupying rooms within the parish to the value of £10 a year unfurnished, will be entitled to attend and vote at a parish meeting, provided only that they are not under age, are not aliens, and have not, within the twelve months preceding the time at which the electoral registers are made up, been in receipt of poor relief. Such persons are now to be technically known as "parochial electors." At a parish meeting each elector is to have one vote and no more, and the same rule holds

to the parishes with a population of less than 300, but the context implies that this limit must be adopted.

[1] "Property" in this sense includes freeholds, copyholds, and leaseholds, which were originally created for sixty years or upwards. Leaseholds originally for less than sixty but for twenty years or more do not qualify unless they are of the value of £50 a year. Certain freeholds of the value of 40s. a year also qualify.

even upon a poll, which, if demanded, is to be taken by ballot.

Every parish meeting is to assemble at least once a year, within seven days of Lady Day, and its proceedings are not to commence before 6 p.m. Other meetings may at any time be summoned by the chairman or any two members of the parish *council*, or by the chairman or any six members of the parish meeting. Usually the chairman of the parish council will be chairman of the parish meeting, but if for any reason he is not present, the meeting will elect a chairman.  {Annual assembly.}  {Chairman.}

Where the parish has a council as well as a meeting, the chief business of the latter body will be the annual election of parish councillors. But it will have other important functions. In the first place, it will act as a critical body, having the right to "discuss parish affairs and pass resolutions thereon." Inasmuch as every parish councillor will know that he must (if he wishes to keep his seat) face the parish meeting in less than a year's time, he will probably pay a good deal of attention to the discussions and resolutions of a parish meeting. But, in the second place, there are certain acts which a parish council will be able to do with, but not without, the consent of its parish meeting; and upon such matters the parish meeting will, of course, have a decisive voice. Such are, for example, the adoption of certain reforms which could formerly only be introduced with the goodwill of a majority of the inhabitants, but which are now left to the decision of the parish meeting,[1] and the incurring of expenditure which will amount in any one year to a sum exceeding a threepenny rate or involve a loan. And, finally, even where a parish council exists, the parish meeting will still exercise certain independent powers.  {Functions of parish meeting:— (a) Where there is a parish council.}  {Consent to acts of parish council.}

[1] These contingencies are discussed at the end of this chapter.

It will be able to forbid the parish council to consent to the stopping up of a public right of way, or to declare that a highway is unnecessary. It will also succeed to the position of those "owners and ratepayers" who, at the present time, are entitled to put in motion the machinery of the Elementary Education Acts and similar statutes. The annual accounts of the parochial charities will have to be laid before it, and its consent will be necessary to enable the parish council to oppose or support any scheme for the readjustment of a parochial charity.

But it is in parishes where there is no parish council that the powers of the parish meeting will be greatest. Then it will, virtually, exercise all the rights which, as we shall immediately see, are usually exercised by the parish council in respect of appointing committees, performing the secular business formerly belonging to the vestry, appointing overseers, assistant overseers, and charity trustees, and in regulating the stopping up of footpaths; but the property belonging to the parish will legally vest in the chairman and overseers, not in the meeting, and the power of the meeting to incur expenses will be limited to a sixpenny rate. It will be possible, however, for the county council to confer on the parish meeting, at its own request, any other of the powers of a parish council. Where there is no parish council the parish meeting must assemble at least twice a year.

The **parish council** will be a representative body which will exist in every rural parish having a population at the last census of 300 souls, and in those other rural parishes or groups of parishes where it may be created by order of the county council. It will consist of not less than five nor more than fifteen councillors, as may be from

# THE PARISH

time to time determined by the county council. Its members will be annually elected by the parish meeting at its Lady Day assembly, and will come into office on the 15th April. Any "elector" of the parish (*i.e.*, any one entitled to take part in the parish meeting), male or female, who has resided for the preceding twelve months within the parish, or within three miles thereof, will be eligible for election, unless— Qualification of members.

(i.) Since a year preceding the election he or she has been in receipt of poor relief, Disqualifications.

(ii.) Since five years preceding the election he or she has been sentenced to imprisonment with hard labour or any greater punishment, or has been made bankrupt or compounded with creditors,

(iii.) He or she holds paid office under the parish council, or is pecuniarily interested in any contract made with the council. (But in the latter case the disqualification may be removed by the county council if it thinks that such removal will be beneficial to the parish.)

Where the full number of places in the council is not filled up at the annual election, such of the retiring councillors as are willing to serve, in order of their votes at the last election, will be entitled to retain their seats until the list is full. Casual vacancies occurring at other times will be filled up, from duly qualified persons, by the council itself. All retiring councillors are re-eligible at any election.

In the absence of special provision, each councillor will be elected by the electors of the whole parish, but, upon the application of one-tenth of the electors, the county council may divide a parish into electoral *wards*, each of Parish wards.

which will, for electoral purposes, constitute a separate parish, with a separate parish meeting, and the councillors will be distributed amongst the different wards. It is a little difficult to tell whether it is intended that the wards shall be considered separate parishes for any other than electoral purposes,[1] but it seems clear that no division into wards can be made in a parish which has not a council.[2] Apparently there is no rule that a councillor must reside in the ward which he actually represents.

The parish council must hold an annual meeting within seven days after coming into office, and at such annual meeting elect a chairman (or chairwoman), who, in the absence of contingencies, will continue in office until his or her successor is appointed. It is his duty to summon the annual meeting and any other (not less than three in the year) which he may think desirable, and he may be compelled by two councillors to summon a meeting at any time. The council may also, if it pleases, elect a vice-chairman, to act in the chairman's absence. A council meeting cannot proceed to business unless at least one-third of its members (with a minimum of three) are present.

Immediately upon coming into office every parish council will become a legal corporation, with power to hold property and to signify its acts by document executed by the chairman and any two members present at a meeting. It will immediately take over certain powers and interests formerly belonging to other bodies or persons, and it will also acquire certain new powers. Perhaps we should distinguish between these two classes of acquisitions.

---

[1] *See* Local Government Act, 1894, § 49 (*b*).   [2] *Ib.*, § 18.

## THE PARISH

**Class A.** The powers and interests now to be *transferred* to the parish council may be summarised thus— *A. Transferred powers.*

(i.) The powers, duties, and liabilities of the **vestry** of the parish (except those which relate to the affairs of the church or to *ecclesiastical* charities, or are specially given to other bodies by the Act). *Of vestry.*

(ii.) The powers, duties, and liabilities of the **churchwardens** (other than those belonging to them *as overseers*), with similar exceptions. *Of churchwardens.*

(iii.) The powers, duties, and liabilities of the **overseers** with respect to— *Of overseers.*

(a) Appeals or objections in respect of valuation list or rates. *Ante*, pp. 32, 33.

($\beta$) The provision of parish books, parochial offices,[1] fire engines, and fire escapes.

($\gamma$) The holding and management of parish or public property (other than ecclesiastical).

(iv.) The powers of the **guardians** in respect of the sale, exchange, or letting of parish property. [This virtually means that the council will be able to dispose of any parish property, subject, in the case of dealing with *land* (other than the letting of allotments), to the approval of the central government, and, in the case of the *sale* or *exchange* of land, to the consent of the parish meeting.] *Of guardians. See post,* p. 89.

(v.) The power of making complaints and representations conferred upon **inhabitant householders** by the Housing of the Working Classes Act, 1890,[2] and on *Of inhabitant householders.*

[1] By the existing law overseers may provide parochial offices at the expense of the poor rate in any parish containing a population of 4000, but only with the consent of the vestry and the Local Government Board. (The Parochial Offices Act, 1861.)

[2] By the provisions of this Act, four or more inhabitant householders

## 44 ENGLISH LOCAL GOVERNMENT

Of parliamentary electors.
**parliamentary electors** by the Allotments Acts, 1887 and 1890[1] (but without prejudice to the rights of such persons).

Of allotment wardens.
(vi.) The powers and duties of any **allotment wardens, committee,** or **managers** constituted by *any* Act of Parliament.

Of Justices.
(vii.) The power and duty, formerly exercised by the **Justices of the Peace,** of appointing *overseers of the poor,* and of appointing and dismissing assistant overseers.[2] Churchwardens are no longer to be *ex-officio* overseers, but overseers appointed by the parish council may take their places. The election of overseers is to be the first business of the annual meeting of the parish council, after the appointment of a chairman. The parish property (other than ecclesiastical) now vested in the overseers, or in the churchwardens and overseers, will pass to the parish council.[3]

B. New powers.
**Class B.** The new powers and interests conferred upon the parish council are chiefly these—

Public buildings and land.
(i.) To provide and manage buildings and land for parish

may compel a medical inspection and report upon buildings alleged to be unhealthy or obstructive.

[1] These Acts enable six registered electors or ratepayers to represent to the sanitary authority (or, failing that, to the county council) the necessity for the provision of land for allotment purposes.

[2] If the parish council does not signify the names of its appointed overseers to the guardians of the poor within three weeks from the 15th April in any year, the guardians may proceed to fill up the vacancy. The same rule holds in the case of casual vacancies.

[3] This rule will apply even where the overseers are jointly entitled with other persons as trustees of a parochial charity; and the council may appoint a similar number of its members as trustees in the place of the overseers.

# THE PARISH

purposes (including recreation), and even (with the consent of the county council) to acquire land compulsorily for such purposes.

(ii.) To utilise any water within the parish for purposes of water supply, to take measures for preventing the spread of danger from stagnant water or refuse, and to acquire by *agreement* any right of way for the benefit of the parish. (But these proceedings must respect private rights, and there is no compulsory power of acquisition.) — Water supply.

(iii.) To hire land for the purposes of allotments. (If necessary, the parish council may obtain leave from the county council to hire land compulsorily for a period of from fourteen to thirty-five years.) — Allotments.

(iv.) To borrow, with the approval of the county council and the Local Government Board, such sums as may be necessary for executing permanent works. — Loans.

(v.) To undertake the repair and maintenance of any public footpaths within the parish, other than footpaths at the side of public roads. — Footpaths.

(vi.) To accept any property offered for the benefit of the inhabitants of the parish, and especially to receive a transfer of their property from any trustees who may hold it "for any public purpose connected with a rural parish, except for an ecclesiastical charity." — Public benefactions.

(vii.) To oppose or support any scheme relating to any charity (other than an ecclesiastical charity) which affects the parish. But to take any such step the consent of the parish meeting is required. — Charities.

(viii.) To complain to the county council in the event of a rural sanitary authority neglecting its duties in the matter of water supply or the repair of highways. — Sanitary authorities.

46     ENGLISH LOCAL GOVERNMENT

Clerk of the parish council.

To enable it to perform these functions the parish council may appoint one of its number to act as clerk, without remuneration; or may impose the duty upon an assistant overseer, or (if there be none) upon a collector of rates or other fit person at a remuneration. The clerk of the council will succeed to the powers of the parish clerk in the matter of the custody of documents ordered by statute or standing order of Parliament to be deposited; but he will not have the right to the custody of the registers of births, deaths, and marriages, and other ecclesiastical or quasi-ecclesiastical documents. When there is no clerk, the chairman of the council acts as custodian of documents. The parish council may also appoint one of its own members to act as treasurer without remuneration.

Parish rates.

See *post*, p. 47.

The parish council will have no direct power to make a rate, but it will be able to incur expenses to an amount not exceeding in any one year a threepenny rate without any special sanction. For expenses involving a larger amount it will require the consent of the parish meeting, but the extreme limit (exclusive of expenses under "adoptive" Acts) will be a sixpenny rate, which will have to include all annual charges payable in respect of loans. If a loan is contemplated, the consent not only of the parish meeting, but of the county council, will be necessary before the expense is incurred. The expenses of the parish meeting will be included in the expenses of the parish council. The amount chargeable on the rates will, presumably, be raised by precept or demand to the overseers, who will include the amount in their poor rate for the year.

This is, in outline, the scheme of the Local Government Act of 1894. Its object is, evidently, to add largely to the powers of self-government possessed by the rural parish,

THE PARISH 47

and to concentrate those powers in the hands of a single authority. How the scheme will work it is impossible to say; but it may be permissible to point out the vast extent of its application. There are about 14,900 civil parishes and separate parts of parishes in England and Wales. Of these 13,235 were at the last census comprised in rural sanitary districts.[1] Allowing for the creation of new urban districts since 1891, some 13,000 rural parishes will still remain. In about 6880 of these parish councils will have to be elected in November next, and then the whole machinery of the Act will be put to the test. It is a great experiment in politics.[2]

Before concluding the subject of the parish, it is necessary to point out that, while the sphere of the normal parish is confined to the subjects previously described or alluded to, a parish *may* be an unit for the regulation or administration of other matters. Whether any particular parish is in fact such an unit, is a matter for enquiry in each case. These matters are, briefly, police, highways, and certain sanitary and educational matters provided for by "adoptive" Acts of Parliament, *i.e.*, Acts which may or may not be adopted by any parish according to its discretion. Of these in order.

Optional functions of the parish.

1. **Police.**—The control of the police arrangements of the country appears originally to have been in the hands of the Hundred, whose *leet jury*, or petty criminal

[1] These figures are taken from a Return furnished to the House of Commons in July 1893 by the Local Government Board.

[2] One of the most curious results of the scheme appears to be that (unless other legislation intervenes), when a rural parish becomes so populous that it has to be made urban, its self-governing powers will largely cease to exist and its council be extinguished.

48 ENGLISH LOCAL GOVERNMENT

court, appointed, or enforced the appointment, of the *constable* and *watch* in each parish or township. This is the primitive institution pourtrayed with such humour in *Much Ado about Nothing*, and it is clear that, even in Shakespeare's day, Dogberry and his companions were regarded as somewhat antiquated machinery. Recent legislation has practically transferred police matters to the authorities of the county and the large borough, but there are still two cases in which, under the provisions of the Parish Constables Act, 1872, a parish may have its own police.

Parish constables.
(*a*) When a county or borough force is certified as insufficient by the authorities, the Justices at Petty Sessions must appoint **parish constables,** who are (in the absence of proper excuse) compellable to serve, and are paid small fees out of the poor rate.

Paid constables.
(β) When the vestry or (in the case of a rural parish) the parish meeting or council, of a parish *which is not within a borough*,[1] resolves that the appointment of a **paid constable** or **constables** is desirable, it may require the Justices to appoint accordingly, and the salaries of such constables will be payable out of the poor rate.

Main roads.
2. **Highways.**—The history of roads in England is somewhat obscure, but the old rule appears to have been that the great high roads of the country were kept in

Footpaths.
repair by the adjoining landowners, while the paths and lanes which practically existed for the convenience of the internal business of the township were looked after by the township or parish officials. Still, a good

[1] It must be carefully remembered that there are many urban parishes which are not comprised within the limits of boroughs.

## THE PARISH

deal of uncertainty prevailed on the subject, and in the sixteenth century it became necessary to deal with the matter comprehensively. After some little hesitation the Tudor policy declared itself in favour of making the parish primarily liable for the repair of all highways, but without releasing any private liabilities which could be proved to exist. This policy was in the main continued until the end of the eighteenth century, though an immense number of local exceptions existed by virtue of various Acts of Parliament. The enclosures of the eighteenth and early nineteenth centuries brought a good many new roads into existence ; but, with the great increase of population, it became necessary to make further provision for the creation and maintenance of new roads. The plan adopted was that of local "Turnpike Trusts," so called from the nature of the gate or barrier erected to prevent the passage of those who had not paid the tolls or dues by which the managers of the trust recouped themselves their expenses. This plan, after being extensively used for upwards of a century, has been thoroughly discredited, and has virtually ceased to operate. The turnpike and other roads in urban parishes have been taken over by the urban sanitary authority, which is now, under the Public Health Act, 1875, the sole authority in the matter; and by the provisions of the Local Government Act of 1894 a similar transfer in favour of the rural sanitary authority is contemplated in the case of the roads in a rural parish.[1] But, inasmuch as this consummation may be

*Highway parishes.*

*Turnpikes.*

*Sanitary authorities.*

[1] The roads in the six southern counties of Wales are under a special scheme of management.

postponed by a county council in any part of their county for a period of three years (or even longer, with the consent of the Local Government Board), it becomes necessary to state very briefly what is at present the machinery employed when a parish maintains its own highways.

This machinery is regulated by the Parish Highways Act of 1835, a fragment only of which is directly repealed by the new Local Government Act. The vestry (now the parish council), at its annual meeting, elects a *surveyor* from among the resident owners or occupiers of property in the parish, and he is bound to serve, unless he has one of the usual grounds of exemption from parochial office. But he may appoint a deputy, or the council, if it pleases, may appoint instead of him a paid professional surveyor.

The surveyor of a parish is bound to maintain the highways in an efficient manner, and, to enable him to do so, he is authorised (with the allowance of two Justices) to make and levy a rate on the basis of the poor rate. But the amount of the rate must not, without the consent of four-fifths of the "inhabitants" of the parish assembled at a meeting specially summoned for that purpose, exceed two-and-sixpence in the pound in any one year. The accounts of the surveyor are open to inspection, and must be produced annually before a district auditor of the Local Government Board.

Moreover, in parishes having a population by the last census of upwards of five thousand, the vestry (or council) may (or might) appoint, instead of a surveyor, a Board of from five to twenty resident ratepaying householders, and such Board and its officials would then have the powers of the surveyor in a smaller parish.

The number of parishes which, at the close of the financial year 1890-91, maintained their own highways was 6501;[1] it will be seen, therefore, that the change contemplated by the Act of 1894 is of a very sweeping character. Highway Parishes in 1891.

We now come to those improvements which it is in the power of the parish to adopt or not, as it pleases.

3. **Burials.**—Where the accommodation provided by the churchyard or other cemetery is insufficient for the wants of a parish, the vestry (in rural parishes, the parish *meeting*) has the power of adopting the "Burial Acts, 1852 to 1885," *i.e.*, a series of statutes aimed at providing increased burial accommodation. If the vestry or council so decides, it appoints a Burial Board of from three to nine ratepayers, one-third of whom retire annually, and this Board provides and maintains a new burial ground under the regulations of the Acts. To pay its expenses, the Board is entitled to demand from the overseers such sums as the vestry or council shall approve, and these sums are raised out of the poor rate in the usual way. The accounts of the Burial Board are audited by two auditors, annually elected by the vestry or council. But an order of the Privy Council may constitute any *urban* sanitary authority the sole burial authority within its district; and, by consent of all parties, without an order, Burial Board.

[1] Report of Local Government Board, 1892-3. Appendix P., p. 409.

a Burial Board may transfer all its property and functions to the *urban* sanitary authority in whose district its parish is situate. At the close of the financial year 1890-1, there were, in England and Wales, 997 Burial Boards, with an expenditure during the previous twelve months of nearly £430,000. Where, on the coming into office of a parish council, the area of a Burial Board is identical with that of a rural parish, the Burial Board will merge in the council;[1] but where parishes have joined (as they may do under the Burial Acts) to provide a cemetery, it is presumed that the provisions above described will still apply.

4. **Public Libraries, Museums, &c.**—Any ten electors in a rural parish may call upon the overseers to ascertain by a poll of the parochial electors whether or not they are favourable to the adoption of the " Public Libraries Act, 1892," and the electors may decide the question by a simple majority. If they decide in favour of adoption, they *may* also (if asked) specify the limit of expense to be incurred in carrying out the scheme; but in any case the expenditure will be limited to a penny rate. Upon the adoption of the Act the parish council will proceed to carry out the scheme by the provision of free libraries and museums, schools for science, art galleries, and schools for art, to the extent of its means. At present, in rural parishes, the scheme is worked by a special body of triennially appointed " Commissioners "; but on the coming into existence of the parish council, the latter body will become the executive authority. When there is no

*Library Commissioners.*

[1] Doubtless the council will appoint a Burial Committee, which will be, virtually, the old Burial Board.

THE PARISH 53

council, presumably the parish meeting will act. In urban areas it is the sanitary district and not the parish which constitutes the Library district.

Other "adoptive" Acts there are, by which a parish can provide itself with conveniences and luxuries, but it is impossible to go into details. The chief examples are lighting and watching (Act of 1833), baths and wash-houses (Acts of "1846 to 1882"), and walks and recreation grounds (Public Improvements Act, 1860). For particulars the reader is referred to the statutes themselves. Enough has been said to show how such parochial machinery works. Broadly speaking, in the urban parish the vestry is the authority for adopting the Acts, whilst they are executed by a special body appointed by the vestry; in the rural disricts, the parish meeting adopts, the parish council executes.

<small>Lighting and watching.
Baths and wash-houses.
Walks and recreation grounds.</small>

# CHAPTER III

### THE SCHOOL DISTRICT

For the history of State education (unless, indeed, we consider the Established Church as part of the State) we need not go far back. Although the State had from time to time made donations toward educational purposes, and likewise from time to time had held enquiries into the working of existing institutions, it did not directly under-
*Elementary Education Act.* take the work of education till the year 1870. Before that time the bulk of such education as there was had been provided by the Established Church and other religious bodies, by eleemosynary foundations, and by private enterprise. But in 1870 was set on foot a great national scheme which, in its main features, is in force at the present day.

*State attitude towards elementary education.* The attitude of the State towards elementary education (for at present the State undertakes little more than elementary or primary education) is double. On the one hand it does not force into its own schools those children who are being properly educated elsewhere. On the other, it insists that every child not thus provided for shall attend its own schools. Thus it is at once artist and critic.

*School Districts.* The whole of England and Wales is mapped out by the Education Department into **School Districts.** Every municipal borough (except Oxford) is a School District; every parish or part of a parish not lying within the limit of a borough is primarily a School District;[1] the metropolis of London is a School District; and the area of the Oxford Local Board is a School District. It might, perhaps, be urged that the borough and not the parish is the true analogue of the School District; but although the borough is the area frequently adopted as the School District, the parish is the model. The machinery employed is mainly parochial in character. It must be carefully noted that a division between boroughs and parishes outside boroughs by no means coincides with our former division between urban and rural parishes; for there are many urban parishes which are not within boroughs.

But School Districts are divisible, quite independently of their geographical position, into two great classes, which correspond with the double functions of the State in respect of elementary education. In the one class the State actually provides the education (or the great bulk of it); in the other, the State merely watches to see that education is properly provided. We may, for the convenience of distinction, call these the *Board District* and the *Committee District* respectively.

### A.—*The Board District.*

In this case elementary education is provided by a public body, called the School Board. A School Board may be brought into existence in any School District in one of two ways. Either the Education Department (*i.e.*, the Committee of the Privy Council on Education) may, {Creation School Board.}

[1] But parishes may, and do, unite for purposes of administration.

of its own motion, after due enquiry, resolve to create a School Board; or local demand takes the initiative. If in the latter case the School District is a borough, the municipal council decides that a School Board is desirable. If it is a parish or group of parishes outside a borough, a meeting of ratepayers, which *must* be summoned by the clerk to the Guardians of the Poor if fifty ratepayers desire it, resolves that a School Board is necessary. The original number of the Board's members (not less than five nor more than fifteen) is fixed by the Education Department, but it may subsequently, with the approval of the Department, be altered by the Board. Apparently there are no special qualifications required for membership,[1] and men and women are equally eligible.

The election of members takes place every three years, and is conducted by ballot if a contest is necessary. In boroughs the burgesses alone have the right to vote,[2] in all other School Districts the ratepayers elect. Each elector has as many votes as there are vacancies to be filled; and may give all or any number of his votes to one candidate. Members of the Board are re-eligible at the expiry of their term of office. Casual vacancies are filled up by the Board itself. It is presumed that the new parish councils will not in any way supersede the School Boards.

Immediately upon coming into existence, a School

[1] But non-attendance without leave for six months, imprisonment for crime, bankruptcy, and composition with creditors vacate a member's seat.

[2] In the ordinary municipal borough the burgess roll includes women, but owing to the special wording of the Elementary Education Act of 1870 (section 37 (6)), women cannot vote in the election of the *City* members of the London School Board.

# THE SCHOOL DISTRICT

Board must elect a chairman and vice-chairman, who hold office during the three years of the Board's continuance. The Board may also (and usually does) appoint a clerk and treasurer, and these officials may be salaried. The Board also appoints the teachers in its schools and, if necessary, "attendance officers," to enforce the law upon the subject of compulsory school attendance. Teachers.<br>Attendance officers.

It is very rarely that a School Board is called into existence unless there is need of further provision of public elementary schools. The primary duty of a School Board is therefore to provide such schools, *i.e.*, schools whose main object is elementary education, and which impose no religious or other unreasonable restrictions upon the entry of scholars, and which satisfy the regulations of the Education Department in the matters of sanitation and efficiency. To enable it to perform this duty, a School Board has power to hire, purchase, or build suitable premises both for schools and offices, and to furnish them with proper equipment and staff. It is, moreover, responsible for the due control and administration of its schools, but it may delegate some or all of its powers in this respect (and in some others) to a body of **Managers** of not less than three, who practically undertake the ordinary administration of the schools. Any persons may (apparently) be appointed managers, but any manager may be removed by the Board, or may resign by notice in writing. Schools.<br><br>Managers.

In addition to providing and maintaining schools, the School Board also acts as a **School Attendance Committee**, *i.e.*, a body to enforce the provisions of the law with regard to compulsory attendance. Broadly speaking, every child between the ages of five and fourteen must (in the absence of reasonable excuse) attend school regularly; and any School Attendance Committee.

58 ENGLISH LOCAL GOVERNMENT

person who employs such a child in a manner inconsistent with the regulations of the local School Board on the subject of attendance, is guilty of a criminal offence, and liable to a penalty. After the child has reached the age of eleven years, however, he may be granted a certificate of exemption or proficiency which will excuse or modify his further attendance. The duty of seeing that the child complies with the law is cast primarily on the parent or other person having charge of him, but its enforcement is left to the local School Board and its officials.

*Income of School Board.* The funds requisite for the performance of its duty by a School Board are obtained from various sources.

(*a*) *Fees*, paid by the children or their parents, the amount being fixed by the local School Board, with the approval of the Education Department. But from the first it has been found necessary to excuse, wholly or partially, the payment of fees in certain cases, for the simple reason that they could not be recovered. Various expedients have been adopted to meet the deficiency thereby occasioned, but the matter has now *Fee Grant Act.* been dealt with in a sweeping manner by the Act of 1891, which provides that a parliamentary grant shall be made to the managers of *every* public elementary school who shall be willing to receive it, at the rate of ten shillings *per annum* for every child between the ages of three and fifteen in regular attendance. If such grant is accepted, no fees may be charged at all, except in cases in which in the year next before the passing of the Act the average fees charged exceeded ten shillings a head, and even then only the excess may be charged. It is probable that Guardians of the Poor will no longer consent to pay the fees of

# THÈ SCHOOL DISTRICT 59

poor children out of the poor rates, and then, if a School Board refuses the grant, it will do so at its own risk.

(*b*) *Parliamentary grants*, which, in addition to the *Fee Grant*, may be made, upon any conditions prescribed by Parliament or the Education Department, towards the purchase of land, buildings, or other permanent objects. The amount so granted during the year 1890-1, amounted in all to £1,445,085.[1]  <small>Parliamentary grants.</small>

(*c*) *Loans*, which may only be raised with the consent of the Education Department, and for permanent objects, such as buildings and plant.  <small>Loans.</small>

(*d*) *The School Rate*, which must be resorted to for final deficiencies. The School Board directs its "precept" to the municipal council in the case of a borough, or to the overseers in the case of a parish, bidding them pay to the Board's treasurer the sum required, and these authorities recoup themselves out of the borough fund or the poor rate as the case may be. The process is beautifully simple and easy—for the Board; and apparently there is no limit to the exten of its demands. But it must be remembered that the members of the Board are elected by the very persons who pay the rates; and extravagance of administration would doubtless have its weight at the elections.  <small>Rates.</small>

All the receipts of a School Board, from whatever source, go into the *School Fund*, the accounts whereof are annually audited by the Local Government Board, and then submitted to the Education Department.  <small>School Fund.</small>

On the 1st April 1893, there were, in England and

[1] Report of Local Government Board, 1892-3. Appendix P., pp. 505-507.

Wales, 168 School Boards, representing as many boroughs, and 2163 Boards representing 3207 parishes. The total population in these School Districts was 18,764,565, or about three-fifths of the total population of England and Wales.[1]

B.—*The Committee District.*

In School Districts where there is no School Board the duty of enforcing attendance at school is undertaken by a special **School Attendance Committee.** But the nature of this committee varies with the character of the District. If the latter is a municipal borough, the committee will be appointed by the municipal council from amongst its own members. If the District is a parish or group of parishes outside a borough, the Guardians of the Poor for the Union in which it is situated will usually appoint the committee from their own ranks. But if an urban sanitary district (other than a borough) consists wholly of parishes which have no School Boards, and whose population amounted to 5000 at the last census, its authority may be empowered by the Education Department to appoint a school attendance committee for its district in like manner as if it were a borough council; and the sanitary authority will be able to raise the expenses of its committee out of the poor rates of its constituent parishes. And even where the urban sanitary district is partly (but not wholly) under the jurisdiction of a School Board or School Boards, or where its population is less than 5000, the sanitary authority may be empowered by the Department to appoint not more than three of its own members to act with the Attendance Committee appointed by the Guardians. Inas-

[1] Report of Education Department, 1892-3, p. xxxi.

THE SCHOOL DISTRICT 61

much as these provisions have been largely acted upon, and inasmuch as, even after the coming into operation of the Local Government Act of 1894, the sanitary authority and the Guardians of the Poor will continue to be identical in rural districts, it is clear that the tendency is to place the appointment of the School Attendance Committee in the hands of the sanitary authorities, or, as they will in future be called, the District Councils. In the absence, however, of express provision by the Education Department, the Guardians of the Poor will continue to appoint the School Attendance Committee in urban districts not comprised within municipal boroughs. But, as will be seen, there will be in the future no *ex-officio* or nominated Guardians.

The duty of the School Attendance Committee is to publish the provisions of the Elementary Education Acts, to report infringements of the "conscience clause" in public elementary schools, and to enforce attendance in the same way as the School Board within its district. Like the School Board, it must frame by-laws upon the subject of school attendance, and, if necessary, it may appoint officials to carry them out; but the consent of its own appointing body is in all cases required for this latter step.

*Duties of School Attendance Committee.*

On the 1st April 1893, there were, in England and Wales, 781 School Attendance Committees, representing the remaining two-fifths of the population. Of these, 131 were appointed by municipal councils, 72 by urban sanitary authorities, and 578 by Poor Law Guardians.[1]

[1] Report, p. xxxi.

# GROUP B.

## THE HUNDRED AND ITS ANALOGUES.

| | | |
|---|---|---|
| 4. THE HUNDRED | . . . | CHAPTER IV. |
| 5. THE PETTY SESSIONAL DIVISION | | CHAPTER V. |
| 6. THE COUNTY COURT DISTRICT | | CHAPTER VI. |
| 7. THE POOR LAW UNION . | . | CHAPTER VII. |
| 8. THE SANITARY DISTRICT | . | } CHAPTER VIII. |
| 9. THE HIGHWAY DISTRICT | . | |

# CHAPTER IV

## THE HUNDRED

THE **Hundred**, or **Wapentake**, has to-day only an antiquarian interest. It is impossible to trace with certainty the origin either of the institution or of the areas which now bear its name. As to the former, historians are divided between views which assign to the Hundred the character of an ancient tribal division, corresponding with the Continental *gau* (the *pagus* of Tacitus), and other views which regard it as the deliberate creation for administrative purposes of a German or English monarch. Perhaps the orthodox view is that the Hundred represents an ancient tribal organization which Frankish kings in the sixth century, and our own Edgar in the tenth, *revived* for police purposes. An institution which needed to be revived in the sixth century must be aged indeed, and the circumstances of the actual hundreds add weight to the theory of the hoary antiquity of the institution; for the arrangement of them seems to be based on no uniform or reasonable plan that we can account for by historical evidence. Their extent and numbers appear to be quite arbitrary. The county of Leicester has but six hundreds, the county of Sussex (less than twice its size) has sixty-four. The small county of Oxford has exactly the same number as the far larger western Shropshire. Devon has thirty-three hundreds;

Distribution of hundreds.

66    ENGLISH LOCAL GOVERNMENT

the adjoining county of Somerset (far smaller) has forty-three. All that one can say is, that apparently the hundreds were more numerous in the parts in which the early Teutonic invaders settled most quickly and thickly. The same presumption of antiquity may be gathered from the fact that the places from which a vast number of hundreds derive their names have dwindled into insignificance, or disappeared entirely; while gigantic towns have grown up beside them. London is locally situated in the hundred which took its name from (or gave its name to) the forgotten village of Ossulston. The great city of Liverpool is within the hundred of West Derby, the latter being a village which, after centuries of obscurity, is again rising into some importance as a suburb of Liverpool. Birmingham appears to be in the hundred of Hemlingford. Where is Hemlingford?

*Names of hundreds.*

As we have said, the Hundred comes first into authentic history as a *police district*, whose inhabitants were made liable for the discovery of the perpetrators of theft and other crimes committed within their district. It was natural, therefore, that their court, or *leet*, should have the power of enforcing and regulating the still older system of *village police*, and that their *hundredman*, or elder, should be looked upon as the head of the police force of his district.

*Police character of early hundreds.*

The hundredman of Saxon times seems to have developed imperceptibly into the *High Constable* of the thirteenth century, an official who, as the leet jury sank into oblivion, gradually acquired great powers. The Tudor policy, however, subordinated him to the Justices of the Peace, by whom (in default of special franchise) he was appointed, whose rates he collected, and whose duties in connection

*The High Constable.*

with the Statutes of Labourers he aided by holding *statute sessions* for the hiring of servants. Meanwhile the old police character of the Hundred survived in the liability of its inhabitants for the repair of certain roads and bridges, and for the making good of damages done by riot. The latter liability was transferred to the *county* or the *borough* by a statute of 1886, but the former remains in a few cases, and is expressly recognised by the Local Government Act of 1888 (the "County Councils" Act). The most important session of the Hundred Court, that of the Sheriff, who held his "Tourn" for the purpose of seeing that the police machinery was in full working order, has, after long decay, now been expressly abolished by statute. But other hundred courts do occasionally exist, and the caprice of the legislature has, within the last half century, made of one or two hundreds special areas for probate purposes. But, virtually, the Hundred is extinct as an institution, and we have only referred to it because its decay has led to the appearance of certain substitutes. The High Constable himself is in process of painless extinction, by virtue of a statute of the year 1869, and while he remains perhaps the utmost one can say of him is—that he is a High Constable. His surviving duties will in future be divided between the clerk of the Petty Sessional Division and the *Chief Constable* of the county. Still, we cannot say that the Hundred is quite dead. Less than a quarter of a century ago it was thought advisable to pass a solemn Act of Parliament for the sole purpose of bringing a part of the hamlet of South Town, in the parish of Gorleston, into the hundred of East Flegg.

Roads and bridges. Riot.

Sheriff's Tourn.

The Sheriffs Act, 1887.

The High Constables Act, 1869.

See *post*, p. 70 and p. 180.

# CHAPTER V

### THE PETTY SESSIONAL DIVISION

THE four great institutions which have taken the place of the decaying Hundred are the Petty Sessional Division, the County Court District, the Poor Law Union, and the Sanitary District. With the exception of the last, each of these institutions serves at least one of the purposes for which the Hundred was formerly used; and the last is so intimately bound up with the Poor Law Union, that it must plainly be treated as a member of the same group. The Sanitary District in most cases (but not all) coincides in area with some older institution, such as the Poor Law Union or the parish; the Petty Sessional Division, the County Court District, and the Poor Law Union have no necessary connection in area, though, for obvious convenience, they are frequently made to approximate, or even to become identical.

33 Hen. VIII., c. 10. **The Petty Sessional Division,** or at least the idea of it, appears to date from 1541. By a statute of that year the Justices of every county were directed to divide themselves according to "Hundreds, Wapentakes, Rapes, Commotes, or Number of Towns and Villages," assigning at least two of their number to each division, and holding frequent sessions therein, in addition to their "ancient Quarter Sessions" for the whole county. Although this statute was

repealed in 1545, the notion which it propounded has constantly been revived, and it gives us a very good idea of the Petty Sessional Division of the present day. The Petty Sessional Division is, primarily, a division of a judicial county made by the Justices of the Peace for that county in Quarter Sessions assembled, and alterable every three years. Although, in theory, every Justice of the Peace can act in any part of his county, in practice, and for convenience' sake, he acts only in that Petty Sessional Division in which he resides, and in the General Quarter Sessions for the whole county. But it will be seen hereafter that there are Justices of the Peace not only for the county, but for some boroughs, and that some boroughs have also professional Justices known as "stipendiary magistrates." And it must be remembered that every "sitting and acting" of borough justices or a stipendiary magistrate is deemed to be a Petty Sessions, and the district for which it is held a Petty Sessional Division. 37 Hen. VIII., c. 7.

When we come to deal with the County we shall consider the nature of the office of Justice of the Peace. At this point we are concerned with the Justice only as the resident magistrate of a Petty Sessional Division, and it is enough to say that a Justice of the Peace is a magistrate with minor criminal and some administrative jurisdiction, appointed by the Crown to act within the limits of a county or a borough, receiving in fact no remuneration for his services, and being, in the majority of instances, without professional training in the law. The Justices who act in Petty Sessional Division are those who reside within its limits, or, in the case of a borough, those who live sufficiently near to be able to act. But this is no rule of *law*, merely a doctrine of practice. In theory (be it again stated) *Post*, p. 152

every Justice can act in every part of his county or borough. There is, however, a real rule of law that for most purposes a Petty Sessional Court cannot be constituted by less than two ordinary Justices; although, by the terms of legal arithmetic, one stipendiary magistrate is generally equivalent to two ordinary Justices. The Justices "acting in and for" a Petty Sessional Division elect their own chairman, either *pro hâc vice* or permanently, and appoint their own clerk, who must not act as clerk to the Guardians of any Poor Law Union in which any part of his Division is situated. The salary of the clerk and the other expenses of the Division are paid by the county or borough council out of the county rate or borough fund.

The jurisdiction of a Petty Sessions is two-fold. It acts as a minor court of justice in criminal and (though rarely) in civil matters; and it also performs the duties of an administrative board. We must keep these two functions distinct.

(a) *Justice*.—There are certain breaches of the law which are taken in hand directly by the State, whether or no they appear to result mainly in damage to individuals. These breaches of the law we call *crimes*. Other offences are left to be remedied upon the application of the injured party; these we call *civil wrongs*. With this latter class Justices' Courts have rarely much to do; with the former they are much concerned.

Crimes again fall, according to English law, into two great classes of (*a*) indictable offences, and (*b*) offences punishable on summary conviction. With each of these classes the Petty Sessional Court has much to do, but its functions differ greatly according to the class of offences involved. Broadly speaking, it may be said the jurisdiction of the Petty Sessional Court with regard to indictable offences is only *preliminary;* in respect of offences punishable upon summary conviction it is *final.*

First, with respect to indictable offences. Here the duty of the Petty Sessional Court is to see whether there is a *primâ facie* against the prisoner who is accused, either by the police authorities or by a private individual, of having committed such an offence within the county. With this object the Court hears the witnesses for the accuser, records their evidence, and makes up its mind whether, in the absence of contradiction, there is reasonable ground for believing that a jury *might* convict the prisoner. The latter is always present at the enquiry, and may, if he pleases, cross-examine the prosecutor's witnesses, or call witnesses of his own. But if there is no reasonable hope that the Court will dismiss the charge as groundless, he usually avoids doing so, preferring not to shew his hand. If the Court thinks that there is a *primâ facie* case, it "commits" the prisoner for trial at the next Quarter Sessions or Assizes (according to the nature of the case), and he is there solemnly accused (or "indicted"), unless indeed the grand jury should decline to allow the proceedings to go on. During the preliminary proceedings the Petty Sessional Court has often to decide whether it will "remand" the prisoner to custody or release him on *bail*,[1] *i.e.*, security to appear again when wanted; and a similar question arises if the Court decides to commit the prisoner for trial. Moreover, other matters of considerable importance, such as the binding over of prosecutor and witnesses to appear at the trial, the disposal of property found on the prisoner, and so on, continually arise to be dealt with in this part of

<sup>Indictable crimes.</sup>

<sup>Committal for trial.</sup>

<sup>Remand. Bail.</sup>

[1] As to the meaning and rules of bail, see *post*, p. 160.

Petty Sessional jurisdiction. Inasmuch as the list of indictable offences includes all the graver crimes in the category—such as murder, arson, rape, burglary, forgery, perjury, and the like—the duties of a Petty Sessional Court involve heavy responsibility. For it would be equally disastrous to commit an innocent man to stand his trial upon a disgraceful charge, and to allow a guilty one to go free. It is satisfactory to know that in the opinion of the late Sir J. F. Stephen (and few persons were better qualified to pronounce an opinion on the subject), innocent persons are very rarely committed for trial by the magistrates. As a matter of fact, about three-fourths of those committed are ultimately convicted; and doubtless a good number of those who escape are really guilty.

In the second place, the Petty Sessional Court has an important *summary* jurisdiction to hear and *decide* petty criminal cases. By virtue of the numerous "Summary Jurisdiction Acts"[1] and other statutes, a long list of offences can be tried and completely disposed of by a Petty Sessional Court. Such offences are common assaults, small wilful injuries to property, small larcenies,[2] offences relating to game, offences against railway and municipal by-laws, minor revenue offences, and many others. These are punishable on summary conviction in all cases. But there is also a growing class of offences which are primarily the subject of indictment, but which, under certain circumstances, may be summarily disposed of. These circumstances may consist

[1] The principal of these are the Acts of 1849, 1879, and 1884; but there have been many amendments.

[2] The reader must not be tempted to use in this connection the obsolete term "petty larceny." It would be very delightful to be able to define petty larceny as a larceny punishable by a Petty Sessional Court. But the facts are against us.

# THE PETTY SESSIONAL DIVISION 73

in the fact that it is the offender's first appearance before a court of justice, that he is a juvenile offender, or that, being an adult, he pleads guilty, or requests to be dealt with at once, and so on. But it would be misleading to attempt to lay down the rules accurately. It is a nice point of casuistry whether the father of an illegitimate child is being punished for an offence when an affiliation order is made against him, or whether he is merely having his pecuniary relations adjusted by a State which has ideas on the subject of paternal duty. But, whatever the view taken of his case, it forms an important item in the cause list of the Petty Sessional Court.

The great difference between the procedure in summary jurisdiction and that upon indictment is that in the former case there is not, while in the latter there is, recourse to a jury. Whatever may be said in defence of the jury system, its advocates cannot argue that it is expeditious. In cases of summary jurisdiction, the Petty Sessional Court hears the advocates and witnesses of prosecutor and prisoner, and comes to its own conclusion upon the evidence. When it has decided, it pronounces sentence forthwith. The decision of the majority is the decision of the Court, the chairman having a casting vote. But there lies an appeal, as a general rule, from every *decision* of a Petty Sessional Court to the Quarter Sessions for the county, by which the case is reheard. Further, *on a point of law*, the opinion of the High Court may in most cases be taken.

We have spoken as though the composition of the Petty Sessional Court were the same in preliminary and summary jurisdiction. In practice it is. But, in theory, much of the preliminary work usually performed by a Petty Sessional Court *may* be done by a single Justice in his own  *[Different legal character of the Court in preliminary and summary jurisdiction.]*

house; while a final *decision* can never be given anywhere but in a court house, and only in rare cases by less than two Justices. A "court house" is either a Petty Sessional Court house, *i.e.*, "a place at which Justices are accustomed to assemble for holding special or petty sessions," or a place appointed by the Justices as an "occasional court house." And the authority of a single Justice, as well as the authority of any number of Justices sitting in an "occasional court house," is limited to awarding a fine of 20s. or imprisonment for fourteen days; while a Petty Sessional Court, sitting in a regular court house, can inflict much severer punishments.

(*b*) *Administration.*—Quite apart from all this judicial business, and in spite of recent changes in the law, to be hereafter noticed, the Justices in Petty or (as it is sometimes called "Special") Sessions perform a good deal of purely administrative or discretionary work. Good examples of this work are the granting and transfer of liquor licences, the hearing of objections to and the sanctioning of rates and valuations, the revision of jury lists, and (where overseers have not been made elective) the appointment of overseers of the poor. At the present time the Justices also grant licences to gang masters, game dealers, passage brokers, and emigrant runners; they issue pawnbrokers' certificates, they regulate fairs, and they enforce the statutes relating to petroleum and infant life protection. But in so far as they have at present power to deal with such matters *out of session*, their power will, on the coming into operation of the Local Government Act of 1894, be transferred to the sanitary authority. As in the case of the preliminary judicial enquiry, much (though not by any means all) of the administrative duty of a Justice which is now done in Petty

# THE PETTY SESSIONAL DIVISION 75

Sessions, might, as a matter of law, be performed by a single Justice in his own house. The advantages of the existing practice are obvious. Had it been adopted a little earlier, the present decided tendency to deprive the Justice of his administrative character might not have set in. In some cases there is, in others there is not, an appeal from a resolution of Petty Sessions upon a matter of discretion. It would be impossible to state details. Where an appeal lies it is to the Quarter Sessions of the Justices for the county or borough, of which the Petty Sessions is, virtually, a local committee.

# CHAPTER VI

## THE COUNTY COURT DISTRICT

THE first thing to be remembered about a modern County Court is that it derives its name, not from the area, but from the nature of its jurisdiction. The County Court District is very much smaller than the county; while there are but 52, or, at the most (reckoning divided counties), 59 judicial counties in England and Wales, there are upwards of 500 County Court Districts. Moreover, a County Court District may cut across the boundaries of a judicial county (which a Petty Sessional Division may never do), and thereby shew its entire independence of the county system. The origin of the name must be looked for elsewhere.

History of the County Court.

For some generations after the village and hundred moots had fallen into decay, the sheriff's court of the county, holden at monthly intervals, was the recognised tribunal for the disposal of petty cases, both civil and criminal. The tide was setting in favour of the royal administration of justice, and the sheriff was a royal official. On the other hand, the old local feeling was strong, and the county court of those days was a more or less popular assembly, in which the freemen of the county took substantial part. But the lawyers who were growing up round the king's central courts at Westminster had no special love for the sheriff. The sheriff fell into disgrace in the twelfth

## THE COUNTY COURT DISTRICT 77

century, and his criminal jurisdiction was strictly limited by the new procedure, which reserved the trial of graver crimes to the king's judges on circuit. In civil business, a statute of the year 1278 practically (though indirectly) limited the sheriff's jurisdiction to cases involving not more than 40s. value. Then the growing importance of the Justices of the Peace swept away the remaining powers of the sheriff as a judge in criminal cases, and left him only the small civil business. Even this was shared by the usurping franchises of the manorial courts, by the mercantile courts of the staple, and by the special local tribunals of the boroughs and other privileged places.

*See post, p. 150.*

*Manorial courts.*
*Staple courts.*
*Municipal courts.*

No wonder that the county court dwindled into insignificance; the startling fact is that its rivals in civil business dwindled too. The manorial courts ceased to decide suits that did not directly affect manorial rights; the organisation of the staple disappeared; the borough courts decayed along with other municipal institutions. And it remains one of the puzzles of English legal history to find out how the yeoman or small tradesman of the seventeenth and eighteenth centuries, who had a petty claim for the value of goods or services, could proceed to enforce it. Had he actually to try the case at assizes?

But, towards the close of the eighteenth century, the cry for cheap local tribunals for civil business made itself strongly felt, and was met in a most unscientific way by the creation of isolated Courts of Requests (or Conscience, as they were sometimes called) in such parts of the country as seemed most to need them. In most cases each court had its own private Act of Parliament, which prescribed its powers, and although these numerous private Acts were, by a statute of 1754, declared to be "public"

*Courts of Requests.*

78  ENGLISH LOCAL GOVERNMENT

(*i.e.*, part of the general law of which judges are bound to take notice, even though their attention is not specially called to it), the evils of the original plan continued manifest. Accordingly, the present uniform system was started by a comprehensive statute of the year 1846, which swept away about a hundred Courts of Requests. The County Court system was, therefore, called into existence, to fill the gap left by the disappearance of the old sheriff's County Court; and hence its name. But its scheme is very different from that of its predecessor. It has had palpable success, its scope has been more than once enlarged, and the law concerning it is now mainly to be found in the provisions of the County Courts Act of 1888.

<small>First County Courts Act.</small>

<small>The modern County Court. Civil jurisdiction.</small>

The modern County Court, as distinguished from the Petty Sessional Court, is a court of *civil*, not of *criminal* jurisdiction. That is to say, it disposes of small disputes between one private citizen or corporation and another; it does not deal with the punishment of offenders by the State. On the other hand, it resembles the Petty Sessional Court in deciding suits which are too small to take up the time of the superior courts; and which, for the sake of litigants and the public alike, require to be dealt with cheaply and speedily. But it has no jurisdiction (or only in a few cases) corresponding with that which the Petty Sessional Court exercises in preparing the preliminaries of a case for the superior tribunal.

<small>Final, not preliminary.</small>

The **County Court District** is, then, an area of local civil jurisdiction, constituted, under powers conferred by statute, by an Order of the Privy Council, which may rearrange or destroy it altogether. The five hundred and odd County Court Districts of England and Wales are grouped into fifty-five *circuits*, each comprising from one to fifteen

## THE COUNTY COURT DISTRICT 79

"court towns," according to the area and density of population. The thickly populated Liverpool circuit, with its small area, has but five court towns; the large and sparsely settled Aberystwith circuit has eighteen.

The County Court judge, who is a barrister of at least seven years' standing, appointed by the Lord Chancellor, is the judge of the *circuit*,[1] not of the district, and holds his sittings at one or other of the court towns of his circuit as often as the exigencies of business demand it. He tries cases upon oral evidence, and, generally speaking, without a jury, although in cases where the value involved exceeds £5, either party may, if he pleases, demand a jury. (If his case be an honest one, he will be very foolish to do so.) But although the judge has jurisdiction over the circuit,[2] the business arising in a district must, as a rule, be disposed of in that same district. That is to say, the district in which the defendant resides or carries on business, or where the property in dispute is situated, or where the bankrupt or deceased lived, is the district in which proceedings must be taken. The plaintiff cannot choose a particular court town in the circuit because he has a fancy for the air of it.

Besides its judge, each County Court has its own Registrar, High Bailiff, and other officials for conducting its clerical and executive business. The *Registrar* is a solicitor of at least five years' standing, appointed by the judge with the approval of the Lord Chancellor, and paid by salary in proportion to the extent of the Court's business. As a rule the Registrar may engage in private

*The judge.*

*Importance of the District.*

*Registrar.*

---

[1] Occasionally, *e.g.*, in the Liverpool circuit, there are two concurrent judges, who divide the business between them by arrangement.
[2] And, if necessary, he may be directed to act in *any* County Court.

practice not connected with the Court, but if the Court business is very heavy, it may be made a condition of his appointment that he is not to practise at all. He may be defined as the chief clerical official of the Court. He issues all summonses and orders, keeps an account[1] of the proceedings which take place, receives and accounts for all fees and other monies paid in, and, generally speaking, is responsible for the routine business of the Court.[2] The *High Bailiff* is appointed by the judge, without special approval of the Lord Chancellor, but the latter may, if he think fit, remove him. The High Bailiff is charged with the *execution* of the orders and proceedings of the Court, *e.g.*, he or his assistant delivers the summonses, warrants, and so on to the parties affected, enforces judgment by seizure and sale of goods, and compels the attendance of witnesses. The High Bailiff is paid partly by salary and partly by fees. No person may be appointed to act as Registrar or High Bailiff in more than one County Court; but it is the policy of the legislature to provide for the future combination in one person of the offices of Registrar and High Bailiff of the same court.

High Bailiff.

The jurisdiction of the County Court has been steadily growing during the last forty years, and is now very extensive. It may be most clearly outlined under six heads—

(1.) "*Common Law*" *jurisdiction—i.e.*, in matters formerly cognisable by the old Courts of King's Bench,

---

[1] The County Court is not, technically, a "Court of Record," *i.e.*, a court whose account of its own proceedings cannot be questioned. Presumably the correctness of a document issued from a County Court might be questioned.

[2] He may even, *on the application of the parties*, and by leave of the judge, decide disputed claims which do not amount to 40s.

## THE COUNTY COURT DISTRICT 81

Common Pleas, and Exchequer. Here the Court has jurisdiction to try any claim not exceeding in value £50, except cases involving

(a) *Ejectment*, *i.e.*, recovery of *possession* of land. Here the limit of jurisdiction is £50 annual value of the land in question, which must be within the District. (The claim to *possession* of land of far greater value may be only worth £50.)

(β) *Title* to land or rights in connection with land.[1] Here the limit is £50 annual value *or* rent, but the property need not be situated in the District. But *with the consent of the parties*, a judge may decide such a question beyond the limits stated. His decision will not, however, be binding on persons not represented in the proceedings.

(γ) Claims for *libel*, *slander*, *seduction*, or *breach of promise of marriage*. These claims can never be brought directly into the County Court.

But claims beyond the £50 limit may be "remitted" by a superior Court for trial in the County Court in certain cases. Thus, in an action brought upon a contract in the High Court to recover a sum not exceeding £100, either party may apply to have the case remitted to a County Court, and the High Court Judge *must*, unless there is good cause to the contrary, grant the request. And in any action of *tort*[2] brought in the High Court, if the defendant

*Remitted cases.*

---

[1] "Corporeal or incorporeal hereditaments . . . toll, fair, market, or franchise." The words in the text are a sufficiently correct rendering for general purposes. It is doubtful, on the wording of the Act, whether a County Court can try the title to a "toll, fair, market, or franchise" of any value, without consent; but it is clear from decisions that at present the view is that it cannot do so.

[2] Civil wrongs fall into two great classes; those which are breaches

F

will swear that the plaintiff has no apparent means of paying costs, should he be defeated, the High Court may order the plaintiff to give security for costs, or to submit to a transfer of the action to a County Court. Moreover, the County Court has a general jurisdiction to try *any* common law cases if both parties agree to submit to the jurisdiction. On the other hand, if a claim on contract exceeding £20, or on tort exceeding £10, is brought in the County Court, the defendant may, if he can persuade the judge that an important question of law or fact is to be tried, and upon giving security, have the proceedings in the County Court stayed. The value of the remitting power of the High Court is shown by the fact that in the year 1892, 1778 cases were compulsorily sent down to the County Court, and that of these only 1070 were tried. For if a plaintiff who brings his action in the High Court is not prepared to enforce it by the simpler and cheaper machinery of the County Court, it is probable that his proceedings are not *bonâ fide*.

(2.) "*Equity*" *jurisdiction*—*i.e.*, in certain matters formerly dealt with by the old Court of Chancery, such as the winding up of the estates of deceased persons, the execution of trusts, the enforcement of mortgages, the "specific performance"[1] of contracts, the rectification and setting aside of contracts, proceedings affecting the conduct of trustees, the administration of the

---

of agreement entered into between the parties, and those which do not arise directly out of agreements. The latter are called "torts."

[1] The rule of the Common Law is that if *A* will not perform his contract with *B*, all that *B* can do is to make him pay damages. But *B* may much prefer to have the contract performed "specifically," *i.e.*, actually; and in a few cases a court of equity will enforce such performance.

## THE COUNTY COURT DISTRICT 83

affairs of infants, and the dissolution of partnership. Many of these matters are not *litigious* at all; the Court acts as genial adviser and supervisor, rather than as judge. And the general rule is that the County Court judge may in these matters do all that a judge of the Chancery Division might do, provided only that the property in question does not exceed £500. Chancery proceedings commenced in the High Court may, as in common law cases, be remitted to a County Court; but the power to remit exists only where the case might originally have been brought in the County Court. During the year 1892 the County Courts dealt with 723 equitable cases, involving property to the value of £83,000.

(3) "*Admiralty*" *cases*—*i.e.*, claims for salvage, towage, necessaries supplied to a ship, seamen's wages, damage by collision at sea, for hire of ship, or carriage of goods. Here the claim, if for towage, necessaries, or wages, must not exceed £150; if on any other account, £300—unless, indeed, the parties agree to submit larger claims. Moreover, it is only those County Courts specially appointed by Order in Council which have Admiralty jurisdiction; and no Order in Council can confer upon a County Court any jurisdiction in prize or slave-trade cases. In the year 1892 there were 23 County Courts (including the City of London Court) having Admiralty jurisdiction; and between them they entertained proceedings in 545 cases, of which 225 were in the City of London Court.

(4) "*Bankruptcy*" *jurisdiction.*—Here, in ordinary cases, the jurisdiction of the County Court is unlimited in

amount, and the County Court has full powers to conduct bankruptcy proceedings. But many County Courts are expressly excluded from bankruptcy jurisdiction by the Bankruptcy Act, 1883, and in the year 1892, apparently only 400 did bankruptcy business, disposing of 2700 cases. Besides the ordinary cases of bankruptcy, the County Court may exercise the rare power of committing to prison a debtor who refuses to obey the order of the Court for payment of a sum of money. The Court, however, will never take such an extreme step unless satisfied that the debtor really can pay if he chooses. A new and useful branch of bankruptcy business is the power conferred upon the County Court by the Act of 1883, in any case in which judgment has been obtained against a man who alleges that he cannot pay and that his total indebtedness does not amount to £50, to make an order for the administration of his estate. 2112 such orders were made in the year 1892, and the Courts succeeded in realising a sum of £3378 for the creditors.

*Imprisonment of debtors.*

(5) "*Testamentary*" *jurisdiction.*—No County Court can grant a Probate, *i.e.*, the official authority to an executor to act, nor can it make an administrator of the estate of a person who has died intestate. *A fortiori*, it cannot collect the "death duties" of any estates. But where there is any dispute as to the existence or genuineness of a will, or the identity of an executor, or the claim of a person to be administrator, the County Court in whose District the deceased died can decide the question, provided that the gross personalty to which the deceased died entitled in his own right did not exceed £200, and his realty did

## THE COUNTY COURT DISTRICT 85

not amount to £300, and provided that the deceased's abode was not in the Metropolitan District. Moreover, by certain useful provisions of recent statutes, where a man or a widow dies intestate, worth only £100 or less, the County Court officials of the District in which he or she lived may fill up the necessary papers and apply for administration on behalf of any applicant who is the widow or child of the deceased, and who lives more than three miles from the Probate Registry having jurisdiction in the matter.

(6) "*Miscellaneous" jurisdiction.*—Finally, by the provisions of a large number of modern statutes, *e.g.*, the Employers' Liability Acts, the Friendly Societies Acts, the Agricultural Holdings Act, and others, jurisdiction in a vast number of special cases is conferred upon the County Court. No generalisations upon the subject can usefully be made; the terms of the jurisdiction can only be learned by reference to the statutes themselves.[1]

Judged by the use made of them, the County Courts have been an unqualified success. In the year 1892, 1,101,075 plaints (*i.e.*, initial steps in legal proceedings) were issued by them. 1,087,300 of these were for amounts under £20, 12,621 for sums between £20 and £50, and

[1] One of the most important branches of the jurisdiction of the County Court is in *replevin* cases, *i.e.*, where goods which have been seized in legal process against *A* are claimed by *B*. If *B* will give security to cover the value of the goods and the costs of the proceedings, the goods will be handed over to him, and he will be bound to commence an action at once against *A*'s creditor to justify his claim. This action may be brought either in the High Court or in the County Court, but in any case the preliminary steps will be taken in the County Court.

1154 for claims exceeding £50. The total sum recovered for litigants was £1,689,824, exclusive of cases settled out of court. It seems possible, on the face of it, that the cry for the localisation of justice will be met by a further increase in the jurisdiction of the County Courts. The great objection to this course is that, at present, County Court proceedings do not pay a fair working remuneration to solicitors, and they are therefore unpopular with the abler members of that profession. Cheap law is good, but law may be too cheap, *i.e.*, nominally too cheap, as litigants in France and America know to their cost.

It is perhaps needless to say that the *law* administered by the County Courts is precisely the same as that administered by the superior courts in parallel cases. It is only the procedure which is different.

## CHAPTER VII

### THE POOR LAW UNION

THE Poor Law Union, as a normal institution of English Local Government, dates from the Poor Law Amendment Act of 1834. But the cost of maintaining separate machinery for the administration of poor relief in every parish, and the other evils attendant upon a too minute subdivision of authorities, had, even before the legislation of 1834, induced the State to sanction and even encourage the union of parishes for purposes of poor law administration. These tentative measures date from the year 1662. *Gilbert's Act.*

Two points should be especially remembered with regard to the scheme of 1834. In the first place it was not compulsory in character. It merely *enabled* parishes to combine together for purposes of poor law administration; and, although the central Government may compel parishes to unite if it appears obviously better that they should do so, there are, as a matter of fact, many large parishes which (either with or without special legislative sanction) still administer their own poor relief. This fact has been recognised by very recent legislation, which defines a Poor Law Union as "any parish *or* union of parishes for which there is a separate Board of Guardians." *Act of 1834 not compulsory.*

*Interpretation Act, 1889.*

In the second place, though the great majority of parishes are united for the purpose of poor law *administration*, there are, practically, none which unite for purposes *Nor did it extinguish individuality of parishes.*

of poor law *maintenance*. The cost of poor relief, and the expenses incident to the machinery of administration, are paid out of the Union's common fund; but this common fund is (in the absence of special order) collected by the overseers in each parish. The amount which a parish contributes depends entirely upon its rateable value, and the authorities of the Union have, *primâ facie*, nothing to do with the sources from which it comes, or the mode in which it is collected. Under the legislation of 1834, the distinction between the several parishes composing a Union was still stronger, for unless they agreed (which they, practically, never did) to consolidate for all purposes of poor relief, each parish contributed only to the extent of the cost incurred in maintaining *its own* poor, *i.e.*, those paupers who, by virtue of the law of "settlement," belonged to its own area, together with a share of the general working expenses of the Union. But the Union Chargeability Act of 1865 abolished this excessive particularity, though it by no means extinguished the individuality of the component parishes of a Union.

The general supervision of the administration of the poor relief throughout England and Wales was placed by the Act of 1834 in the hands of a body known as the Poor Law Commissioners. This body was superseded in the year 1847 by a new Commission, generally known as the Poor Law Board; and this again, on the formation of the Local Government Board in 1871, gave up its powers to the newly created body, which now remains the central authority in Poor Law matters.

The **Poor Law Union** then (of which there appear to be 648 in England and Wales[1]) is an area for the administra-

[1] Report of Local Government Board, 1892-3. App. P., p. 490.

tion of poor relief, being usually a combination of parishes formed either by agreement or by order of the central government, but occasionally still a single parish. A comparison of figures shews that there is an average of between twenty-two and twenty-three parishes to every Union; but such a result is necessarily fallacious. The actual number of parishes in a Union is purely arbitrary, being settled by such considerations as those of size, density of population, and the like. Whether the Union be a single parish or a number of parishes, the poor law authority is always a **Board of Guardians**, and at the present time a Board of Guardians (in the absence of special legislation) consists of the Justices of the Peace resident in the Union (who are *ex-officio* members) and a number of representative guardians elected by the owners and ratepayers of the constituent parishes of the Union, upon a cumulative vote ranging from one to six, according to the value of the property for which they are respectively rated. There must be at least one elective Guardian for each constituent parish containing a population of 300, but smaller parishes may be united. A property qualification for the elective Guardians (not exceeding a ratal value of £40) is fixed by the Local Government Board, and the Guardians sit for one year only, unless the Board, with the consent of a majority of the ratepayers, resolves that it will sit longer. Even under the present law women are (it is said) entitled to act, both as electors and Guardians. Present system.

But by the law which will come into force in November next (1894) great changes will be introduced into the constitution of Boards of Guardians. In the first place, there will be no more nominee or *ex-officio* Guardians; and the property qualification for the office is impliedly (though not expressly) swept away. The scheme of 1894. No *ex-officio* Guardians. No property qualification.

90  ENGLISH LOCAL GOVERNMENT

Parochial electorship.
Residence.

See *ante*, p. 41.

No one will be eligible as a Guardian for any parish unless he is either a parochial elector of or has for twelve months resided in some parish (not necessarily that for which he is standing) within the Union; or unless, in the case of a candidate for a parish wholly within a borough, he is qualified to be a member of the borough council. On the other hand, neither sex nor marriage will disqualify for voting or for election, but, generally speaking, the disqualifications for the office of parochial councillor apply to that of Guardian,[1] and, in addition, the fact of serving as a paid Poor Law officer *anywhere* is a bar. It is said that the office of a Guardian is not compulsory.

Election of Guardians.

*Ante*, p. 38.

Again, all Guardians (with the exception to be hereafter noted) will be elected on an uniform plan by the parochial electors of each parish, or, if the parish is very large, of the wards into which it has been subdivided for purposes of election. In the case of Guardians for a rural parish, the parochial electors will be the persons who will elect the parish councillors;[2] and, in an urban parish, the persons who, if the parish were rural, would elect the councillors. Who those persons are we have already seen. As in the case of parish elections, each elector will have one vote for each vacancy, and cumulation will not be allowed. If there is a contest, the poll will ·be taken by ballot, and not, as at the present time, by voting papers left at the houses of the electors.

[1] The disqualification for crime is wider than in the case of a parish councillor. Any conviction for felony, fraud, or perjury, however long ago, will, apparently, disqualify a candidate for the office of Guardian.

[2] There will not, in fact, be any election of Guardians *as* Guardians in a rural parish, but there will be an election of (rural) District Councillors who will act as Guardians. (See *post*, p. 105.)

# THE POOR LAW UNION 91

Once more, the term of office of a Guardian will be three years, and, usually, one-third of the Board will retire annually; but, upon the application of the Board, the County Council will be able to sanction the simultaneous retirement of all the members.   *Term of office.*

Finally, by a curious provision, intended, doubtless, to soothe the feelings of the ejected *ex-officio* guardians, a Board of Guardians will be able to elect its chairman and vice-chairman, and not more than two other persons, as "additional" members of the Board, from outsiders who are qualified to hold the office of Guardian; but if, on the first of such occasions, there are existing *ex-officio* or nominated Guardians (who have actually served), and they are willing to accept office, the preference must be given to them.   *Additional Guardians.*

Thus much for the constitution of Boards of Guardians. A word now as to their powers and duties.

The primary object of the existence of Guardians is, of course, the relief of the poor. If we leave out of account the very limited powers of granting relief still vested in the overseers, all the *distribution* of the seven or eight millions annually spent in the official relief of the poor is in their hands. Roughly speaking, there are two ways in which a pauper may be relieved, and opinion is very much divided as to their respective merits. Either he may be taken into a workhouse or asylum provided by the authorities, and there housed, clothed, and fed at the expense of the rates; and this either as a casual occurrence, on occasions of temporary necessity, or as a permanent provision. Or, relief may be granted by doles, provision of work, or other means, to applicants who live in their own homes. Certainly it may be said that it   *Poor relief.*   *Indoor relief.*   *Outdoor relief.*

never was the intention of the law that any but the "impotent poor," *i.e.*, those persons who had no reasonable prospect of earning their livings independently, should be permanently isolated from ordinary life, and maintained at the expense of the rates. But "impotency" is, of course, a relative term, and the extreme difficulty of gauging the genuineness of applicants for outdoor relief has inclined the authorities to strain somewhat the interpretation of the term, and to use admission to the workhouse as a test of real *bonâ fide* poverty. Needless to say, the inmate of the workhouse is not entitled to spend his days in idleness; but the low standard of task work, combined with the unwillingness of Poor Law authorities to compete with independent labour, and the growing feeling of industrial organisations against allowing protected goods to be put upon the market, tend to reduce the value of the workhouse output. Notwithstanding, however, the feeling of Guardians in favour of indoor relief, its amount, both actually and relatively to the amount spent in outdoor relief, has shewn a perceptible diminution in the last few years.

Relief must be given. The extreme importance of the subject of *indoor relief* is that it cannot legally be refused to those who genuinely stand in need of it, and shew the necessary title. This title is technically known as **settlement** within a parish comprised in the Union. The law of settlement, at any rate in its simpler form, dates from the very beginning of the Poor Law itself, but its evil reputation arises from the complications introduced into it during the seventeenth and eighteenth centuries, and there can be small doubt that grave suffering and wrong were inflicted in its name for many generations. So long as a parish administered its own poor relief, so long even as it was responsible for the actual cost of the paupers who claimed "settlement" in it, the object of the parish authorities was to reduce by every possible means the number of its inhabitants who were at all likely ever to fall into poverty. A certain statute of the year 1662 gave the parish authorities power to apply to two Justices of the Peace for an order to remove from the parish, within forty days after their arrival, all persons likely to become chargeable to the poor rate, unless they inhabited a tenement of the annual value of £10, or gave security to the satisfaction of the Justices. By refusing to build or allow to be built any cottages of less annual value than £10 (a safe margin in days when the average yearly wage of a labourer was about the same sum), the landowners of a "close" parish (*i.e.*, a parish in which all the land belonged to one or two large proprietors) could pretty effectually keep down the increase of population, and the zeal of the parish officers would do the rest. Since the abolition of specific parochial liability in 1865, the desire of a parish to rid itself of possible paupers has been less marked, but as the law of settlement still determines the liability of a Union, it is necessary to state it here in bare outline. The grounds upon which settlement in a parish may be claimed are— {Removal statute of 1662.}

(i.) *Birth.*—In the absence of proof of any other settlement, the old rule holds, that a man is legally "settled" in the parish in which he was born. But if, in the case of a child under the age of sixteen, it be proved that its father or (if he be dead) its widowed mother has or had a settlement in another parish, the presumption is shifted to the parish of {Derivative settlement.}

settlement of the parent in question.¹ A similar rule holds with regard to the settlement of a married woman, who takes that of her husband instead of that of her birth. But, of course, in either of these cases of "derivative" settlement, the pauper may have acquired a settlement of his or her own by any other title.

(ii.) *Ownership of property.*—Towards the end of the seventeenth century it was decided by the Courts that a man could not be removed under the statute of 1662 from a parish in which he had an estate in land. If, therefore, such a man resided in the parish for forty days (the limit of time allowed by the statute for application for an order of removal), he acquired a legal settlement. And the rule still holds; but the Poor Law Amendment Act of 1834 has provided that a settlement acquired by the ownership of property shall last only so long as the claimant resides within ten miles of the parish.²

(iii.) *Occupation of a tenement of the yearly value of £10.*— By a similar course of reasoning, a man who came to occupy a tenement of the value of £10 a year could not be removed under the statute of 1662, and he, therefore, acquired a settlement after forty days. And this rule still holds, modified, however, by the provisions of the Poor Law Amendment Act of 1834, which requires one year's payment of poor rates in respect of the qualifying tenement.

¹ In the case of an illegitimate child the settlement derived is that of the mother.

² The wording of the section left it doubtful whether the limit of residence was ten miles from the *parish* or from the *estate*. But it has been decided that the view stated in the text is the correct one.

## THE POOR LAW UNION

(iv.) *Apprenticeship* under a deed, followed by residence for forty days under its provisions in any parish, confers a settlement.

(v.) *Residence.*—Finally, after a voluntary residence in a parish for a period of one year, a person cannot be *removed;* and, after a similar residence for three years, he is to be deemed to be settled in the parish of residence until he has *acquired* some other settlement.

There were formerly other means of acquiring a settlement, *e.g.*, by payment of highway rates, hiring and service, service of office, and so forth; but these have all been abolished. The chief difficulty of the law of settlement now appears to be in ascertaining the priority of liabilities. If a man or a single woman applies for relief, and he or she can be proved to have resided in a parish of the Union for a year, there cannot, as a general rule, be any removal. If this cannot be proved, the enquiry must be directed to find the parish in which the applicant last resided for three years. Failing this, settlement by ownership, occupation, or apprenticeship may be proved, the latest being (presumably) the test of liability. If no such settlement can be established, the place of birth is the last resort. Wives, as we have seen, take the settlements of their husbands, and children under sixteen of their father, in the absence of proof to the contrary. But the Guardians are not allowed to postpone the giving of temporary relief on the ground that the applicant is not settled in the Union. They must give immediate relief in cases of urgency, and then apply for an order of removal.

*Outdoor relief* may take the form of medical attendance in cases of sickness, payment of funeral expenses, allowance in money or kind to widows, women deserted by

Outdoor relief.

their husbands or whose husbands are in the army or navy, payment of expenses of children attending pauper schools, or the provision of work for able-bodied males. The last-named form of relief is rendered almost compulsory by an old-standing Order of the Poor Law Board, which directs that "every able-bodied male person, if relieved out of the workhouse, shall be set to work by the Guardians and be kept employed under their direction and superintendence so long as he continues to receive relief." This Order has been somewhat liberally construed, and of late years there has been a growing tendency on the part of the "unemployed" artisan or labourer to demand the institution of relief works as a right. So long as a Board of Guardians (either in their primary capacity or in their character of rural sanitary authority) can really find useful work, not branded with the stigma of pauperism, for decent men who are in temporary difficulties, they will perform a great service to the community. But it may well be questioned whether Boards of Guardians are exactly the authorities best fitted to introduce an era of collective production. And it is quite certain that, as the law at present stands, no man has a legal *right* to outdoor relief of any kind. He may go into the workhouse if he pleases, and (subject to certain exceptions) come out when he pleases. More than this he cannot claim.

Poor rates.

See *ante*, p. 31.

To provide themselves with funds for carrying out their duties the Guardians of a Union are entitled to make such demands upon the overseers of their constituent parishes as may be necessary. The proportionate liability of each parish being settled beforehand by the valuation list drawn up by the assessment committee, the question is merely one of distributing the amount required at any time in

## THE POOR LAW UNION

accordance with the rateable value of the constituent parishes as shown by the list. Overseers who fail to comply with an order of the Guardians for payment of money can be proceeded against in a summary way, either by conviction and fine, or by levy against their goods. The Guardians have a similar right to proceed summarily against any person through whose neglect or default they have been put to expense. Absconding husbands, absent soldiers and sailors, and others who have failed to provide for the maintenance of their relatives, can be proceeded against by the Guardians for the recovery of the expenditure incurred in relieving those for whom the defaulters should have made provision.

Moreover, for the performance of works of permanent value, a Board of Guardians is sometimes entitled to raise money by way of loan, repayable by instalments. Such works are workhouses, hospitals, ambulance stations, asylums, schools, and the like, objects whose benefit will obviously last over a long term of years. The security for the repayment of these loans is the prospect of forthcoming poor rates. But no loan can be raised without the sanction of the Local Government Board, and the total indebtedness of the Guardians must not exceed one-fourth of the annual rateable value of the Union, or, in cases specially considered by the Local Government Board, one-half of such value. *Loans.*

The ministerial duties of a Board of Guardians are performed by a staff of paid officials, medical officers, relieving officers, valuers, masters and matrons of workhouses, collectors, and clerks. These officials are appointed by the Guardians with the consent or by the direction of the Local Government Board, but they can only be dismissed by the last-named authority. This provision is necessary *Union staff.*

in order to secure the independence and safety of the officials. But it renders it sometimes very difficult for a Board of Guardians to get rid of an incapable servant.

Other functions of a Board of Guardians.

In addition to their primary duties in connection with the administration of poor relief, Guardians of the Poor have or may have various duties in connection with sanitary matters, highways, elementary education, and other subjects. But these either have been or will be discussed in connection with the subjects to which they specially relate. It may, however, here be remarked that upon the Guardians falls the somewhat invidious task of enforcing the provisions of the Vaccination Acts. The Poor Law Union constitutes *primâ facie* the **vaccination district**, which may, however, be divided if the necessities of the case require it. The vaccination officers are the officers of the Guardians, and at least one paid vaccination officer must be appointed for each Union. Finally, the Poor Law Union constitutes the district for the registration of births, deaths, and marriages, presided over by a Superintendent Registrar, who is usually the clerk to the Guardians. Each Union is divided into as many sub-districts as the Registrar General may deem necessary, and a Registrar is appointed for each by the Guardians. But both Superintendent Registrar and Registrar may be dismissed by the Registrar General, who is, of course, an official of the central government, having his headquarters in London.

Registration of births, deaths, and marriages.

# CHAPTER VIII

### THE SANITARY DISTRICT AND THE HIGHWAY DISTRICT

IT is no light task to attempt even the barest outline of the vast and complicated scheme of English sanitary administration. Even if we put aside (as we must do) the special peculiarities of Metropolitan management, in themselves almost sufficient for the study of a lifetime, we are bound to face the fact that the Legislature has deemed it impossible to state the law on the subject in less bulk than a great codifying statute of 343 clauses, and some forty amending Acts, to say nothing of Orders in Council innumerable. If we add to this reflection the consideration of the fact that in a few months the whole existing scheme will be cut across and re-shaped by legislation which is not yet in force, we shall realise something of the magnitude of the task before us. *Public Health Act, 1875. Local Government Act, 1894.*

But there is one gleam of comfort. The Law of Public Health is statutory, not traditional. Our forefathers were not morbidly anxious about drains, offensive trades, contagious diseases, overcrowding, and the like. Their sanitary efforts rarely extended beyond feeble and spasmodic attempts to provide a system of usable roads, if indeed unsewered roads can be deemed a department of sanitation. It was not until the cholera had more than once wrought havoc in the land that any decently com- *Health Law is modern and statutory.*

100   ENGLISH LOCAL GOVERNMENT

Act of 1848.

prehensive scheme of sanitation was adopted. The Public Health Act of 1848 (brought into existence by the cholera of 1847), which constituted a Board of Public Health with numerous local authorities working under it, is the first great sanitary statute on the English statute book. It was followed by revised schemes in 1858, 1866, and 1872, till, in the year 1875, the great statute, which is the basis of the present law, came into existence. Consequently, the law upon the subject of sanitation, complex and voluminous as it is, is modern and easily accessible. It is not necessary to pore over Littleton and Coke to discover the duties of a Local Board of Health. Patience, not great antiquarian learning, is the essential qualification for the task.

Every square inch of land in England and Wales (with the exception of the metropolitan area) is supposed to lie within the area of a **sanitary district**. All sanitary districts are either *urban* or *rural*, but, by virtue of special provisions of the Public Health Act, a sanitary district of a peculiar kind, known as a *Port* sanitary district, may be constituted by Order in Council, and its administration will be of such a special kind that it will, practically, constitute a third class. Sanitary districts may then be classified as *urban*, *rural*, and *port*.

(1) An *Urban Sanitary District* may at the present time consist of any one of the three following areas, each with its different sanitary authority.

(a) A *Municipal Borough.*—We have not yet considered the nature and constitution of a municipal borough; but for present purposes it may be defined as an area subject to the jurisdiction of a town or city council, exercising its functions by virtue of a Crown *Charter*. Almost every

See *post*, cap. xii.

municipal borough is an urban sanitary district, and the borough council (of the constitution of which we shall have to speak later on) is its sanitary authority. Legally speaking, the borough council acts in the double capacity of municipal council and urban sanitary authority; practically, it is one body whose powers come from various sources. There are at present some 300 municipal boroughs in England and Wales; consequently some 300 sanitary districts and sanitary authorities already provided for.[1] The Local Government Act of 1894 makes practically no change in the case of the urban sanitary district which coincides with a borough, except, perhaps, that it will be more correct in the future to speak of "urban district" than of "urban sanitary district," and that it will be lawful to *describe* a town council, when acting in its sanitary capacity, as an "urban district council." But it will not be lawful to alter the "style or title of the corporation or council of a borough."

(β) An *Improvement Act District*, *i.e.*, an area constituted, prior to the passing of the Public Health Act, 1875, as a separate sanitary district,

[1] This statement is not strictly true. When a borough, at the passing of the Public Health Act, 1875, lay wholly within a larger urban sanitary district, the authority of the larger district is continued. Thus Oxford, Cambridge, Blandford, Calne, Wenlock, Folkestone, and Newport (Isle of Wight) are within larger urban sanitary districts. This rule appears to reduce the actual number of borough sanitary districts to 292. (Report of Local Government Board, 1892-3, Appendix P., p. 490).

by virtue of a local Improvement Act, and not since transformed into a borough or a Local Board District. Here the sanitary authority is the local *Improvement Commissioners*, appointed in manner provided by the local Act, and charged with the duty of carrying out its provisions. Quite naturally, these provisions differ in various cases, but as only thirty-four Improvement Act Districts remain, and as their distinctive constitutions will be swept away when the Local Government Act of 1894 comes into force, it is hardly worth while dealing with them in detail. Examples of existing Improvement Act Districts are Lytham, Fleetwood, Birkdale, Downham Market, Hove, Llandudno, and Maryport.

(γ) A *Local Board District*, *i.e.*, an area, other than a borough, constituted as an urban sanitary district by the Local Government Board (which has succeeded to the functions formerly exercised by the Board of Public Health), under the provisions of some *general* Act of Parliament, such as the Public Health Act, 1875, or its predecessors. Here the sanitary authority is a *Local Board of Health*, consisting of a number of members fixed by the Local Government Board (but always divisible by three), elected by thirds in each year, and serving for three years. A member of a Local Board of Health must, at the present time, be qualified by residence within seven miles of the District, *and* by the possession of property or by the payment of rates within the District to an amount varying with the population of the District.[1] Apparently there is no disqualification on account of sex, or on any other ground than existing insolvency; but a member of a Local Board who absents himself from the meetings for six months (unless in case of illness), or accepts paid office under the Board, or has an interest in a contract with the Board, thereby loses his seat. The Local Board is elected by the registered owners and ratepayers of the District (not necessarily resident), who vote in accordance with the amount of property owned or occupied by them in the District, on a scale which rises from one to six votes.[2] The District may be divided into wards for election purposes, and, if there is a contest, the poll is taken by means of open voting papers left at the houses of the voters, and collected by the returning officer's messengers. Local Board Districts may be united under *Joint Boards* for administrative purposes. In the year ending Lady Day, 1891, there appear to have been 682 Local Boards and thirty-three Joint Boards in England and Wales.[3]

[1] The exact figures are—in districts containing less than 20,000 inhabitants, £500 (realty or personalty), or £15 rating; in larger districts, £1000 ownership, £30 rating.
[2] Both for ownership and occupation property rated at less than £50 confers one vote, and each additional £50 an additional vote. Six is the limit for ownership or occupation; but electors who are both owners and *bonâ fide* occupants may vote in both capacities. Apparently the possessor of six votes may give six each to as many candidates as there are vacancies, but not twelve to one candidate.
[3] Report of Local Government Board, 1892-3, Appendix P., p. 490.

Changes by the Act of 1894.

No property qualification.

See *ante*, p. 38.
Election by parochial electors.

Triennial office.

The Local Government Act of 1894 aims at providing an uniform scheme of constitution for all urban sanitary authorities *other than borough councils*. Every such authority is to be an "urban district council," and to consist wholly of elective councillors, who are either parochial electors of some parish within the District or who have *resided* in the District for the whole twelve months preceding their election. No property qualification whatever will be required, and neither sex nor marriage will disqualify; but the same disqualifications which apply to the parish councillor will apply to the district councillor. Urban district councillors will be elected by the parochial electors of their district, or, if the district is divided into wards, of their ward, and each elector will have one vote and no more for each vacancy. The urban district councillor will hold his office for three years, and, generally speaking, the councillors will retire by thirds in each year; but upon a resolution passed by two-thirds of the members of an urban council present at a meeting, the county council may order that all the district councillors shall go out of office together in every third year. Finally, it must be remembered that the fact of being within an urban district (borough or otherwise) constitutes a parish an "urban parish," and, generally speaking, excludes it from those provisions of the new Local Government Act which relate specially to parishes.

(2) *A Rural Sanitary District* may at the present time be defined as the area of any Poor Law Union which is wholly outside the boundaries of all urban sanitary districts, or, in the case of a Poor Law Union partly coincident with an urban sanitary district or districts that part of it which is outside

## THE SANITARY AND HIGHWAY DISTRICTS 105

such district or districts. The sanitary authority in a rural sanitary district is the Board of Guardians of the Union with which it is identical or in which it lies. But the *ex-officio* member of a Board of Guardians, who is resident in an urban parish of the Union, is not entitled to act in sanitary matters for the Union, unless he has property in a rural parish of the Union, which would qualify him as elective Guardian therefor; and an elective Guardian who represents an urban parish cannot act at all for the Union in sanitary matters.

The Local Government Act of 1894 does not make much change in this state of affairs. The rural sanitary authority will henceforward be known as a "rural district council," and its district as a "rural district." There will be no *ex-officio* members of the council, and all property qualifications will cease. But the identity of the rural district with the rural area of a Poor Law Union will be preserved, and likewise the identity between the rural Guardians and the rural district councillors. In point of fact the rules relating to the election, qualification, term of office, and retirement of a Guardian of the Poor, will apply equally to the rural district councillor, and, *in rural parishes*, the Guardians will be elected as district councillors and not as Guardians. Only, it is presumed that when a Board of Guardians is acting as a sanitary authority, those of its members who represent urban parishes will retire, although it seems clear that the "additional" Guardians (if any) elected by the Board itself will take part in the proceedings of the rural district council.

*The scheme of 1894.*

See *ante*, p. 89.

See *ante*, p. 91.

Powers of sanitary authorities.

So much for the constitution of ordinary urban and rural sanitary districts and their respective authorities. Reserving the special "Port" Districts for the end of the chapter, we come now to the powers exercised by sanitary authorities. It would be, of course, a hopeless attempt to aim in this place at anything like a complete statement of the vast powers exercised by local authorities in sanitary matters. All that can be done is to enumerate a few of the more important heads of their jurisdiction, taking first the objects for which local powers exist, and, subsequently, the machinery by which they are exercised. We must be careful to bear in mind that the urban authority possesses a good many powers which cannot be exercised by a rural authority.[1]

Urban.

(a) *Roads.*—For some years the urban sanitary authority has been the exclusive local authority in the matter of maintaining and making highways within its district. It may agree to take over private roads, either from turnpike trustees or from private owners, and all streets within an urban district which are repairable by the inhabitants at large vest *ipso facto* in the urban authority.

Rural.

Hitherto, however, the rural sanitary authority has not *necessarily* had any jurisdiction in highway matters. The rural highways not falling under the care of the parish or the county, and not being the subject of Turnpike Trusts, have been administered by **Highway Boards** formed under the provisions of the Highways

[1] But it must be also remembered that upon the application of a rural sanitary authority *or* of the ratepayers representing one-tenth in value of the rateable property of the district, the Local Government Board *may* confer any one or more of the special powers of an urban authority upon a rural authority.

## THE SANITARY AND HIGHWAY DISTRICTS 107

Acts, 1862 and 1864. These statutes empowered the county authorities to combine parishes into **Highway Districts**, governed by Highway Boards, consisting of the resident Justices of the Peace and of "waywardens" annually elected by the inhabitants in vestry assembled of the constituent parishes. The Highway Board has its own treasurer, clerk, and district surveyor, and is entitled to impose a *Highway Rate*, payable by the overseers of the constituent parishes upon precept of the Board. It may, moreover, with the approval of the Local Government Board, raise money by way of loan upon the security of its rates. At present there are, apparently, 360 of such Highway Boards in England and Wales. Waywardens.

But there has for some time been an evident desire on the part of the legislature to get rid of the Highway Board as a separate body. By a significant provision of the Highways Act of 1878, it was enacted that county authorities, when forming or altering a Highway District, should, so far as possible, follow the lines of the rural sanitary districts; and, by another section of the same statute, it was provided that, upon the application of a rural sanitary authority whose area was identical with that of a Highway District, the sanitary authority might be constituted the highway authority for the district, and the separate Highway Board be extinguished. Under these provisions, forty-one rural sanitary authorities have taken over the powers of Highway Boards, and the Guardians of the Union have in these cases become the highway authority. Disappearance of the Highway Board.<br>The Act 1878.

The Local Government Act of 1894 puts the finishing stroke to this policy. By its provisions the The Act 1894.

rural district council will in every case take over the powers not only of the Highway Board,[1] but of any other highway authority within its district, and will, moreover, acquire all the powers previously stated as belonging to the urban sanitary authority in the matter of the management, making, and taking over of highways.[2] Further than this, it will be the special duty of both urban and rural district councils to protect all public rights of way, and prevent encroachments upon, or obstructions to, all roads situated in or serving their districts, and being within the limits of their county. But, with regard to the newly conferred highway powers, it is expressly provided that the operation of the statute may be deferred by a county council in any part of their county for a period of three years, and even (with the consent of the Local Government Board) for a longer period. It is, therefore, still necessary to know the outlines of the existing system. But, subject to this reservation, we may say that when the new Local Government Act comes into operation, the sanitary authority, urban and rural, will be, saving the jurisdiction of the county (of which more hereafter), the sole authority in the matter of public roads within its district.

(β) *Sewers.*—For upwards of four hundred years the English legislature has dealt with the subject of sewers; but we must not therefore suppose that

---

[1] It is expressly provided that "highway boards shall cease to exist." (Sec. 25).

[2] Apparently the roads will not become the property of the rural district council, for the powers conferred by the new Act do not include that section (149) of the Public Health Act, which vests the urban highways in the urban authority.

sanitary legislation has had so long a history. Until the close of the eighteenth century, a sewer was simply a ditch or cutting containing nothing worse than fen water; and the various "Commissions of Sewers" which have from time to time been created, were merely concerned with the reclamation or (as it was called) "inning" of marsh and fen lands, and the maintaining of them against the encroachments of the sea. The cesspool and the midden were almost the only sanitary contrivances, and the notion of the sewer, as of a pipe or channel to carry away the impurities of domestic existence, is as modern as the Public Health Acts themselves. But, broadly speaking, one may now lay it down that all sewers and drains[1] within any sanitary district,—except those constructed by private persons or companies for their own profit, irrigation channels made and used for draining land under a special Act of Parliament, and sewers under the control of Commissioners of Sewers,—belong to and are managed by the sanitary authority. The same authority enforces the provision and proper management of privy accommodation in all inhabited buildings,[2] and an urban authority (but not, apparently,

[1] A "drain" appears, for Local Government purposes, to be a pipe or channel used merely to communicate between a single building or block of buildings, and a general receptacle for sewage matter; a "sewer" includes all channels for the carrying off of refuse except "drains," and except pipes under the control of a special road authority. "Main drain" would therefore appear to be an incorrect expression.

[2] Including factories and workshops. But the special provisions of the Factory Acts, with regard to overtime, employment of women and children, and the like, are not enforced by the sanitary authority, but by inspectors directly appointed by the Local Government Board.

a rural) is entitled to provide urinals and other accommodation for the use of the public. The sanitary authority may (and if ordered by the Local Government Board, must), either by its own servants or through contractors, undertake the removal of refuse from houses, and the cleansing of ashpits and privies in its district, and construct proper sewage works for the disposal of such refuse matter. Moreover, the sanitary authority, in making new sewers, may carry them through any land laid out as a street, and even (if necessary) through strictly private land. Every owner or occupier of premises is entitled to drain into the sewers belonging to the sanitary authority of his district, subject to the observance of proper conditions; but there are various statutory regulations to prevent occupiers turning into sewers any matter likely to cause an obstruction, or any chemical refuse, or even hot water, which is likely to create a nuisance. The sanitary authority itself is not permitted to foul a natural stream by allowing the escape into it of sewage matter.

(γ) *Infectious Diseases.* — The Local Government Board has power, by virtue of various statutes, to make regulations for preventing the spread of epidemic, endemic, or infectious disease, and in particular, to order such steps as the speedy interment of dead bodies, the visitation and inspection of houses believed to contain persons suffering from contagious diseases, the provision of hospitals and other medical attendance for relief purposes. Upon the sanitary authority is cast the duty of enforcing such regulations. But, even in the absence of special regulations applying to its district, a sanitary authority may provide itself with hospitals and medical officers for the reception and treatment of any sickness. Moreover, it may enforce the disinfection of houses and conveyances which have been occupied by persons suffering from infectious disease; and may provide mortuaries and places for *post mortem* accommodation. It may call upon any Registrar of deaths to supply it with information as to the particulars of any death registered by him. And where the sanitary authority has expressly adopted the provisions of recent legislation,[1] it will have even wider powers of compelling heads of households and medical practitioners to notify its officers of the existence of any cases of infectious disease in their families or practices, of inspecting and controlling dairies suspected to be the source of disease, of ordering the disinfection of houses, bedding, and clothing, and of making temporary provision for the shelter of persons who have been compelled to leave their homes for purposes of disinfection. Under the head of infectious disease, we may also refer to the important powers possessed by the officers of a sanitary authority to inspect and examine at all reasonable times any meat, vegetables, milk, fruit, flour, and the like, exposed or prepared for sale, and to obtain from a Justice of the Peace an order for the destruction of such of it as shall prove to be unfit for human food. Similar powers exist under the Adulteration Acts in cases in which the articles in question are not necessarily in-

Food inspection.

Adulteration.

[1] The Infectious Disease (Notification) Act, 1889, and the Infectious Disease (Prevention) Act, 1890. The provisions of the Acts are *ipso facto* in force in London; elsewhere they require special adoption.

jurious to health, but are so different from their apparent character as to constitute a fraud upon the public.

(δ) *Water Supply.*—Every rural sanitary authority *must* see that there is a due supply of water to every house within its district, and, if necessary, provide such a supply at the expense of the owner, unless the cost would exceed a sum which, at 5 per cent., would produce twopence a week. An urban sanitary authority *may*, unless there is in existence a public company authorised by Act of Parliament which is able and willing to supply the district at a reasonable cost, provide or contract for the supply of water, and may charge water rents or rates upon the occupiers of the houses supplied. Moreover, the obligation resting upon a rural authority in the matter of water supply may be imposed also upon any urban authority by the Local Government Board, and this obligation includes the duty of periodically inspecting the condition of the supply. Any sanitary authority whose water is fouled by any person, has the remedies belonging to an ordinary waterworks company under the "Waterworks Clauses Acts," and the sanitary authority may enforce the provisions of the Rivers Pollution Prevention Act, and other statutes intended to prohibit the fouling of running water by sewage, rubbish, and other nuisances.[1]

(ε) *Housing of the Working Classes.*—A great consolidating statute of the year 1890 has collected together the scattered provisions of the law upon the various sub-

---

[1] Concurrent jurisdiction now belongs to the county council by virtue of the Local Government Act, 1888. But the power of the sanitary authority is not taken away.

## THE SANITARY AND HIGHWAY DISTRICTS 113

jects included under this head. The general result may be said to be that the sanitary authority is in every case the body entrusted with the execution of the provisions of the statute applicable to its area. But the powers of urban and rural authorities are not the same.

It is the duty of every sanitary authority to inspect its district periodically with a view to the discovery of houses unfit for human inhabitation, and upon such discovery or upon representation by their medical officer of health, or by four inhabitant householders, and upon due proof of the facts, to order the house in question to be closed, and ultimately, if the defects are not remedied, to be demolished. Even though a building is not in itself unfit for human habitation, if it prevents due ventilation, or otherwise causes or prevents the removal of a nuisance in other buildings, the sanitary authority may compel the owner to sell to it both the building in question and its site for purposes of demolition, unless the owner chooses to retain the site, in which case he gets compensation only for the demolished building. In the case of the insanitary house the owner who executes improvements to the satisfaction of the sanitary authority merely gets a charge upon the property to the extent of his outlay as against other persons interested. Where buildings have been demolished, or are about to be demolished, the sanitary authority may, with the approval of the Local Government Board, and after enquiry held, take up a scheme for reconstruction and re-arrangement of the area in question. If a *rural* or Metropolitan sanitary authority declines to pull down an unhealthy or obstructive building after

<small>Insanitary houses.</small>

<small>Obstructive buildings.</small>

due representation, the county council in whose county the district is may order it to do so, and, in the event of further neglect, may itself do the work at the expense of the sanitary authority. But this rule does not extend to the undertaking of a scheme of reconstruction, nor does it, apparently, affect the ordinary *urban* authority.

Unhealthy areas.

Furthermore, any *urban* sanitary authority may, if satisfied that any part of its district constitutes an "unhealthy area," that is, an area so unhealthy that its defects cannot be remedied otherwise than by a comprehensive scheme of improvement, including rearrangement and reconstruction of streets and houses, adopt a scheme accordingly, and, having given notice of the fact to every owner or occupier affected, and advertised the existence of the scheme, may apply to the Local Government Board for a provisional order confirming the same. The Local Government Board, if satisfied that the preliminaries have been duly complied with, may hold an enquiry, and, being satisfied of the soundness of the scheme, may make an order accordingly, which, upon being confirmed by Act of Parliament, will be carried out by the sanitary authority.

Working-class lodging-houses.

See *post*, p. 117.

Finally, any sanitary authority which adopts Part III. of the Housing of the Working Classes Act, may purchase or build working-class lodging-houses, and manage them according to regulations made under the general conditions affecting local sanitary legislation. But no *rural* sanitary authority can adopt Part III. without the consent of its county council, and before the expiry of a certain time after that consent has been given. The provisions in Part III. are, however, in addition to and not in derogation of the duties imposed upon *every* sanitary authority by the Public Health Act of 1875, with respect to the registration, management, and inspection of all common lodging-houses kept by private persons within its district. Even houses of a superior class let in private lodgings may be placed by the Local Government Board partially under the control of a sanitary authority.

*Common lodging-houses.*

(§) *Recreation and general public convenience.*—Under this somewhat elastic description we may class a miscellaneous group of powers, exerciseable, generally speaking, only by an *urban* sanitary authority, and which aims at providing something more than the bare necessaries of civic life. For example, an urban sanitary authority may acquire, either by purchase, gift, or hire, public walks and pleasure grounds, and may even contribute to the expense of maintaining such places though they belong to private individuals. It may fix up clocks in conspicuous places, plant trees in public roads, provide boats to be used in a place of public recreation, and erect baths and wash-houses for public use.[1] The statues and monuments in any street or public place within its district are under its control, and it may authorise the erection of new ones. It shares to some extent with the Justices the duty of protecting the public against danger from defects in places of public entertainment. It may (under certain conditions) provide and manage public markets.

Finally, a special word must be given to the new powers conferred upon the sanitary authority by the Local Govern-

*Certain powers of Justice transferred to sanitary authorities.*

[1] In rural districts the power to provide public baths and wash-houses may be acquired by the parish council.

ment Act of 1894. They have been before incidentally referred to, but it is well also to state them directly. All sanitary authorities will, then, after the coming into operation of the new Act, take over the powers at present exercised by the Justices of the Peace *out of session* in respect to the licensing of gangmasters, dealers in game, passage brokers, and emigrant runners, and the granting of pawnbrokers' certificates, the abolition and alteration of the days for holding fairs, and the execution of the Acts relating to petroleum and infant life protection.[1] They will also acquire the powers of Quarter Sessions with respect to the licensing of knackers' yards. And by an important, though not very generally known section of the new Act, the Local Government Board will have power, on the application of any *urban* council outside the Metropolis, to confer on that council, *or any other representative body within the district*, any of the powers, duties, and liabilities of a parish council, including the important power of appointing overseers, and of appointing and dismissing assistant overseers. If this section of the Act is used to any extent, it will go far to remove the differences which will otherwise exist between the urban and the rural parish, for, at least outside boroughs, the urban sanitary district is often coincident in area with a parish.

<small>Power to confer rural powers on urban parishes.</small>

We have now spoken of the objects for which sanitary authorities exist. It remains to say a few words of the machinery by which they seek to accomplish these objects.

---

[1] It is difficult to say shortly what is done by magistrates in and out of sessions respectively in regard to these matters. Perhaps it may be accepted that, as a rule, the grant of a licence is made in sessions, but that revocation or endorsement may be ordered by magistrates out of sessions.

# THE SANITARY AND HIGHWAY DISTRICTS 117

This machinery may be considered under the three heads of legislation, officials, and finance.

*Legislation.*—A sanitary authority has a general power (within defined limits) of enacting local legislation for the purpose of enabling it to fulfil the objects of its existence. Such legislation may take the name of *by-laws* or of *regulations*, according to its nature, and, although the differences between these two methods of local legislation are not great, they have some distinctive characteristics of their own.

(a) *By-laws* may perhaps be defined as the normal type of local sanitary legislation, the form adopted by the authority which is acting upon its general powers. By-laws are, practically, the statutes or general rules laid down by a local authority [1] for the guidance of its subjects, just as Acts of Parliament are the great means by which the central authority controls the conduct of its subjects. No by-law must, of course, conflict with "the laws of England," *i.e.*, with the law recognised by the courts of the central authority, and this rather elastic rule practically gives the central authority a fairly tight grip upon the vagaries of local legislation.[2] And, particularly, the sanitary by-law must, both in letter and spirit, conform to the provisions of the great statute from which the bulk of sanitary powers are derived, the Public Health Act of 1875. But beyond this, the latitude allowed to sanitary

[1] It is said that the term by-law is derived from the Danish word *by* (township or hamlet), so often found as the termination of place-names (Whitby, Ferriby, &c.). The by-law, if this derivation be correct, is the law of the *by* or town.

[2] The central courts have long established their right to quash a by-law for "unreasonableness," consequently a litigant must always be prepared to defend the validity of a by-law upon which he relies.

authorities is, in theory, considerable. Only, every sanitary by-law requires confirmation by the central government, generally by the Local Government Board, occasionally by the Board of Trade,[1] and public notice of intention to apply for such confirmation must be given. Moreover, every by-law must, so far as possible, when made, be brought to the notice of the public. In particular, every by-law of a sanitary authority must be printed and hung up in its office, and a copy given to every ratepayer who applies for it, while every *rural* sanitary authority must send copies of its by-laws to the overseers of its constituent parishes, to be deposited among the parish records. Moreover, all by-laws must be authenticated by the common seal of the authority which makes them,[2] and no sanitary by-law can impose a penalty of more than £5 for a single offence, or, in the case of continuing offences, a further penalty of 40s. for each day during which the offence is continued.

(β) *Regulations* may be defined as being special rules made by a sanitary authority by virtue of particular powers conferred upon it, and applicable only to a limited area or class of people within its jurisdiction. Thus, when a new street is being built, an urban sanitary authority may prescribe the line of frontage to be followed by those who build houses in the street; any sanitary authority may make regulations for the use of its own *post-mortem* rooms, or for the perfor-

---

[1] *E.g.*, in the matter of telegraph wires.
[2] But a copy of such by-laws, certified by the clerk to the authority, is evidence in all legal proceedings until its genuineness is disproved.

mance of their duties by its own officials. Such regulations do not primarily affect the general public, and do not (as a rule [1]) require the sanction of the Local Government Board, nor the official publication demanded of a by-law.

*Officials.*—There are some officials which every sanitary authority must appoint, others which an urban authority must appoint, but which a rural authority need not, and others whose employment is optional with either class of authority. The chief officials of a sanitary authority are—

(i.) *The Chairman.*—The rules as to the election of chairman, both in urban and rural sanitary authorities, are in the main untouched by the new Local Government Act. And as, according to the existing law, the chairman of a Local Board is elected annually under the provisions of the Public Health Act, and the chairman of the Guardians for a similar period by virtue of the Order of the late Poor Law Commissioners, it is presumed that the chairman of the ordinary urban or rural district council will continue to be so elected. The Local Government Act of 1894 indeed expressly provides that neither sex nor marriage shall disqualify for election, and it is therefore quite possible that we shall have chairwomen of district councils as well as chairmen. But whereas every chairman of a district council will be *ex-officio* a Justice of the Peace for the county within which his district is situated, a chairwoman will enjoy no such privilege. The mayor of

---

[1] But regulations compelling the removal to a particular hospital of foreign patients arriving in the district by water, require the approval of the Local Government Board.

a borough will of course continue to be the chairman for all purposes of the borough council; and we must remember that a *rural* council may elect its chairman from outside its own body. Every urban council (not being a borough council) and every rural council may appoint a vice-chairman, and in the case of the rural council, the vice-chairman may also be imported from outside.

(ii.) *The Medical Officer of Health*, who is an essential official of every sanitary authority, though he need not be specially appointed by the authority if he is already acting in the district for some other body. He must be a legally qualified medical practitioner, and his special qualifications are now prescribed by statute, while the Local Government Board may to some extent define the manner in which his duties are to be discharged.

(iii.) *The Inspector of Nuisances*, likewise, is essential both to the urban and the rural authority, but the functions of medical officer and inspector of nuisances may be combined in one person.

(iv.) *The Surveyor*, whose appointment is only incumbent on the urban authority, and even here the same person may unite the offices of surveyor and inspector of nuisances.

(v.) *The Clerk*, who is specially appointed only by an urban sanitary authority which is not also a borough council. In the case of the rural authority the person who acts as clerk to the Guardians acts also as clerk to the sanitary authority, and may receive an extra allowance on that account. In the case of the borough, the Town Clerk is clerk of the council for all purposes.

## THE SANITARY AND HIGHWAY DISTRICTS

(vi.) *The Treasurer*, who, similarly, is specially appointed only for the non-borough urban sanitary district, the treasurer of the Guardians, as in the case of the clerk, acting in a double capacity. It is, however, specially provided that no one individual may in any way, wholly or partially, combine the duties of clerk and treasurer of a sanitary authority.

But beyond these officers, every sanitary authority has power to employ such officials, expert or clerical, as shall be necessary in its particular circumstances; and some sanitary authorities, whose districts are densely populated, are obliged to maintain a most elaborate and costly staff. To all sanitary officials certain rules apply. No official may directly or indirectly be concerned in any contract made with his authority. Every official entrusted with money must give security for his honesty, and must account, whenever called upon, for all moneys received by him. Any officer failing in his duty in this respect is liable to severe punishment on summary conviction, in addition to his ordinary civil liabilities. One feature of special importance in the position of the sanitary official is that he may be (and generally is) entrusted with the personal duty of enforcing, as representative of his authority, the various provisions of the law upon the subject of sanitation. Inasmuch as there is now an express statutory duty upon every local authority to exercise the powers conferred upon it in such a manner as to secure the proper sanitary condition of all premises within its district, the duties of the sanitary official have lately become increasingly onerous. Unless the law otherwise specially provides, all sanitary offences must be prosecuted within six months of their commission, and the tribunal which enforces the complaints of sanitary

Other sanitary officials.

Must not be interested in sanitary contracts.
Must give security.
And must account.
Executive duties.

Prosecution of sanitary offences.

officials is a court of summary jurisdiction, consisting of at least two Justices of the Peace sitting in Petty Sessions, or of a stipendiary magistrate. There is, however, an appeal to Quarter Sessions, which may, if it thinks fit, state a case for the opinion of a superior court. A sweeping protection, of a kind very rare in English law, exempts the members of a sanitary authority and their officials from personal liability for acts *bonâ fide* done in the execution of their public duties and with the sanction of their respective authorities ; and all proceedings against a sanitary authority, its members, or officials, must be commenced within six months of the happening of the act or default complained of, while due opportunity must be given for the tender of amends.[1]

*Protection to members of sanitary authorities.*

*Finance.*—The subject of sanitary finance is complicated by the differences between the constitution of the urban and the rural sanitary district. For whilst the urban district is as a rule a single or consolidated area, the rural district is a composition of more or less disconnected units, whose separate individuality, especially in the matter of finance, has always to be reckoned with. Nevertheless it is possible, with care, to treat the subject of sanitary finance as a whole. The income (using the word in its largest sense) which a sanitary authority may possibly receive is derived from five sources—

*Income of sanitary authority.*

(i.) *Property.*—Rents of land and houses, market and
    bridge tolls, harbour dues, water and gas rents,
    may be regarded either in the light of income from
    investments or as cash equivalents for work and

---

[1] The rule as to time of commencing proceedings and allowing tender of amends has been very recently extended to all public authorities by the Public Authorities Protection Act, 1893.

## THE SANITARY AND HIGHWAY DISTRICTS 123

labour done. It is but rarely, of course, that any sanitary authority except a borough council owns invested property to a large extent; but a few parishes have land devoted specially to the maintenance of highways, and this will (indirectly) become the property of rural councils under the new Act, while any sanitary authority may be allowed by the Local Government Board to retain permanently any land which it has been obliged to acquire for sanitary purposes, even though it may no longer be actually needed for such objects.

(ii.) *Subsidies.*—Until the institution of county councils it had long been the practice for the central government to assist local authorities by direct treasury subventions towards the maintenance of roads, lunatic asylums, sanitary officials, teachers in poor law schools, registrars of births and deaths;[1] and the practice, though there are objections to be urged against it, is likely to continue in some form. One of its great merits is that it enables the central government to maintain the standard of local administration by laying down conditions of efficiency as the basis of grant. For the future, however, the subventions to the local authorities will not come (except in the case of county councils themselves) directly from the treasury, but through the county councils to whom the "local taxation grant" is now, as will be seen in a later chapter, payable by virtue of the provisions of the Local Government Act of 1888. See *post*, p. 164.

---

[1] Many of these sums are payable to Poor Law Guardians, rather as Guardians than as sanitary authorities, but it is difficult to separate the two functions.

The sums actually received by the non-metropolitan sanitary authorities (other than boroughs) under this head during the year 1890-1 amounted to upwards of £170,000.

(iii.) *Penalties.*—The fines inflicted by the courts of summary jurisdiction for ordinary sanitary offences, as well as those larger sums which in the case of certain graver offences are directly recoverable as debts by the sanitary authorities,[1] are, after payment of the informer's share where a private person brings the matter to light, payable into the general funds of the sanitary authority.

(iv.) *Loans.*—Where a sanitary authority deems it necessary to undertake works of permanent utility, for the expense of which its ordinary income is insufficient, or which it is obvious ought in fairness to be at least partly paid for by future ratepayers, it may, but always with the sanction of the Local Government Board, borrow, either from private individuals by the issue of debenture stock or certificates, or from the Public Works Loan Commissioners, such sums as may be necessary to effect the desired improvements. The money so borrowed will be repayable by instalments at dates agreed upon (with the sanction of the Local Government Board) between the sanitary authority and its creditors, and are, in the meantime, a charge upon the rates. But no loan

---

[1] *E.g.*, if any person deliberately fouls any public water with gas washings, he incurs a penalty of £200 for the first offence, and £20 a day during its continuance, and these penalties may be directly recovered in any of the superior courts by the sanitary authority or the person primarily injured.

## THE SANITARY AND HIGHWAY DISTRICTS 125

may extend over a longer period than sixty years, and the total unsecured indebtedness of a sanitary authority must not exceed two years' assessable value of the district.[1] A sanitary authority may, however, mortgage its sewage land or plant in much the same way as an ordinary owner of property, and up to three-fourths of the cost of such works the money borrowed upon them will not be counted in reckoning the unsecured debt of the authority. The extent to which sanitary authorities have availed themselves of their borrowing powers may be gathered from the fact that at the close of the financial year 1890-1 their total outstanding indebtedness exceeded one hundred millions sterling, which sum did not include the debts of metropolitan sanitary authorities.[2]

(v.) *Rates.* — Finally, any sums required by a sanitary authority, after all its other sources of income have been exhausted, must inevitably be obtained from the ratepayers of its district. This rule holds for urban and rural authorities alike, but the methods employed by the two classes of authority differ considerably.

In the case of the urban authority the sums required are assessed and levied directly by the authority either as a *General District Rate* or as a *Private Improvement Rate*. The expenses included in the General District Rate comprise all those expenses incurred by an urban sanitary authority

[Urban sanitary rates.]

---
[1] A loan which would bring the total debt above *one* year's value of the district must not be sanctioned by the Local Government Board before it has held a local enquiry.
[2] Report of Local Government Board, 1892-3. Appendix P., p. 511.

126     ENGLISH LOCAL GOVERNMENT

<small>Does not require allowance of Justices.</small>

which are not, either by established custom or the express provisions of some statute, payable out of a special fund. The General District Rate is assessed and levied by the urban authority upon the basis of the poor rate, and is published, both before and after making, in much the same way as the poor rate. But the allowance of the Justices is not required for any rate made by an urban authority, and the sums due from the ratepayers are collected by the agents of the sanitary authority, not by the overseers. As in the case of poor rates, the General District Rate is primarily payable by occupiers, but provisions somewhat similar to those which affect the poor rate enable the sanitary authority to rate the owner instead of the occupier of premises which are either of small value or are let on short tenancies or in apartments. But a very important section of the Public Health Act provides that the owners of tithes, and the occupiers of lands used exclusively for agricultural, pastoral, or horticultural purposes, or as a canal towing path, or as a public railway,[1] shall be assessed for sanitary rates only to the extent of one-fourth of the net annual value of their properties, on the ground, presumably, that sanitary improvements are chiefly for the benefit of occupiers of dwelling-houses. A General District Rate may be made for the purpose of covering expenses incurred or to be incurred; but in the former case the liability must have arisen within six months before the making of the rate.

<small>Partial exemption of agricultural land.</small>

---

[1] Recent statutes have included orchards and allotment gardens in the partially exempted list.

## THE SANITARY AND HIGHWAY DISTRICTS 127

*A private Improvement Rate* is a rate imposed upon the occupier or (if there be none) upon the owner of premises in respect of which the expenses which the rate is designed to meet have been specially incurred.[1] But an occupier who holds at rack rent is entitled to deduct from the amount payable to his landlord three-quarters of the amount paid by him on account of private improvement rate, and an occupant who holds at less than a rack or full rent may make a proportionate deduction. The private Improvement Rate may be payable by instalments, and it remains a charge upon the premises until it is paid off; but it may be redeemed at any time by the owner or occupier.

A rural sanitary authority has no direct power, except in the case of private improvement rates, as to which it stands in the same position as an urban authority, to make and levy its own rates. The sums which an urban authority would raise by direct levy, the rural authority obtains by means of precepts directed to the overseers of the "contributory places" within its district, *i.e.*, to the separate parishes of which it is composed, or to the special drainage districts formed within its area by the rural authority itself with the sanction of the Local Government Board. But the expenses of a rural sanitary authority (other than private improvement expenses) are divided by the Public Health Act into two classes of "general" and special rates.

Rural sanitary rates.

General and special rates.

---

[1] A common example of a private Improvement Rate occurs when a new street of houses is built upon what was formerly a field, and the owners of the houses do not properly make the roadway, which is thereupon completed by the sanitary authority, at the expense of the owners.

"special," the former including the cost of establishment and officials, of disinfection, and the conveyance of infected persons, and, in fact, all other expenses not expressly directed to be charged in some particular area. General expenses are paid out of a "common fund" raised equally from each contributory place in proportion to its assessable value. Special expenses are a separate charge on the contributory place in respect of which they are incurred, and every precept directed by the rural authority to the overseers of a contributory place must specify whether the sum demanded is on account of general or special expenses. The sums demanded of the overseers in respect of general expenses are paid by them out of the poor rate of their parish; and the sums demanded in respect of special expenses are raised by the overseers by the levy of a separate rate in the same way as a poor rate, except that the rule previously mentioned, exempting the occupiers of non-residential land from three-quarters of their assessable value, is observed in the levy of a separate rural rate.[1]

Finally, it may be observed that the accounts of every urban sanitary authority, not being a borough council, and of every rural authority, are audited annually by an officer of the Local Government Board.

*The Port Sanitary District.*

Although for the purposes of the Public Health Act with respect to nuisances, infectious diseases, and hospitals, any

[1] An appeal lies to the Court of Quarter Sessions against the making of any sanitary rate. In rural parishes the parish council will henceforth be entitled to appeal.

## THE SANITARY AND HIGHWAY DISTRICTS 129

ship lying in waters within the district of an ordinary sanitary authority is deemed to be within the jurisdiction of that authority, yet the peculiarities of port towns frequently require a special method of treatment, more particularly where, as is usually the case with river ports, the town is subject to two distinct sanitary jurisdictions. In order to obtain this special treatment, the Local Government Board may provisionally [1] or even (if there is no opposition) finally order that the area of any port recognised as such by the Customs Acts shall constitute a separate *Port Sanitary District*, to be governed in manner provided by the Order. But in selecting its port sanitary authority, the Local Government Board must choose either an existing sanitary authority whose district abuts on the port, or must make a port sanitary authority by a combination of two or more such riparian authorities. The port sanitary authority thus created may exercise within its district such of the powers of the Public Health Act as are assigned to it by the order of constitution; but no port sanitary authority can, in that capacity, directly raise any revenue. If it is already a sanitary authority, it can raise within its own district such parts of its expenses as are fairly chargeable to it in respect of its interest in the port; but for the shares of the other parts of the port area, it must resort to the sanitary authorities within whose districts those parts happen to lie, and such authorities must respond to the claim. If they do not, the amounts claimed can be recovered from them as debts. Under the provisions of the Public Health Act there are at present constituted 58 port sanitary authorities, 10 temporary, 48 permanent. The port of London is under the control of the Corporation of the city.

[1] A provisional Order requires confirmation by Parliament.

I

GROUP C.

# THE COUNTY.

10. & 11. THE PARLIAMENTARY, JUDICIAL,
 AND MILITARY COUNTY . . . CHAPTER IX.

12. THE ADMINISTRATIVE COUNTY . . CHAPTER X.

13. THE JOINT COMMITTEE . . . CHAPTER XI.

# CHAPTER IX

## THE SHIRE OR COUNTY—PARLIAMENTARY, MILITARY, AND JUDICIAL

THE terms "county" and "shire," though now almost synonymous, have not by any means the same history. Shire (*scir*) appears to be an Anglo-Saxon (or at least Teutonic) word, originally used to signify any district or jurisdiction under the control of a special or distinctive authority, possibly with a notion of subdivision from a larger unit. Thus a bishop's diocese is called his "scir"; the hundreds of Cornwall were at one time known as "shires"; at the time of Domesday there were seven "shires," that of the archbishop and six others, within the city of York. Distinct traces of this vague use of the term survive in the purely nominal shires of the present day—Hexhamshire, Hallamshire, Richmondshire, Allertonshire.

Gradually, however, the word shire became peculiarly appropriated to the district ruled by an earl or ealdorman, or, as he was called by the Latin-writing chroniclers and clerks, the *comes* or count; and, before the Norman Conquest, the existing English counties had for the most part made their appearance. The actual origins of these differ considerably; one thing only we may assert with tolerable confidence, that their boundaries were not fixed arbitrarily, in the way that a modern colony is mapped out, nor even

*County and shire.*

by natural geographical features, though these may have been remotely connected with their original formation. Thus, some of our existing counties (Sussex and Essex, for example) represent heptarchic kingdoms, kingdoms of the south and east Saxons. Dorsetshire, Wiltshire, and Somersetshire are probably ancient tribal settlements, which once had an independent or semi-independent existence. Yorkshire and Cheshire stand for the territories governed from great Roman cities, and show the difference between the Roman and the Teutonic methods of colonisation. Durham is the patrimony of the great Cathedral of St Cuthbert, and long maintained its peculiar individuality.

Even before the Norman Conquest, too, the county had acquired a peculiarly *royal* character. No doubt the shire moot or county court was, to a certain extent, a popular institution ; no doubt the historic background of the shire tended to keep alive strong feelings of independence. But the earl or count, though probably designated by local popularity or claims of blood, was formally appointed by the Witan of the kingdom, in which the royal influence was great, and the sheriff (*shire-reeve*), whose growing importance is one of the special features of late Anglo-Saxon history, was a purely royal official.

The Norman policy added powerfully to the existing tendency. The great idea of the greatest Norman kings— the Conqueror, his son Henry, and (so far as he can be called a Norman) Henry II.—was to make the county court the great engine for bringing the native population into conscious touch with the royal government. To the great ecclesiastics and landowners licence of exemption from attendance at other local gatherings was freely granted ; but from the half-yearly county court, where the sheriff proclaimed the king's dues, and the royal judges administered the king's justice, no one was allowed to absent himself. The great landowners and ecclesiastics came in person, the villagers were represented by their reeve and four men. Edward I., the great organiser of English political life, did but strengthen still further the tendency when he added to the duties of the county court the election of knights of the shire to serve in the newly-created Parliament. His grandson, when he brought into existence his Justices of the Peace, added yet another storey to the edifice of royal county administration; and the Tudor monarchs, who built up a new county aristocracy on the ruins of the plundered church, to replace the old feudal families which had gone to pieces in the Wars of the Roses, put the coping stone upon the great political fabric. From Tudor times to our own, the Justice of the Peace, who is above all things a royal county official, has been the great governmental factor in the life of rural England. Lancashire and the other northern counties were definitely arranged soon after the Conquest; six of the Welsh counties emerged from the conquest of Wales by Edward I.; the remaining six and the border county of Monmouth were formed by the Parliament of Henry VIII. By the middle of the sixteenth century the tale of the counties was complete, and though survivals of old palatine privileges have lingered to our own time, for upwards of four centuries the county system has been, in the main, uniform and definite. Oddly enough, the race of kings which did most for the county, abolished the count. The count or earlbecomes, after the Conquest, a mere titular grandee, with a pension out of the revenues of the county from which he takes his title. The sheriff is in

*The Planta-genets.*

*The Tudors.*

*Complet of count system.*

name *vice-comes* or earl's deputy, but practically he is an official of the royal Exchequer. Presently, he too sinks into comparative insignificance, and the king's travelling judges and his resident Justices rule the county in the king's name.

The county has at the present day at least four distinct political aspects—parliamentary, military, judicial, administrative. The first is foreign to our present purpose, and may be briefly dismissed. The second and third may be treated together. The fourth, by reason of recent legislative changes, will require separate handling.

### A.—*The Parliamentary County.*

This, as we have said, is the creation of Edward I., or of the politicians whose ideas he borrowed. It is no part of this enquiry to deal with the subject of Parliament, the great organ of central government. It is sufficient to say that the idea of a Parliament representing the local units of counties and boroughs seems to have grown out of the troubles of the Barons' War, and to have been definitely realised by Edward I. or his ministers at the close of the thirteenth century. When the scheme appears in its complete form, it is found that the national Parliament is a collection of lay and ecclesiastical grandees, and of elected deputies from counties, boroughs, and dioceses. In theory it is so still; but the clerical deputies have practically disappeared, and the lay deputies, though still retaining the names of county and borough members, are no longer elected by Quarter Sessions or even County Council, still less by burgesses acting as such. The sheriff is still returning officer for the county, and the mayor for the borough;[1] but each member of Parliament is member for a mere geographical area which may or may not coincide with a local government district, and the distinction between county and borough member tends rapidly to disappear. According to the Census Returns there are now fifty-seven Parliamentary counties for England and Wales, viz., the fifty-two traditional or (as they have been well called) "geography book" counties,[2] two extra for the "ridings" of Yorkshire, and three extra for the "districts" of Lancashire; but a reference to the Redistribution of Seats Act, 1885, the statutory authority on the subject, apparently discloses only forty-five. It may be mentioned that the Local Government Act of 1888 has transferred the powers formerly exercised by the county justices in the matter of Parliamentary polling and registration arrangements to the new county councils. Further than this it is not necessary to go.

B.—*The Military and Judicial County.*

From time immemorial the constitutional defensive force of the country, the *fyrd* or militia, has been a county force. An ancient theory, pertinaciously adhered to, laid it down that while every freeman was bound, if need were, to serve the state in arms, his service could not be demanded beyond the limits of his own county, at least unless the safety of his county was threatened from without. In ancient days the county militia was led by the earl in

The ancient militia system.

[1] As a matter of fact it is only during the present century that the mayor has acquired the position of returning officer. For centuries the sheriff acted for the boroughs in his county.
[2] Maitland, *Justice and Police*, p. 112, n. 1.

138 ENGLISH LOCAL GOVERNMENT

person; when the local earldoms disappeared, the sheriff took his place as leader of the county force. But when, after the chaos of the Wars of the Roses, the Tudors set about the re-organisation of the militia, they determined to create new officials of greater social dignity than the sheriff to command the county forces. Hence we begin our list of county officials with—

(1.) **The (Lord) Lieutenant**,[1] who is recognised as a normal official of the county by a statute of the year 1559, but whose duties are now mainly regulated by the Militia Act of 1882. By the latter statute the Lieutenant is deprived of almost all authority in connection with the militia, except the power of recommending candidates for a *first* commission to Her Majesty's notice, and the power of conducting any ballot which may be necessary to fill a deficiency in voluntary enlistment. In other respects the militia is under the control of the War Office, in the same way as the professional army. In spite, however, of this diminution of his authority, the Lieutenant may still appoint *deputy-lieutenants*, in fact must appoint twenty, if so many there be duly qualified in his county. This is almost like saying that, the Lieutenant having nothing to do, must appoint twenty people to help him to do it. And, in fact, the office of deputy-lieutenant is more ornamental than important. It is reserved for peers or heirs apparent of peers having a place of residence within the county for which they are appointed, and for persons possessing a life interest at least in property within the United Kingdom producing £200 a-year, or the heirs apparent of such persons. The Lieutenant must not finally grant the commission of his deputy until he hears that the latter is "not

Deputy-lieutenants.

[1] The " Lord " is a mere courtesy addition not officially recognised.

disapproved by Her Majesty." And Her Majesty may signify to any Lieutenant Her pleasure that any of his deputy-lieutenants be dismissed. On the other hand, Her Majesty may appoint any three deputy-lieutenants of the county to act in the place of the Lieutenant during his absence, and the Lieutenant himself may, with Her Majesty's approbation, appoint any deputy-lieutenant to act as *vice-lieutenant* during his own inability to act.   Vice-lieutenant.

But, besides his military position, the Lieutenant occupies important posts in the county as head of the *Commission of the Peace* and *Custos Rotulorum*. In the former capacity he has the right to recommend to Her Majesty the names of candidates for the office of Justice of the Peace; in the latter he is officially entrusted with the care of the county archives. The position of *custos rotulorum* is often spoken of as identical with that of Lieutenant, but as a matter of theory it is quite distinct, having been in existence long before the Lieutenancy was created. It was as *custos* and not as Lieutenant that the official head of the county formerly appointed the clerk of the peace.

(2.) **The Sheriff**, an official whose exact origin it is impossible to trace, was at an early date, as we have said, the special permanent representative of royalty within the county. At first, perhaps, he was merely a local taxgatherer, who collected the gifts of food and other produce due to the king by immemorial custom—a relic of the days when the king was entitled to be entertained by his subjects in his royal progresses, and long surviving in the vexed claim of *purveyance*. But as the power of royalty increased, the power of the sheriff increased with it. He held the *tourn* or *view of frankpledge*, for inspection of the police system of the Hundred invented or re-organised by   Increase of sheriff's power.

Edgar. He administered the vast estates which, by the great confiscations of the Conquest, had become the *demesnes* (or direct property) of the Crown. He ferreted out and enforced the growing feudal claims of the Crown to treasure-trove, wrecks, strays, deodands,[1] royal fish, and the like. He exacted the fines for breaches of the king's peace, and the other penalties imposed by the new criminal jurisdiction of the king's courts. For all these receipts he accounted twice a year at the king's Exchequer, and his accounts and reports were the means by which the king kept himself informed of the state of the country. As the feudal system hardened, and the claims of the Crown as lord paramount to wardships of heirs, to escheats and forfeitures, to fines for leave to sell, and the like, became a chief part of the royal revenue, it was the sheriff who reported to the Exchequer officials the windfalls which chance had brought in their way. As the Saxon ealdorman disappeared, the sheriff took his place as marshal and leader of the county militia. But, most of all, as the criminal jurisdiction of the Crown ousted the old popular system of wer-gilds[2] and purgation oaths, the sheriff became, not merely an administrative official, but a criminal judge, who tried the pleas of the Crown, as well as presided in the popular court of the shire. The middle of the twelfth century may be regarded as the culminating point of the

*Accounts at the Exchequer.*

*Acts as criminal judge.*

---

[1] A *deodand* (a thing to be given to the gods) is the instrument by which homicide (wilful or accidental) is committed—the axe which wounds a man, the arrow which pierces his heart. Heathen piety devoted it to the gods; royal reforms secured it for the Crown. The deodand only disappeared in 1846.

[2] A *wer-gild* was a payment in the nature of compensation for a wrong committed. Its great importance in the history of law is that it is almost the first successful step in the supersession of the blood feud.

sheriff's history. He was then, indeed, as has been well said, a "resident provincial viceroy," a king in his own county. What he could become was shown, even so late as the early thirteenth century, by the career of the turbulent Falkes de Breauté, the sheriff of six midland counties, who, during the minority of Henry III., set at nought the authority of Hubert de Burgh, Regent of the kingdom, and actually imprisoned the king's judges in Bedford Castle. It is hardly too much to say that, up to the close of the twelfth century, the history of the sheriff is the history of central government.[1] {Falkes de Breauté.}

The outbreak of Falkes de Breauté was, however, a mere spasmodic revival of anarchy, due to the bad reign of John and the weakness of his successor. The death-blow to the sovereignty of the sheriff had been dealt by the second Henry, who would tolerate no rival in power. Even before his day the itinerant judges of his grandfather had created a powerful counter-influence to the sheriff's authority, but the famous enquiry held by Henry II. in 1170, and the policy which followed upon it, are the real turning-points in the history of the sheriff. From that time the decline of the sheriff begins. He ceases to be a prosecutor of offenders against the king's law; that duty is handed over to a local jury. By the Great Charter he is roundly forbidden to hold any pleas of the Crown. He ceases to be a criminal judge, he sinks into the position of an executive official. The change was vital, not only to the history of the sheriff, but to the history of England. Another reign such as that of Stephen, and England would have been covered with {Decline and fall of the sheriff.} {Inquest of the sheriffs.}

[1] A list of the sheriff's iniquities may be read in the articles of the enquiry of 1170, printed in Stubbs' *Select Charters and other Illustrations of English Constitutional History.*

hereditary sheriffs of the Gascon type, defying royal authority, bent upon petty local independence, only to be crushed at last by an absolutism like that of Louis XI. From this fate England was saved by the reforms of Henry Fitz-Empress.

*Fall of the sheriff.* The decline of the sheriff continued. Such shadow of judicial power as he possessed at the close of the thirteenth century disappeared before the new Justices of the Peace created by Edward III. The growth of direct Parliamentary taxation deprived his fiscal position of much of its importance, and although, as Parliamentary returning officer, he had opportunity for a good deal of quiet misbehaviour, his illegality was no longer open and avowed. Finally, the creation of County Lieutenants by the Tudors deprived him of his duties as leader of the county militia, and left him, as he now is, the shadow of a great name, a splendid wreck.

It seems almost an insult to say that the position and duties of an official with such a history are regulated by the provisions of a mere modern statute. Yet such is the case. *The Sheriffs Act.* The Sheriffs Act of 1887, which repealed, wholly or in part, some eighty previous enactments, is our main source of information concerning the present position of the sheriff. There is a sheriff for each of the fifty-two traditional counties of England and Wales, except that Cambridge and Huntingdon may be united in one Shrievalty. It is said that there once was a woman sheriff of Westmoreland,[1] but

[1] The Shrievalty of Westmoreland was long an anomaly. From the reign of John to 1849 it was hereditary in the family of the Veteriponts, sometime Earls of Thanet. In 1849 the male line became extinct, but the last male holder of the office endeavoured to devise it by will. This attempt, however, was defeated, and the appointment of sheriff placed on a normal footing by a statute of the year 1850.

the precedent has not been repeated for many years, and judicial opinion is inclined to hold that a woman cannot be appointed sheriff. Every sheriff (save the sheriff of Lancaster and the sheriff of Cornwall[1]) is appointed— "pricked" is the correct term—by Her Majesty in person, on the nomination of a court which sits every year on the 12th November at the Royal Courts of Justice. This court, in theory the mere creation of a modern statute, is one of the most interesting survivals in English history. It consists of the Lord Chancellor, the Chancellor of the Exchequer (representing the vanished Lord Treasurer), the President "and others" of the Privy Council, and the Chief Justice, or any two of these persons, assisted by two judges of the High Court. This apparently arbitrary collection of great personages is really a desperate attempt (thoroughly characteristic of English law) to reproduce the old Royal Exchequer of the twelfth century, where the sheriffs laid their accounts before the royal revenue officials after the manner of a game of draughts ("chequers"), upon a cloth marked out into squares by rods, where little heaps of money represented counters in a game. The old court of Exchequer has gone, even its colourless substitute, the "Exchequer Division" has disappeared, and no more Exchequer "barons" will be created. But the intense tenacity of official conservatism is marked by the fact that, when possible, one of the seats allotted to the "two judges of the High Court" at the nomination of sheriffs, is always

*Pricking of sheriffs.*

*The nominating Court.*

[1] Till the year 1888 the Corporation of London, by immemorial custom, elected the sheriff of Middlesex. Really, the two sheriffs of London acted as the sheriff of Middlesex. This little anomaly escaped the besom of the Act of 1887, but was swept away by the Local Government Act of 1888.

occupied by the learned judge who is now affectionately termed the "last of the Barons."

*Office compulsory.* Service in the office of sheriff is compulsory upon any one who cannot plead a legal exemption, but a man who has once served must not be chosen again within three years if there are other suitable persons in the county. No one may be appointed sheriff unless he "have sufficient land within his county to answer the Queen and her people," *i.e.*, to be responsible for any damages which may be awarded against him for neglect of duty. Apparently there is no other positive qualification; but an officer of the regular forces on the active list is incapable of serving, and a militia officer, whilst actually on duty, may execute the office through his under-sheriff.

*Duties of the sheriff.* At the present day the sheriff may be described as the chief executive official of the superior courts, civil and criminal, and as still, to some extent, an agent of the *Arrest.* Treasury. In the former capacity he arrests, either with or without warrant, any person suspected to have committed a felony, and every person in the county must be prepared, *Keeping the Assize Courts.* if called upon, to assist him in so doing.[1] When the assizes are being held, the sheriff is responsible for the maintenance of order in the court, unless the Quarter Sessions has specially committed the duty to the police. *Jurors.* The sheriff prepares the "panel" or list of jurors, taken from the jury lists already prepared, and sees that sufficient *Execution.* jurors are in attendance. The sheriff also executes the judgment of the superior court, whether criminal or civil, either by enforcing the sentence of death or imprisonment,

---

[1] The inhabitants so assisting are known as the *posse comitatus*, and it is express modern law that, for default of being "ready and apparelled" to assist the sheriff, any person may be fined.

PARLIAMENTARY, ETC., COUNTY 145

by levying fines, by selling goods under "execution," or, in the rare cases in which a committal order is made against a man for a civil debt, by arresting the body of the debtor. The sheriff also may have to hold an "inquest" for the assessment of damages under a judgment of a superior court,[1] or under the statutes giving compensation to a man whose land is wanted for public improvements, but he is expressly forbidden to hold any inquest whereby any one is indicted. *Inquiry as to damages.*

As a revenue official, the sheriff collects debts which are due to the Crown under recognisances, fines, bonds, and other instruments. As a rule, the Crown has the privilege of enforcing its claims in a summary way, without the formality of an action. This course is never adopted where there is any reasonable doubt as to the amount owing; but there rarely is any such doubt, and the Crown, after "forfeiting" or "estreating" the bonds or recognisances, simply directs its officer to collect the amount due. In theory there is still a "ferm of the shire,"[2] or rather a shire revenue (for the sheriff is expressly forbidden to let his county "to ferm," and he never receives it to ferm); and *Crown debts.*

---

[1] Thus, if there is an undefended case in which the plaintiff claims "unliquidated," *i.e.*, non-specific damages, the court may give judgment generally for the plaintiff, and direct an enquiry to ascertain the amount of damages. The defendant may appear before the sheriff and give evidence in mitigation of damages, but he may not dispute the correctness of the judgment.

[2] In the Middle Ages the practice of commuting a number of miscellaneous liabilities of uncertain value for a fixed amount (*firma*) was very common, and the sheriff generally accounted for the normal receipts of his office at a fixed sum, known as the "ferm of the shire." The practice was the origin of our modern word "farmer"—*i.e.*, the man who pays a fixed rent, as opposed to the bailiff who accounts for the balance of income and outgoings in detail.

K

## 146 ENGLISH LOCAL GOVERNMENT

Accounts. the accounts thereof are to be presented for audit at the Treasury within two months after the expiry of the sheriff's office.

Sheriff's liability. The most unpleasant part of the sheriff's position is that he is personally liable for mistakes committed either by himself *or by his officials*, in the performance of his office. One section of the Sheriffs Act is so thoroughly characteristic of what we have called the "common-law" character of our local government, that it may be quoted in full. "A person unlawfully imprisoned by a sheriff or any of his officers shall have an action against such sheriff in like manner as against any other person that should imprison Wrongful him without warrant."[1] He is liable, not only for wrongful imprisonment. imprisonments, but for escapes of persons imprisoned in Escapes. civil actions, and for unlawful executions against property. Improper For misconduct of a positive character, he may be summarily punished by any of the superior courts. On the Allowances. other hand, the sheriff is entitled to a percentage on Crown debts collected by him,[2] and to certain fees and poundages in the course of his other duties.

As a matter of fact, the sheriff performs none except the purely ceremonial duties of his office in person, and takes none of its remuneration. Every sheriff must appoint an Under-sheriff. under-sheriff and a deputy-sheriff. The former is the local representative of the sheriff in all legal business, [3] and receives the fees and commission, giving security to the

[1] Presumably, however, the Sheriff would be entitled to the protection afforded by the Public Authorities Protection Act, 1893. (See *ante* p. 122).

[2] One shilling and sixpence in the pound up to £100, one shilling beyond.

[3] As a matter of fact, even the duties of under-sheriff may, and generally are, put out to a firm of solicitors accustomed to do them, upon

sheriff to indemnify him from all claims arising from non-performance or improper performance of official duties.[1] The latter, the sheriff's London agent, having a residence or office within three miles of the Inner Temple Hall, and receiving and answering writs. Other officials of the sheriff are bailiffs and sub-bailiffs, who do the purely ministerial work of the office.

*Deputy-sheriff.*

Finally, it may be mentioned that there are still a few exceptional "franchises" or "liberties" in which the duties normally belonging to the sheriff are vested in some other person, known as the "bailiff." In such cases the sheriff is not responsible for mistakes which occur in the execution of process; but the Sheriffs Act contains provisions by virtue of which he may obtain practical control of the machinery, and it is express law that the sheriff, with or without his *posse*, may pursue a felon within the limits of a franchise.[2]

*Franchises.*

(3.) **The Coroner** appears first in the year 1194 as part of the new machinery devised to check the power of the sheriffs; but he, unlike the sheriff, was from the first an *elective* not an appointed official, although, as his name implies, he was principally concerned with the interests of the Crown. The Great Charter includes him in the clause which prohibits the sheriffs from *holding* pleas of the Crown; but it is noteworthy that the petitioning barons, upon whose "Articles" the Charter is founded, had no wish to exclude

such terms as may be agreed between them and the real under-sheriff. The latter appears on ceremonial occasions only.

[1] It need hardly be said that this practice does not relieve the sheriff of personal liability to the public. It is merely a private arrangement between himself and his under-sheriff.

[2] So far as regards *police*, the powers of the exceptional franchises have been swept away by modern statutes.

the jurisdiction of the coroner. A statute of the year 1276 enumerates the duties of the coroner, and shows him to have been, even at that early date, a merely inquisitorial officer, having no power to award punishment. Very recent legislation has transferred the election of the coroner from the freeholders of the shire or district (for there may be more coroners than one in a county) to the members of the county council; but in many respects the coroner retains the ancient characteristics of his office. Apparently the only qualifications demanded by the law are that he be "a fit person, having land in fee sufficient in the same county whereof he may answer to all manner of people." He appears still to hold his office for life, or rather, during good behaviour, being removable by the Lord Chancellor or the convicting court, on conviction of offence in the performance of his duties. Every county coroner must appoint, in writing, a deputy, approved by the chairman of the county council which elected him, to act in case of his own incapacity.

It is the duty of a coroner to hold an enquiry or inquest by the oaths of at least twelve and not more than twenty-three good and lawful men in all cases of sudden and unaccounted for deaths where there is the least suspicion of foul play, in all cases of death in prison (whether sudden or not), and in cases of deaths in a lunatic asylum or a baby farm, unless certain medical certificates are forthcoming, and in all cases of treasure trove occurring within his district. It is said also that, by strict law, the coroner must hold an inquest in cases of housebreaking, but in practice this duty has long been neglected.

The jury finds the cause of the death, or the fact of the discovery of treasure, but the verdict need not be unanimous, provided only that twelve oaths concur. If the verdict is "murder" or "manslaughter" by any person, the coroner must apprehend the person named and commit him for trial at the next assizes. In the case of manslaughter, the coroner may, if he thinks fit, release the accused on bail.  See *post*, p. 160.

The coroner also acts as substitute for the sheriff in certain cases in which the sheriff is personally interested.

(4.) **The Justice of the Peace.** — The judicial power formerly belonging to the sheriff has now largely passed to the Justices of the Peace in their corporate capacity. Herein, possibly, lies the explanation of the fact that the Crown, after its experience of the sheriff's misdemeanours, was once more willing to entrust judicial duties to local officials. The sheriff was a single person, and could take secret counsel with himself when on evil bent; the Justice of the Peace could only act in important matters as member of a body of his fellows, and in the multitude of counsellors there lay safety—for other people.

But the Justice of the Peace was not, originally, a judicial officer at all. Historians trace the beginnings of his existence in the knights assigned by Hubert de Burgh to enforce the taking of the oath of peace proclaimed in the year 1195. Less than a century later, guardians of the peace (*custodes pacis*), one for each county, are regularly elected in the shire court, to carry out the provisions of the great statute of Winchester,[1] issued in the year 1285. But the commencement of the reign of Edward III. saw these officers turned into royal nominees, and this character they have ever since retained.  Early history of office. The peace oath. Guardians of the peace.

[1] This statute revived many of the decaying institutions of Saxon England—such as the *fyrd*, the watch, the hue and cry, &c.

Later in the same reign, the guardians of the peace are empowered by statute to hear and determine felonies; and thus, before the fourteenth century has run out, they acquire their present title of Justices of the Peace.

The career of the Justice from the days of Edward III. to our own has been one long triumph, at least if growing importance can be regarded as a test of success. Towards the end of Edward's reign came the terrible visitations of the Plague, shaking the social fabric to its very foundations. The working classes, reduced to half their former numbers by the pestilence, seized the opportunity of demanding enhanced prices for their labour. The old *régime* of lord and serf broke down; the era of free labour had come. Quite naturally, and, to some extent at least, in perfect good faith, the capitalist classes attempted by repressive legislation to check what they deemed to be the outrageous demands of the manual workers. One Statute of Labourers after another provided an elaborate system for the regulation of wages and hours of labour, and the enforcement of these statutes was invariably committed to the Justices of the Peace. Sometimes they were merely directed to enforce the scale of wages definitely fixed by statute; oftener they were entrusted with the more delicate task of "assessing" and proclaiming, at annual intervals, the limits beyond which wages, either by piece or time, might not rise. This latter policy, after vibrating backwards and forwards during the two centuries and a half immediately following the Black Death, was definitely affirmed by a great Elizabethan statute of the year 1563, and continued in practice till the middle of the eighteenth century, in theory till the beginning of the nineteenth. Not only were the Justices the authority for the assessment of wages; to them was committed all jurisdiction in disputes between master and workman.

The break up of medieval society which followed upon the Black Death ultimately led to the appearance of the great Poor Law question. We have seen in an earlier chapter how, when the statesmen of Elizabeth's reign definitely placed the administration of poor relief on the basis which it continued to occupy till the beginning of this century, they deliberately made the Justice of the Peace the corner stone of the system. The Justices appointed the parochial overseers and approved the poor rate made by them, or heard objections against it. The Justices compelled negligent parishes to do their duty, and helped the feeble parish with "rates in aid." Later on, the Justices enforced the law of settlement by ordering the removal from a parish of new-comers who seemed likely to come upon the rates. And, as we have seen, the position of the Justice in the Poor Law system remains almost untouched at the present day; although the appearance of factories and trades unions, county courts and Boards of Conciliation, have robbed him of much of his importance in industrial matters.

*The Poor Law.*

*Overseers' Poor rates.*

*Settlement and removal.*

Generally it may be said that the Justice of the Peace was, until the passing of very recent legislation, the presiding deity of that religion of parochial self-government and county administration which was initiated by the Tudors and developed by their successors. In addition to his judicial or quasi-judicial duties in criminal matters, the Justice of the Peace was the great maintainer of order, religion, and morality in his neighbourhood. He enforced the statutes for uniformity of worship, hunted out dissenters,

*Enforcement of morality.*

licensed alehouses, repressed profanity and disorderliness, prohibited Sunday trading and the like. It is the custom for poets and novelists to speak of the squire as though he were, *quâ* squire, the " God Almighty of the country side." This is a mistake. Since the disappearance of feudal rights in the Wars of the Roses, the mere landowner has had no other advantages than those which wealth and social status could give him. It was as Justice of the Peace and not as squire that he reigned. Let him but be obnoxious to the Government, let him be excluded from the Commission of the Peace, and his power was gone. The governing caste in English country life since the Reformation has not been a feudal but an *official* caste. The first great blow struck at the position of the squire has not been an attempt to deprive him of his acres. It has been a great shearing away of the powers of the Justice of the Peace. Let us see what is left.

The Justice of the Peace is now appointed by the Crown, upon the advice of the Lord Chancellor,[1] and the recommendation of the (Lord) Lieutenant, who is himself the head of the Commission of the Peace for the county. Various suggestions have been made as to the motives which do, or should, influence the Lieutenant in his recommendations; but they are foreign to our purpose. Only it is to be observed that no one can be appointed a Justice for any county unless he have an income of £100 a year in possession, or £300 in expectancy[2] from freehold, copyhold, or long leasehold property within the county, or

[1] In the palatine counties the advice is tendered to Her Majesty by the chancellor of the duchy.
[2] That is, of course, legally secured expectancy, not merely anticipation.

unless he have occupied for two years previously to his appointment a dwelling-house within the county, in respect of which he is duly rated and taxed, and which is assessed to Inhabited House Duty at £100 per annum. But peers, privy councillors, judges, law officers, and eldest sons of peers do not require any special property qualifications; nor are such qualifications demanded of persons who are by virtue of their offices Justices of the Peace, a notable example being the chairmen of district councils. There is still a theory that the Justice of the Peace must be resident in his county, but in practice the rule is disregarded. In theory, also, the county Justice can claim four shillings a day for attendance at sessions; in practice he does not, any more than the Member of Parliament, claim his wages. He holds office simply "during pleasure"; and can be struck off the roll by Her Majesty at any time, without reason assigned. We use the masculine pronoun throughout our description of the Justice, and rightly, for no woman can be a Justice of the Peace. Neither can a man found guilty of corrupt practices at elections, a person who is an uncertificated [1] bankrupt, nor a solicitor practising in the county; and a sheriff, during his year of office, may not act as a Justice, though his name remains on the commission. *Residence.*

Formerly there was a highly appreciated distinction between Justices *of the Quorum* and not of the Quorum, as witness the well-known scene in Sheridan's *Scheming Lieutenant*. For in days when the education of a country *Quorum.*

---

[1] The mere fact of *discharge* from a bankruptcy does not remove the disqualification, unless the bankrupt has received a *certificate* exonerating him from personal blame. But a disqualification by bankruptcy only lasts for five years from discharge.

Justice was apt to be peculiar rather than extensive, it was the habit of the Crown officers, in framing the Latin Commission of the Peace (the authority for the execution of his office by the county Justice), to draw a line between those simpler duties which any Justice was thought capable of performing, and those more difficult functions which required the handling of the more skilled. More especially was this the case when the duty in question required the presence of more than one Justice (as most of the heavier duties did). The Commission then, in conferring the performance of such duty upon "you or any two of you," would add, "of whom" (*quorum*) "X, Y, Z," &c., "shall be one." The persons thus flatteringly distinguished held their heads a shade higher than their less honoured brethren at Quarter Sessions, and much jealousy was the result. As the education of Justices (or, perhaps one should say, of Justices' clerks) has improved, the practice has fallen into abeyance; though, again with the famous conservatism of English law, the tradition is kept up by the omission of *one* unfortunate name from the list of the favoured Quorum.

Of the multitude of duties which still fall to the lot of the Justice of the Peace, it will only be possible to give the barest outline. They can be most conveniently treated of under two heads—those which are performed in Sessions, and those which are performed out of Sessions. Inasmuch as we have already discussed the position of the Justice when acting in Petty (or Special) Sessions, we can here confine our remarks on Sessions to the great Quarter (or General) Sessions of the Peace for the county.

**Quarter Sessions.**—By a statute of the year 1362, it is provided that all Commissions of the Peace shall expressly direct the Justices to "make their Sessions four times by the year," viz., at Epiphany, Lent, Pentecost, and Michaelmas; and from that day to this, the Quarter Sessions has been an established institution of English county life. Strictly speaking, there should be sixty courts of county Quarter Sessions in England; for the three ridings of Yorkshire and the three "Parts" of Lincolnshire, the *soke* or liberty of Peterborough, the Isle of Ely, and the two divisions of East and West Sussex, have each a separate Commission of the Peace and Court of Quarter Sessions, while Suffolk, though having but a single Commission of the Peace, has two Courts of Quarter Sessions.[1] Nevertheless, the unity of the traditional county was, until lately, preserved in the special *Gaol Sessions* which were held every year in the divided counties, and at which the Justices of all the Divisions attended to exercise jurisdiction in the matter of the maintenance and due regulation of the county gaol and house of correction, as well as the reformatories and industrial schools. But a statute of the year 1877 has transferred the control of prisons and houses of correction to the Secretary of State, and the Local Government Act of 1888 has handed over to the county councils the management of reformatory and industrial schools; so that Gaol Sessions are no longer necessary. Gaol Sessions.

Since the Local Government Act of 1888 has expressly taken away from the Justices in Quarter Sessions the greater part of the vast administrative duties which they formerly exercised, the main bulk of Quarter Sessions work has become of a judicial character. Nevertheless, in spite of Quarter Sessions work.

---

[1] On the other hand, Hampshire appears to have two Commissions of the Peace (one for the Isle of Wight), but only one Court of Quarter Sessions.

the Act, some administrative duties remain, and will require a word of reference.

But first, let it be premised that the Court of Quarter Sessions, consisting as it does of all those Justices for the county who choose to attend, is often a numerous body, incapable of conducting proceedings in an orderly manner without some organisation. Accordingly it elects a *chairman*, usually some one having special legal knowledge, who acts as president and mouthpiece of the Court. But the decisions of the Court are the decisions of the majority of its members, even where, as in Middlesex, the chairman is a professional judge, appointed by the Crown, and paid by the County Council.

The judicial business of the Quarter Sessions falls into two great branches, which require separate treatment. These branches may be defined as *original* and *appellate*.

(i.) The *original* or *primary* jurisdiction of the Court is chiefly concerned with the trial of those crimes which are deemed too serious for disposal by a court of summary jurisdiction, but not serious enough imperatively to demand trial by a judge of assize.[1] " Indictable offences not specially reserved for the assizes," we may term them. It is a theory of English law that no offence can be tried by Quarter Sessions unless there be express statutory authority for the practice. As a matter of fact, the statutes which confer general jurisdiction upon Quarter Sessions are so wide in their terms that the Justices try all indictable offences

---

[1] Presumably, an assize judge has a perfect right, if he pleases, to try all criminals awaiting trial by a court of high criminal jurisdiction; but prosecutors and prisoners have no longer the right to insist on a trial before a judge of assize of offences triable at Quarter Sessions.

PARLIAMENTARY, ETC., COUNTY 157

except those which are expressly reserved by statute for the assizes.[1] These offences are treason, capital felony, felonies punishable with penal servitude for life on a first conviction (such as manslaughter, arson, burglary), also perjury, bribery, bigamy, forgery,[2] and many others.

Offences properly triable at Quarter Sessions are tried in very much the same way as offences tried at assizes. The accusation is (in the majority of cases) first examined by the "grand" or accusing jury, who find a "true bill," or "throw out the bill" accordingly as they believe or do not believe, after reading the evidence taken before the committing magistrates, that there is a reasonable probability of conviction. If the grand jury find a true bill, the prisoner is then tried by a petty jury, the magistrates, that is, virtually, the chairman, acting as judge and pronouncing sentence in accordance with the finding of the jury.[3]

[1] Principally by a statute of the year 1842.
[2] Some forgeries are punishable with penal servitude on a first conviction, but others are not.
[3] It seems almost necessary to say a word about the duty of the citizen to serve on juries. The matter is now regulated mainly by two statutes, of the years 1825 and 1870. In counties, all male persons between the ages of twenty-one and sixty, having £10 a year in freehold or copyhold lands, or £20 in leaseholds above twenty-one years, all householders assessed to poor rate or inhabited house duty at £20, or who occupy a house of not less than fifteen windows, are qualified and bound to serve on all petty juries in trials held by superior courts, and on both grand and petty juries in sessions cases tried in the county where they reside. In boroughs all the burgesses are qualified and liable to serve both on grand and petty juries. Qualifications in Middlesex and London are slightly higher. "Special" jurors (for civil cases) must be either esquires, bankers, or merchants, or persons of higher degree, or occupants of premises of value varying with the place in which they are

158     ENGLISH LOCAL GOVERNMENT

Appellate. (ii.) The *appellate* jurisdiction of Quarter Sessions is perhaps equally important with its primary jurisdiction. Generally speaking, there lies an appeal to Quarter Sessions from every order of a court of summary jurisdiction which inflicts a sentence of imprisonment, as well as from many other magisterial decisions. Appeals also lie from orders allowing rates or approving valuation lists, and in these cases, too, the appeal lies to Quarter Sessions. Appeals to Quarter Sessions are in the nature of rehearings, and the appellant is entitled (subject to certain provisions as to giving notice) to deal with matters of fact as well as of law. The Court of Quarter Sessions may reverse or amend the order appealed from, and award costs. In fact, an appeal to Quarter Sessions is a strong illustration of the truth that the Petty Sessional Court is really only a local committee of the county Justices, whose proceedings may be varied in any way by the full body. Beyond Quarter Sessions there is no direct appeal; but the Sessions may voluntarily state a case on a point of law for the opinion of a superior court, or the latter may itself order the court of Quarter Sessions to do so. When sitting as a court of appeal the Quarter Sessions acts without a jury.

Administrative work of Quarter Sessions.
The administrative side of Quarter Sessions has, ad- situated. County Court jurors are taken from the ordinary jurors' book, but there is a limit to the number of times they may be called upon to serve. Jurors at an ordinary coroner's inquest require no special qualification. There are numerous exemptions from the duty of serving, *e.g.*, barristers, conveyancers, solicitors, medical practitioners in actual practice, clergymen and Nonconformist ministers, peers, members of Parliament, &c. Burgesses of a borough which has its own Quarter Sessions are not liable to serve at Quarter Sessions for the county.

PARLIAMENTARY, ETC., COUNTY  159

mittedly, been robbed of the bulk of its importance by the Local Government Act of 1888. Still, Quarter Sessions has certain administrative work to do. It appoints a "county licensing committee" from amongst its own members, a committee without whose approval no *new* liquor licence is good. It appoints another committee to visit and inspect the county gaol and to bring any abuses found there to the notice of the Secretary of State, as well as to carry out the regulations laid down by the latter for the conduct of prisoners and the prison. It appoints a third committee to carry out the provisions of the Lunacy Act, 1890, with respect to non-pauper lunatic asylums. By a curious irony it was the body entrusted with the marking out of the electoral divisions for the first elections under that scheme which did so much to diminish its own importance—the County Councils scheme of 1888. And, although its powers in relation to Parliamentary election matters have been transferred to its new rival, it is presumed that Quarter Sessions still retains the right of marking out its county into Petty Sessional divisions. But the financial duties of Quarter Sessions, once so important, have now absolutely gone.

*[margin: Licensing Committees. Prison Visiting Committee. Asylums Inspection Committee.]*

**Single Justices.**—The duties which a Justice of the Peace may be called upon to perform out of Sessions are still very numerous and important, though they are tending, perhaps, to diminish. Strictly speaking, all the preliminary enquiry which we have previously described as preceding the committal for trial of an alleged offender, though it usually takes place at Petty Sessions, may be done by a single Justice sitting in his own parlour. And the very fact that so much of this preliminary work goes to Petty Sessions, has rendered the duty of the single magistrate with regard to one important subject more critical than

160   ENGLISH LOCAL GOVERNMENT

Bail.

ever. This is the subject of *bail*. The law of England is rightly tender of the liberty of the subject, and refuses to allow a man to be detained in prison, even for a few days, merely because he happens to be charged with some offence. The rules on the subject of *Habeas Corpus* are familiar, at least in outline, to most Englishmen, but the Habeas Corpus procedure requires the interference of a superior judge, and, in the vast majority of cases, the procedure by simple application for bail is quicker and cheaper. The Justice (in some cases the mere police-officer) before whom an alleged offender is brought, at any time before his actual trial, may (in some cases must) allow him to go at large on bail, that is, upon the undertaking of certain sureties to pay a sum named if he is not forthcoming when wanted. The law upon the subject of the right to bail is very simple. When a man is charged with treason, no magistrate may grant bail without an order of a Secretary of State or the Queen's Bench Division. When the charge is of felony, or some one of about a dozen specified misdemeanours,[1] the magistrate may grant or refuse bail according to his discretion. In all other cases of alleged misdemeanours, the magistrate *must* grant bail, even though he be perfectly aware that the accused is contemplating flight to America. But he may fix the sum to be given as security at a pretty high figure, the only restraint on his power being the somewhat vague declaration of the Bill of Rights, "that excessive bail ought not to be re-

[1] The distinction between *felony* and *misdemeanour* is arbitrary, and can only be found by reference to law books. Formerly every conviction for felony involved forfeiture of the offender's goods. Almost all the more serious offences are felonies; but sometimes the line is very arbitrarily drawn. Forgery is a felony, perjury is not.

PARLIAMENTARY, ETC., COUNTY 161

quired." And he may enquire sharply into the solvency of the proffered sureties. Moreover, the surety may lay forcible hands on the accused if he be evidently attempting an escape; for, in legal theory, the body of the accused has been *bailed*, *i.e.*, handed over to him—the accused is, in fact, his bondsman.

Also, the single Justice issues warrants to arrest alleged offenders, to compel the attendance of witnesses, and to search suspected places. Various statutory declarations or assertions may be made before him, and he may even administer oaths in matters within his own jurisdiction. He is the authority in the matters of billeting and impressment of carriages for military purposes under the Army Act, 1881. He is entitled, notwithstanding the transfer of prisons to the Secretary of State, to visit and inspect the prisons within his county. In the matter of his ancient and original duty, the keeping of the peace, he is still the first resort of the law-abiding citizen; we see him reading the Riot Act before the sterner hand of the central Government takes up the reins of authority. Although the control of the county police as a whole is now vested, as we shall see, in a newly created body, the single Justice is still entitled to command the allegiance of the individual constable, and the latter is quite safe in acting upon the Justice's warrant, unless it is manifestly illegal.

By reason, no doubt, of the facts that he is practically an unremunerated official, and that he is, in the majority of cases, not a professional lawyer, the Justice of the Peace enjoys a special protection somewhat anomalous in English law. No action may be brought against a Justice on the mere ground that he has wrongly exercised a discretion given him by statute; in order to succeed, the plaintiff

L

must prove that the Justice acted *maliciously and without probable cause*. No action at all will lie against a Justice for an act which he was ordered by a superior court to do, nor for the granting of a warrant of arrest or distress, where the grant has been confirmed on appeal. Even where the plaintiff alleges the doing by a Justice of a wholly illegal act, he must wait until the act has been formally quashed by a superior authority before bringing his action. And yet he must, as must all persons bringing actions against public authorities, bring his action within six months after the doing of the act complained of, or from the ceasing of the damage which accrued therefrom— for in all cases the plaintiff must prove actual damage— and he must give the offending Justice opportunity of tendering amends. If he does not, he is liable to be condemned in costs.

We may conclude our account of the judicial county with a brief word concerning—

(5.) **The Clerk of the Peace**, whose statutory history reaches back to the middle of the sixteenth century, and who was formerly appointed (apparently during pleasure only) by the Lieutenant of the county in his capacity of *custos rotulorum*. It was his duty to take charge of all documents belonging to the county, amongst others, papers deposited pursuant to Standing Orders of Parliament or the Lands Clauses Consolidation Acts, the warrants of the appointment of sheriffs of his county, the accounts of public water-works, and so on. Moreover, he set in motion the machinery for filling up the lists of county jurors and voters, and kept the lists when completed. Further than this, he was not only the mouthpiece of the county for business purposes, its agent in legal proceedings, and the

Custody of documents.

Jurors' and voters' lists.

registrar of its Quarter Sessions; but the property of the county was deemed to be legally vested in him. But the Local Government Act of 1888 has transferred his appointment to the Joint Committee of Quarter Sessions and County Council, his salary is paid by the County Council, and in the latter is now vested all the property of the county save certain ornamental possessions such as portraits. The Clerk of the Peace is expressly disqualified from acting as clerk to any bench of Justices for a division of his county.

*Trustee of county property.*

# CHAPTER X

### THE ADMINISTRATIVE COUNTY

THE administrative county, as a separate unit of local government, is the creation of the Local Government Act, 1888, a statute which had for its obvious (though not avowed) object, the transfer of county business from Quarter Sessions to elective councils.

The division of England and Wales into administrative counties is supposed to follow the boundaries of the parliamentary counties, except that, for purposes of coordination with judicial boundaries, there are additional administrative counties for Suffolk and Sussex, the Isle of Ely, and the soke of Peterborough, making sixty in all, or, with the addition of the Metropolitan area, which ranks as a separate administrative county, sixty-one.

In each administrative county there is an elective **county council**, consisting of such a number of persons as the Local Government Board directs. Each county is divided for election purposes into two classes of constituencies — boroughs and county divisions,[1] but each

---

[1] The number of combinations now possible with the name "county" is apt to be rather bewildering. A "county division" under the Act of 1888 must be distinguished from a "county district" under the Act of 1894, and yet the county division is, so far as possible, to follow the lines of the county district. The "county at large" appears to be the "geography-book county"; the "entire county" is much the same

borough which, in the allotment of seats, is entitled on the basis of population to more than one member, must be sub-divided into as many "wards" or "electoral divisions" as there are members, so that there may be one member and no more for each ward or electoral division. In the boroughs the sub-divisions follow the lines of the municipal wards, and the county divisions those of the county districts (*i.e.*, sanitary districts), and where it is necessary to sub-divide a county district, the boundaries of parishes are, where possible, followed.

The electors to the County Council are likewise divided into two classes, corresponding with the distinction between boroughs and county divisions. In the borough constituencies the electors will be the burgesses enrolled under the Municipal Corporations Act of 1882 as electors to the borough council; in the county divisions, persons who, if their place of abode or occupation were a borough, would be qualified to be enrolled as burgesses, together with £10 occupiers of property within the division. We need not here discuss the nature of burgess qualification — that will come later on. But it may be said generally, that under the Local Government Act of 1888, all persons who have for twelve months occupied rated premises within a borough or parish (as the case may be), who have paid their rates, and who have resided within seven miles of their borough or parish, are, if registered on their borough or parish roll of electors, entitled to vote at County Council elections. The only general disquali- *Local Government electors.*

*Disqualifications.*

thing, but the expression is only used of a county at large in which there are more than one administrative county. The expression "division of a county" appears to be reserved for the older institutions, such as hundred, lathe, wapentake, &c.

fications appear to be infancy, alienage, and receipt of poor relief. It must, however, be remembered, that the burgesses of certain large boroughs, known as "county boroughs," will take no part in elections for the county council of their "county at large"; their borough being for most purposes independent of the council for the county at large, being, in fact, almost an administrative county in itself.

See *post*, p. 228.

Besides the elective councillors, the County Council contains "county aldermen" and a chairman. The aldermen, one-third in number of the ordinary councillors,[1] are elected by them for six years, but retire by halves, so that there is an election of aldermen every three years. The chairman is elected annually by the whole council. The ordinary councillors are elected for three years, and retire together. Chairman and aldermen may be chosen either from among the existing councillors, or from other persons qualified to be councillors. But whereas the election as alderman vacates the seat of an ordinary councillor, election as chairman does not.

County aldermen.

Chairman.

This brings us to the qualifications of councillors. No one can be elected an ordinary councillor nor (therefore) an alderman or chairman of a county council, unless he be either qualified to be councillor of a borough within the county, or be a peer owning property in the county, or be a parliamentary voter registered as such in respect of the ownership of property in the county. To be qualified as a borough councillor a man must be either entitled, by virtue of burgess qualification, to be registered as an elector, or be qualified in all respects save that of residence within the

Ordinary Councillors.

See *post*, p. 202.

[1] This virtually makes it necessary to fix the number of the ordinary councillors at some multiple of three.

## THE ADMINISTRATIVE COUNTY 167

seven mile limit, and (being resident within fifteen miles) be entitled to or rated in respect of property of a certain value.[1]

The only disqualifications for election as a councillor, other than those which disqualify as an elector, appear to be— Disqualifications.

(a) *Sex.*—It has been expressly decided that no woman can be a county councillor.

(b) *Office.*—No person holding paid office in the gift of the council can be a member thereof.

(c) *Contractorship.*—No person who has any interest, direct or indirect, in a contract with the council can be a councillor.

(d) *Bankruptcy.*—No uncertificated bankrupt can be a member of a county council for five years after his discharge from bankruptcy.

But possession of Holy Orders is not (as with a borough councillor) a disqualification.

The matters entrusted to county councils by the Act of 1888 and subsequent statutes may be grouped under nine heads—

(1) *Locomotion.*—All *main* roads within the area of an administrative county belong to and must be maintained by the county council, unless an urban council should expressly insist on maintaining that portion which runs through its district. It seems somewhat difficult to define a main road otherwise than by saying that it is a road which a county authority has declared to be such; but probably there will be no Main roads.

---

[1] Ownership of £1000 value (realty or personalty) where the borough has four wards, £500 where it has less; rating in respect of £30 a year where it has four wards, £15 where it has less.

great anxiety on the part of county councils unduly to enlarge their liabilities in this respect. A county council has, in respect of its main roads, all the powers of a highway board with respect to ordinary highways. And even where an urban council insists on maintaining its portion of a main road, the county council must contribute towards the expenses of maintenance. A county council is also the authority for the management and repair of existing county bridges, and for the purchase and erection of new ones.

(2) *Health.*—Besides having a general power to make bylaws for the prevention and suppression of nuisances, not otherwise summarily punishable, the County Council is expressly constituted an authority for the prevention of river pollution within its county, and for the execution of the statutes relating to the contagious diseases of animals and to destructive insects. It is also the fish conservancy authority, and the protector of wild birds for the county, though these functions may possibly have more regard to sport than to health.

(3) *Education.*—The management and support of reformatory and industrial schools is now transferred from Quarter Sessions to the County Council. But, in addition to this, the position of the County Council as an educational organ has been rendered very important since the passing of the Act of 1888, not merely by the entrusting to it of a general power (shared by the urban council) of assisting technical instruction by means of a "rate in aid," but also by the practice adopted by Parliament during the last

## THE ADMINISTRATIVE COUNTY 169

three or four years of making large grants to it from the general Inland Revenue, with the object of enabling it to subsidise or organise technical instruction.

(4) *Poor.*—Although the County Council is not, technically, a poor-law authority, it has duties which touch very closely upon the administration of poor relief. It provides and maintains pauper lunatic asylums for its county, it may advance money for the purpose of assisting emigration, it may contribute towards the expense of holding enquiries by the Charity Commissioners, and it may, in default of action by a district council, take over the powers belonging to that body in the matter of providing allotments. *Pauper lunatics. Emigration. Charity enquiries. Allotments.*

(5) *Records.*—The County Council is a great recording body for various purposes. It has taken over the functions formerly belonging to the Quarter Sessions in respect of the registration of the rules of scientific societies,[1] the particulars of charitable gifts,[2] the existence of places for religious worship;[3] and it confirms and records the rules of loan societies.[4] *Scientific societies. Charitable gifts. Places of worship. Loan societies.*

[1] By an act of the year 1843, learned societies whose rules have been duly certified to the clerk of the peace for their county, are exempt from payment of rates.

[2] By the Charitable Donations Registration Act, 1862, trustees who hold property for charitable purposes are required to register particulars with the clerk of the peace or Quarter Sessions.

[3] By various statutes of the end of the last and the beginning of the present century, dissenters who desired protection for their places of worship were required to register them with, and get them certified by, Quarter Sessions. But they have now the option of transmitting particulars to the Registrar General.

[4] By the Loan Societies' Act, 1840, the rules of a loan society must be transmitted by the certifying barrister to the clerk of the peace to be laid before Quarter Sessions.

Moreover, it is now the polling and registration authority for the county in parliamentary elections.

<small>Music halls. Race-courses.</small> (6) *Public amusements.*—The granting of music and dancing licences, and of licences for race-courses, is now vested in the County Council.

(7) *Trade.*—The County Council is the local authority for the enforcement of the statutes which aim at ensuring <small>Weights and measures.</small> the uniformity of weights and measures throughout the kingdom, and, by a very recent statute, it is empowered to purchase the peculiar "franchise" or privilege claimed within its county by any other person or body in respect of examining, testing, and regulating any weights or measures.

(8) *Supervision of other local authorities.*—This is a very important branch of the County Council's jurisdiction, which recent legislation has made somewhat prominent. The Local Government Act of 1888 gave the County Council a substantial voice in the constitution <small>New boroughs. Boundaries. Wards.</small> of any new borough within its county, in the alteration of district and parish boundaries, in the division of urban districts into wards, and in the conversion of rural into urban districts. But the new Local Government Act has gone much further. Under the provisions of that statute, the County Council fixes the number <small>Parish councils.</small> of members of the parish councils within its county, decides whether certain small parishes shall or shall not have councils, lends money to the parish council or authorises it to borrow money elsewhere, hears complaints of the parish council against the district council, divides parishes into wards, is the general boundary authority in disputed questions within

# THE ADMINISTRATIVE COUNTY 171

the county, and, broadly speaking, has to do its best to bring the somewhat complicated scheme of the Local Government Act of 1894 into working order.

(9) *Finance.*—But perhaps the most important duties of the County Council are, after all, those connected with finance. For its financial powers are not merely those which are given to all public bodies, to enable them to fulfil their primary duties; the County Council is a financial authority even for matters with which it is not immediately or exclusively concerned. Not only has it to find money for its own proper wants, the payment of its own officials, and the performance of its own special work; but it has to provide for the wants of judicial authorities, of assizes and Quarter Sessions, Justices' clerks, coroners, police, and petty sessions, for poor-law officials, and even for some officials of the central government.

To enable it to fulfil these functions, in the County Council is vested all (or nearly all) the property belonging to the county, the power to borrow money for county purposes, to make, assess, and levy all county rates, to examine and pass the accounts of all county officials, and to fix the fees which they may take; to appoint, remove, and determine the salaries of all county officials, except the clerk of the peace and the Justices' clerks. It must, at the beginning of every financial year,[1] consider an estimate or budget Budget. of probable income and liabilities for the current year, and must again consider the budget at the expiration

[1] The financial year of the county begins on the 1st April.

of the first six months of the year. All its financial business is in the special charge of a finance committee, which it is bound "from time to time" to appoint; and no payment (except in pursuance of an Act of Parliament or an order of a competent court) can be made by the county treasurer without an order of the council signed by at least three members of the finance committee; nor can any liability exceeding £50 be properly incurred without an estimate submitted by the finance committee.

The question naturally arises: Whence does the County Council get the money for all these purposes? And we may say that, apart from its revenue from property, which may come in the form of rents, tolls, royalties, and so on, and from such casual sources as penalties for breach of statutes and by-laws which it is entitled to enforce, the County Council derives its revenue from *loans, contributions*, and *rates*. A word as to each of these.

(i.) *Loans.*—For any purpose of permanent utility within the scope of its duties, such as the consolidation of existing debts, the purchase of land and buildings, and even for the assistance of emigration from its county, the County Council may, with the sanction of the Local Government Board, borrow money by way of loan, repayable by instalments extending over a period not longer than thirty years. But even the Local Government Board cannot, without the express approval of Parliament, sanction any loan which will bring the total debt of a county above a tenth of the rateable value of the property within its area. The loan may be secured either by "county stock" issued under the provisions of the Local Government Act of 1888, by debentures or annuity certificates under the Local Loans

THE ADMINISTRATIVE COUNTY 173

Acts, 1875 (a statute which prescribes general rules for the management of loans to local authorities), or by mortgage under the provisions of the Public Health Act ; but every loan must be repaid by means of equal yearly or half-yearly instalments, or by means of a sinking fund.

Mortgage.

Instalments.

Sinking fund.

(ii.) *Contributions.*—One of the most important financial duties of a County Council is to receive and distribute certain sums of money which, though in many cases actually raised within its area, are collected by the officials of the central government,[1] and subsequently handed over by the Exchequer. The chief of these sums are (1) the proceeds of "local taxation licences," *i.e.*, licences for the sale of intoxicating liquors, for dealing in game, for keeping or using dogs, horses, guns, armorial bearings, and many other purposes, (2) a proportional share, amounting to about two-fifths of the whole amount collected, of the sum received during the year for probate duty by the central government, and (3), by a statute of the year 1890, certain specified Customs and Excise duties. The amount actually distributed under this head to county councils during the year 1890-1 was upwards of a million and a-half of money; and, at the end of that year, there remained a still larger sum undistributed, which has by this time probably found its way to the county treasurers.[2] But sums received in this way from the central government are not applicable to the general purposes of the county fund. They must be paid into a separate account known as the "Exchequer Contribution Account," and are primarily devoted to pur-

Local taxation licences.

Probate duty grant.

Inland Revenue grant.

Exchequer Contribution Account.

[1] It is expressly provided, however, that Her Majesty may, by Order in Council, on the recommendation of the Treasury, transfer to County Councils the power to collect the proceeds of "local taxation licences" within their respective counties.

[2] Report of Local Government Board, 1892-3. App. P., pp. 505, 507.

poses prescribed by statute, such as poor law officers, medical officers of health for districts within the county, registrars of births and deaths, pauper lunatics, police, and, in the case of the Customs and Excise duties, to technical instruction. Only in the event of all these claims being satisfied is the Exchequer Contribution Account liable to be devoted to general purposes, or even divided among the district councils within the county.

(iii.) *Rates.*—Again, in the event of prior sources of income failing, resort to the ratepayers is the ultimate method adopted by a County Council to make both ends meet. The provisions on the subject of county rates are mainly to be found in a statute of the year 1852, known as the County Rates Act. Only it must be remembered that the statute treats the Justices in Quarter Sessions as the rating authority; whereas, as we said, all the powers formerly exercised by Quarter Sessions in the matter of making, levying, and assessing rates are now bodily transferred to the County Council. The basis or standard of rating is fixed by an "Assessment Committee" of the County Council, which may either adopt the existing valuation made by the Guardians for the purposes of the poor rate, or may direct a new valuation; and any valuation adopted may be changed from time to time when necessary.[1] The Council then directs a "fair and equal" rate to be made and assessed upon every parish in proportion to its value as appearing in the Valuation List, and the amount for which each parish is liable is primarily obtained by precept of the Council directed to the Guardians of the Union in which the

[1] The liability is the same as that for poor rate; but, of course, county and poor law authorities may take different views as to what is the rateable value of a particular property.

THE ADMINISTRATIVE COUNTY 175

parish is situated, who collect the sums demanded from their various constituent parishes in the same manner as the poor rate. But if the Guardians fail to pay the sums demanded within the time specified in the precept, the Council may order the amounts to be collected by the overseers of the parishes from which they are due, at the expense of such parishes. And if the overseers fail to do so, the sums in question may be exacted from them personally by distress and sale.[1] But although the right to make, assess, and levy county rates now belongs to the County Council, appeals in the matter of rates, either against a proposed valuation, or against an actual rate itself, or its manner of distribution, still go, as heretofore, to the Justices in Quarter Sessions assembled. The total amount of rates levied during the year 1890-1 by the County Councils exceeded one million and a-half sterling, being an average of about £28,000 for each county; but it is interesting to notice that the transference of the power to levy rates from Quarter Sessions to the County Councils has not as yet resulted in any increase of demands upon the ratepayers. In fact the tendency is the other way. The county rates for 1890-1 were, on the average, lower than in any previous year of the decade save one.[2]

Rating appeals still to Quarter Sessions.

The accounts of every county council are made up and published at the close of each financial year; and any ratepayer may inspect and verify them. They are then audited

[1] It is perhaps as well to state here, though we are rather anticipating matters, that the power of the county authorities to levy rates does not extend to the larger "Quarter Sessions Boroughs"—*i.e.*, boroughs which have their own courts of Quarter Sessions. But even these may have to contribute indirectly to county expenses. (See *post*, p. 219.)
[2] Report of Local Government Board for 1892-3. App. P., p. 503.

at the expense of the county by a district auditor appointed by the Local Government Board.

Finally, it is necessary to say a few words respecting the machinery by which a County Council effects the objects of its existence. This machinery may be considered under the two heads of *by-laws* and *officials*.

*By-laws.*—A County Council possesses, in addition to its power to make *by-laws* for the suppression of nuisances not otherwise summarily punishable, a general power of legislation "for the good rule and government" of its county. By-laws made under this power must observe the rules followed by a municipal council in making by-laws for its borough; that is to say, they must be passed by a meeting consisting of at least three-fourths of the members of council, they must be published for at least forty days before coming into operation, and all by-laws (except those made for the suppression of nuisances under the Public Health Act) must be submitted to a Secretary of State before they become legally valid. Offences against a county by-law are punishable on summary conviction; but no by-law may appoint a penalty exceeding £5 for any one offence, and no county by-law has any force within a municipal borough.

*Officials.*—Every County Council *must* have (in addition to its chairman, who is a constituent part of the Council) a clerk and a treasurer, and it may (and always does) have

Clerk.
Clerk.
Treasurer.

certain other officials. The *clerk* of the Council is the same person as the Clerk of the Peace for the judicial county,[1] but the *treasurer*, through whom alone payments out of the county fund can be made, is specially appointed by the Council, apparently on such terms as may be agreed between them. But the Council may also appoint medical

[1] This rule does not apply to the administrative county of London.

officers of health, public analysts, surveyors, auditors, and such other officials as it may deem necessary ; and, although the Local Government Act of 1888 made provision for the transfer to the County Council of existing officers of the county, and for the maintenance of existing claims, in future appointments the Council will have an entirely free hand. It should be noted that no paid official in the permanent employment of a County Council, who is required to devote his whole time to his county duties, is eligible as a member of Parliament.

# CHAPTER XI

## THE STANDING [1] JOINT COMMITTEE

THE standing Joint Committee of the Quarter Sessions and the County Council of a county is a statutory body created by the Local Government Act of 1888, for the purpose of dealing with matters jurisdiction in which is shared by Quarter Sessions and the County Council. These matters include the appointment and regulation of the duties of the Clerk of the Peace, the control (but not the appointment) of the Justices' clerks for the Petty Sessional Divisions within the county, and the sharing of buildings which both Justices and Council require to use. But its chief and most important function is the control and management of the **county police**.

Clerk of the Peace.
Justices' Clerks.
Buildings.

Constitution of the Joint Committee.

The Joint Committee is a body consisting of an equal number of county Justices and members of the county council appointed by Quarter Sessions and County Council respectively. The precise numbers are agreed between Quarter Sessions and the Council, or, failing agreement, are fixed by a Secretary of State. There is, apparently, no statutory rule as to the term of office of a Joint Committee, but, as a County Council only lasts for three years, it is

[1] This adjective is (doubtless) inserted by the Act to distinguish between the joint committee of the Quarter Sessions and the County Council, and the joint committees which may from time to time be appointed by the councils of neighbouring counties.

presumed that its portion of members at least will require to be triennially appointed.

It was not until the middle of the present century that England finally gave up her cherished theory that the parish constable was the normal and adequate guardian of law and order throughout the realm. Even so late as the year 1833 a comprehensive attempt was made to revive the decaying system of parish constables; but the attempt was a failure, and in the year 1856 the legislature at last faced the problem of a new and uniform police system for the whole kingdom—that is, with the exception of the metropolitan area, which was already specially provided for. The new scheme is to be found in the "County and Borough Police Act, 1856," a statute which, in spite of alterations, still continues to be the ruling authority on the subject. There were originally two great difficulties in the way of an uniform scheme—the expense, and the special privileges of certain "franchises" or "liberties,"[1] which claimed the right to maintain their own police. The latter difficulty had been already partly got rid of by an earlier statute, the County Police Act of 1839; but that Act had been only permissive in its operation, while the new one was to be compulsory and universal. The difficulty of expense was met by a promise of Treasury contributions towards the cost of maintaining those county and borough forces which should be kept in a due state of efficiency. This plan has since been continued, and we may say now that, in addition to the central police Superannuation Fund,

*Police.*

*Parish constable*

*County and Borough police.*

*Franchis*

---

[1] The terms "franchise" and "liberty," originally applied to the peculiar privileges or exemptions possessed by a certain locality, have long since become equally applicable to the localities in which they are exercised. The change has many parallels in the English language.

established in the year 1890, the Treasury pays (through the County Councils) one half of the cost of maintaining the efficiently kept county and borough police forces.

*Police areas.* The scheme of the Act of 1856 was to establish a separate police force in every county and in every borough possessing a certain population. Leaving the borough force for future consideration, we may here sketch in outline the constitution of a county force.

*County police.* The police of a county is under the general control of the Joint Committee of Quarter Sessions and the County Council. This Committee, with the sanction of a Secretary of State, increases or diminishes the numbers of the *Police districts.* county force, divides the county into "police districts," and assigns the proper number of constables to each, appoints *Chief Constable.* the *Chief Constable* for the county, and provides the necessary buildings for the discharge of the police duties. The rules as to the clothing, pay, and accoutrements of the police are, with a view to uniformity, prescribed by the Secretary of State; but the carrying out of these rules is in the hands of the Joint Committee. The ChiefConstable of the county, with the approval of Petty Sessions, appoints the specified number of constables in each police district,[1] *Superintendents.* with a *Superintendent* at the head of each, and has even considerable powers of dismissal and punishment; but in these and most other matters, he is subject to the general control of the Joint Committee, which may, with the approval of the Secretary of State, organise and distribute the county force in such manner as to it may seem fit, providing for gradations of rank, pay, allowances, promotions, and other details.

[1] Although there does not seem to be any direct statutory provision on the subject, the lines of the police district must follow those of the petty Sessional Division.

But it is here very necessary to observe that, although the general administration of the county force has been transferred to the Joint Committee, the control and authority of Quarter Sessions and even of single Justices over individual constables has been specially retained by the County Councils Act. It would be impossible for daily business to be done if a magistrate had invariably to appeal to the Joint Committee before obtaining the services of a single constable. And so it is expressly provided by the Act of 1888 that the Quarter Sessions and even the County Council may exercise, concurrently with the Joint Committee, the power of ordering constables to perform "such duties in connection with the Police," in addition to their ordinary duties, as they may think fit.[1] Moreover, it is also expressly laid down that the change is not in any way to affect the primary powers and duties of the Justice as conservator of the peace, nor the obligation of constables to obey his lawful orders given in that capacity. And it is presumed that the statutory duty formerly laid upon the chief constable to attend every Quarter Sessions court of his county, and upon the District Superintendent to attend every Petty Sessional court in his district, is not in any way abolished by the new Act, though probably the Joint Committee will prescribe the manner in which it is to be exercised. *Quarter Sessions and Justices.*

As we have said, one-half of the cost of maintaining the county police force is paid by the Treasury through the medium of the Exchequer Contribution Account of the County Council. An elaborate statute of the year *Cost of maintenance of police.*

[1] This is a delightfully vague power, and might, if exercised by all three bodies concurrently, lead to some friction. The Act of 1888 refers to the Act of 1856, but the latter is equally vague.

1890 has now provided a scheme by which every constable who serves a specified time or is incapacitated by accident or sickness, is entitled to a pension or superannuation allowance as a matter of right; and the source

*Pension fund.* from which such pension is to come is the "pension fund" directed to be established in every area for which a police force exists. This pension fund is made up partly of deductions from pay, partly of fines imposed on the constables of the force for neglect of duty, partly of payments made by other authorities for extra services rendered, and partly by direct contributions from the Treasury. If at any time a pension fund is unable to meet the existing claims upon it, the deficiency must be

*Police fund.* made good by contributions from the "police fund" of the same authority, *i.e.*, from the fund available for the maintenance of the existing force. This police fund, as we have seen, is partly provided (in the case of efficient forces) by Treasury subvention; the remainder is found

*Police rate.* by the imposition of a "police rate," that is to say, a special rate for police purposes assessed by the County Council upon each police district within its county in proportion to the number of constables employed in it.[1] The police rate is calculated on the basis of the valuation for the ordinary county rate, and is collected in the same way as, and along with, the county rate.

*The constable.* Finally, a word as to the position of the individual policeman. But we must first point out that the word "policeman" is, if not actually unknown to, at least very rarely used by English law. The law knows of "police forces," "police regulations," "police authorities," and so

[1] There are, however, some general police expenses to which the whole county contributes indescriminately.

# THE STANDING JOINT COMMITTEE

on; and the word "police" is used to qualify those persons or institutions who or which are managed by the legislation we have recently been discussing, to distinguish them from the older institutions of the parish constabulary. Our modern policeman is technically known to the law as a "constable," more properly, as a "police constable," which qualification distinguishes him from the "parish constable" or "paid constable" appointed under the Act of 1872, from the "special constable" temporarily appointed by two Justices in apprehension of a riot under the Special Constables Act of 1831, and from the "special constables" appointed annually in every municipal borough for use in case the ordinary force prove insufficient. *See ante, p. 48.*

The position of police constable involves some considerable disabilities, as well as substantial privileges. The constable may not engage in any private occupation; and although his former incapacity to *vote* at parliamentary and municipal elections has been recently removed, he may not canvass at either parliamentary or municipal elections within his county or borough. He is subject to special punishments which cannot be applied to the ordinary citizen. On the other hand, he is absolutely protected from suits when acting upon a Justice's warrant,[1] even though the warrant turn out to be defective; he is exempted from service in the militia and on juries; assaults made upon him in the execution of his duty are punished with special severity; he is entitled to arrest any one without warrant on suspicion of committing a felony, and, if he act *bonâ fide*, is not liable for damages, even though it turn out that no felony was, in fact, committed; and a superintendent or inspector of police has almost magisterial

*Constable's special disabilities.*

*Privileges.*

[1] The constable must observe certain rules as to showing his warrant.

authority in being entitled to release on bail a person charged with an offence punishable upon summary conviction who cannot at once be brought before the Justices. Generally speaking, we may say that the ordinary police constable looks first for orders to his superior officer; but that he is bound to obey the warrant of any Justice of the Peace who professes to be acting in the scope of his duty.

GROUP D.

# THE BOROUGH.

14 & 15. THE PARLIAMENTARY AND
    MUNCIPAL BOROUGH. . . CHAPTER XII.
SPECIAL TYPES OF BOROUGH . . CHAPTER XIII.

# CHAPTER XII

### THE BOROUGH—PARLIAMENTARY AND MUNICIPAL

ALTHOUGH it seems probable that the body of traditional usage which the earliest Teutonic invaders of Britain brought with them made no special provision for large centres of population, although the roaming Saxon hated the confinements of what we now call town-life, yet it is hardly possible to find authentic records of a time when there was in England nothing in the way of settlement beyond the typical agricultural village. Long before the Norman conquest, we get traces of that *burh* from which both the character and the name of the modern borough are derived. There is a curious and suggestive similarity between the original names of the village and the borough; for while the *tun*, the original village, was, as we have seen, the hedged or stockaded place, the *burh* was the strong or fortified place. And it is not a little curious that, just about the time when the country districts became fairly peaceful and safe under the strong hand of the Tudor monarchy, the name *town* should pass, in common language, from the village to the borough. With us, "town" is opposed to "village"; so late as the fifteenth century the town was the village. {Town and burh.}

When we ask ourselves the origin of the historic centres of population in England, we can give, in many cases, no {Origin of English towns.}

definite answer, certainly no rule of general application. Artizan and merchant life may have lingered on in the old Roman cities, such as London, York, and Chester, and been gradually reinforced by in-drift from the country. Some German scholars bid us find the earliest symbol of citizen life in the market cross; but although, doubtless, facilities for the exchange of goods often led to the growth of a borough, many other causes were at work. Small groups of houses grew up round the castle of a powerful official with a reputation for clemency, around some famous shrine which extended the peace of the church to those who lived under its shadow.[1] And thus, ere Domesday Book was drawn up, there had established itself in the land a special class of burghers (*burgenses*), who lived in what we should now call towns, usually under the protection of some great noble, spiritual or secular, who allowed them special privileges in return for pecuniary assistance.

*Roman cities.*

*Markets.*

*Castles.*

*Shrines.*

*Burgesses.*

*Servile origin of boroughs.*

But one very remarkable feature is to be found in all these cases. There was always a flavour of *serfdom* attaching to the burgess, however wealthy. Whether it was that the earliest burgesses had really commended themselves as serfs to the lord or religious house under whose ægis they had come to dwell, or whether it was that the peculiar privilege, possessed by many boroughs, of freeing from his lord's claims the rustic who dwelt unmolested in them for a year and a day, had branded the borough as a refuge for escapees, it is certain that the theory prevailed that every

---

[1] Those who wish to realise how a town grew up round a shrine in the Middle Ages should visit the chapel of St Anne of Auray, in Brittany. A few years ago it was a solitary landmark, round which, at pilgrimage times, a few booths were temporarily erected. Now the booths have become shops and the pathways streets of houses.

burgess had something servile about his position, and that practical consequences were drawn from this theory. Not only did the borough-member occupy a position far inferior to that of the knight of the shire in Parliament, when Parliament had come to be; not only was the cringing burgess held up to the mockery of the stout yeoman on the Elizabethan stage; but, in earlier days, the servile taint which clung around burghership had subjected the boroughs to the bitter tax of *tallage*, and in the struggle against tallage lies the critical point in the earlier history of boroughs.

Now, *tallage* was a tax peculiarly hateful on two grounds. First, that payment of it involved the stigma of serfdom. Second, that there were no limits to the number of times which it might be levied, nor to the amount which might be claimed under it. The lord who tallaged "did what he would." In theory, he was only taking from his serfs a part of those chattels, the whole of which legally belonged to him, but which his clemency allowed his serfs to retain the use of. No doubt the theory was glaringly untrue in fact, but long after the "aids" and "scutages" to which the free man was subject had been strictly limited by the Great Charter and by other statute law, the burgess remained subject to the indefinite tallage.

Naturally the burgess revolted against the hateful imposition, and set himself to remove it. His first step was to buy off the liability to indefinite taxation by a promise of a fixed annual sum (*firma burgi*) in its stead. There was *The firma burgi.* at first probably no definite body of persons responsible to the lord for this annual render; but the lord was quite secure, for, if the sum were not paid, his bailiff simply harried the burghers under the name of tallage. In this way several boroughs had won the first step towards freedom before Domesday. Chester paid ten marks of silver (to king or bishop); Lincoln one hundred pounds of silver by tale, half to the king and half to the earl; Oxford sixty pounds. But there is no hint [1] as to who actually paid the sums, or how they were collected inside the walls. Some one found the money, or king's sheriff and earl's bailiff would know the reason why.

So the process went on for some two centuries. But meanwhile, a most formidable theory made its appearance.

Boroughs in the King's hand.

It often happened that, owing to deaths or failure of a feudal line, or perhaps because in reality the borough had grown up without special protection, the burgesses of a particular place had in fact no feudal superior who claimed tallage. It might have been thought that their position was peculiarly fortunate. But it must be remembered that Norman William had firmly established the theory that the land which had a private lord had also an overlord in the king, while the land which had no private lord was directly "in the king's hand." So ran the feudal maxim: "No lord, no land." And where no private lord claimed to tallage a borough, that borough could be tallaged by the king.

For a long time the only way out of the difficulty was for these boroughs to do as the private boroughs did, viz., to buy off the liability to tallage by agreeing to pay a fixed annual sum. Very often such a bargain was solemnly

Charters.

recorded in a *charter*, *i.e.*, simply, a parchment scroll, in which, in return for the annual payment, the king or lord granted to the borough freedom from all other claims, and

[1] Except the vague statement that certain houses in the borough were "tax-paying" (*geldantes*).

the uses of certain special privileges carefully specified in the charter. Thus the whole land gradually became dotted over with chartered boroughs, each relying upon its own special charter. Thus, too, the history of municipal privileges acquired that peculiarly anomalous character which it retained down to the great reform of 1835. But the boroughs which received no charters (and, it is to be feared, sometimes those which did) were still in evil plight.

At last brighter days came. A national parliament was established, and, from the very first, set itself steadily to acquire the sole right of taxation throughout the land. That any authority should now attempt to tax Englishmen without the approval of Parliament is so impossible, that we are apt to forget the slowness and the bitterness of the struggle which brought this result about. Though the Great Charter laid down the rule that the free man should not be taxed save by the consent of a " Common Council of the realm," the wording of the clause was narrow, and the royal officials found many a loophole in it. Still, by the end of the thirteenth century, Parliament had won the battle as regards freemen's taxes, only to find its flank turned by a daring use of the claim to tallage. For, if the king could fill his exchequer by tallaging the boroughs, where was the Parliament's dream of complete control of taxation, and pressure upon the king by means thereof? *The parliament.*

So once again the issue was joined. The kings, fighting inch by inch, fell stubbornly back, and, at last, before the fourteenth century had run out, the victory was gained, tallage without consent of Parliament was declared illegal, and the theory of the serfdom of burgesses had gone for ever. *Fight over tallage.*

But this was, after all, only a negative position. The borough was exempt from tallage, and, probably, from *The corporation.*

feudal jurisdiction, but it was too vague an entity to have much positive power—to be able to govern its own members. The earliest charters are very general in their terms, when they attempt to describe the persons to whom their privileges are granted. The king grants privileges to "my citizens of London," to "my barons[1] of the Cinque Ports," to "my burgesses of Nottingham," and so on. There seems to be no definite body capable of acting as trustee of the town's privileges, no **corporation**, as we should say. The townsmen were not *organised*. It is, in fact, one of the very hardest things to say what constituted burghership in the eleventh or twelfth century.

But, although there was no one organism which summed up and expressed the whole life of the borough, there were often germs which might well form the nucleus of such an organism. Even where the borough had grown up out of a single township, there would still be the old town-moot of the original settlers or their descendants, who still held the ancient homesteads of the town. Around them, in more recently built dwellings, jealously excluded, no doubt, from the sacred circle of ancient householders, was the constantly increasing group of newcomers, whom hopes of profit had attracted towards the borough. In these cases mere ownership of one of the old tenements, without proof of descent, often gave to the owner and his descendants a right to be considered members of the privileged class. Where the borough was originally a group of townships, it seems, in many cases, to have organised itself spontaneously on the model of a *hundred*, with a representative moot and a leet jury of the twelve senior landowners. Here again would be opportunities for further development, as

Town-moot.

Leet jury.

[1] The word "baron" originally meant simply "liege man."

the town court and the jury acquired more and more
distinctness. Most important of all, the borough may  *Gild.*
have originally owed its importance to its position on one
of the great trading routes; and then, in all probability,
there would be a *gild* or *hanse* of merchants, an association
for the purposes of commerce, existing by licence of the
king; and this gild would have its elder brother or
*alderman*, as well as its ordinary members.

Out of these scanty materials there gradually grew up, Mayor,
by a process so silent that we cannot trace its definite aldermen,
lines, our familiar organisation of *mayor, aldermen*, and burgesses.
*burgesses*—not necessarily as the universal type of borough,
but as the orthodox type, to which others tended to
conform. The *burgesses* include all the privileged dwellers
in the borough, sometimes acting in a primary body, as
in the old township moot, more often through an elective
council, like the courts of hundred and shire. The
*aldermen* are the senior members of the gild or gilds,
sometimes chosen by the burgesses at large, sometimes
only by the gild brethren, who, however, must often have
been identical with the burgesses. The *mayor (major)*,
though his name probably comes from Latin-speaking
countries, is either the lord's bailiff or reeve, or else the
elected foreman of the leet jury—the *major et jurati*.
Between these two alternatives the distinction is, of course,
vast; it implies all the difference between the Government-
appointed *maire* of the French *commune*, and the elective
mayor of the modern English town. Gradually England
declared in favour of the present model. London, which London.
at William's death had only a "portreeve" (probably
appointed by the bishop), wrings from John Lackland the
right she has ever since possessed of electing her own

194   ENGLISH LOCAL GOVERNMENT

mayor. But London is, of course, far in advance of other boroughs, and we must probably allow at least another hundred years before the leading type of mayor, aldermen, and burgesses becomes, not universal, but even general.

1295. The fact that Edward I., in organising his Parliament, gave separate representation to the boroughs, seems to prove the importance which the latter had acquired by the end of the thirteenth century, though there is a certain very plausible theory which denies that, in the original scheme of Parliament, it was ever intended to give separate representation to any but *royal* boroughs, *i.e.*, boroughs in the hand of the king.[1] On the other hand, the fact that the sheriff and not the mayor was made the returning officer in the parliamentary boroughs, goes far to shew that there was no well recognised type of borough constitution, even at the end of the thirteenth century.

Legal personality of the borough.   And even after mayor, aldermen, and burgesses had made their appearance, there yet remained one most important step to be taken before the borough organisation could be considered complete. This was the recognition of the borough as a legal personality, a *corporation*, or, as the lawyers called it, *persona ficta*. Until this point was established there would be endless difficulties about power to hold lands, power to make by-laws, power to use a seal, power to sue and be sued,—about those ordinary business acts which an individual can do without question.

[1] Certain it is that, for the first century of its existence, the borough representation in Parliament vacillates in a most mysterious way. In one year a borough will send members, in another not. Some historians are inclined to attribute this to purely casual circumstances, prosperity or otherwise of the borough in question. This is very unlike medieval notions. The position of the Scotch "royal burghs" considerably strengthens the theory in the text.

Suppose, for example, a dying citizen left part of his land "to the good town of X." Who would be legally entitled to enforce performance of the will? The existing burgesses? Suppose one of them died, what about his heirs? Again, according to legal theory, if land belongs to several persons jointly, none of them can commit trespass upon it. In this way a handful of citizens might appropriate the whole benefit of the gift. It was not until the existence of the fictitious person, or corporation, comprising all the burgesses for the time being, and yet, in the eye of the law different from all of them, not until this legal personality was recognised, that the position of the borough could be deemed really safe. And we cannot put this consummation much before the close of the fifteenth century.

Curiously enough, its realisation was almost immediately followed by a dark period in municipal history. The great opportunities for individual enterprise offered by the discoveries of the sixteenth century, and the expansion of trade consequent thereon, seem to have thrown the municipal offices into the hands of inferior men. The rich merchant found himself quite able to stand alone; he ceased to care much for the small affairs of his borough. Naturally, municipal politics tended to become timid and corrupt, and the tendency was accentuated by the new practice, adopted by the later Tudors, of manipulating the borough representation to check the growing independence of the House of Commons. Since the reign of Edward IV. it had become the practice to grant the right of sending members to Parliament in borough charters; and the Tudors shrank from forcibly cancelling these chartered rights. But it was easy, in the then state of constitutional

*Decay of municipal life.*

*Rotten boroughs.*

law, for the Crown to create new borough constituencies out of little towns in which royal influence could easily intimidate or buy over the municipal officials, who would practically control the elections. It is to the saintly Edward and the glorious Elizabeth that we owe our first wholesale creation of "rotten boroughs"; and James and Charles followed suit.

<small>Close corporations.</small> But there was even worse to come. For, after the heroic attempt and failure of the Long Parliament and Cromwell to purge the parliamentary constituencies, the Restoration made of the municipal boroughs not merely hot-beds of political corruption, but elaborate engines for the extortion of money and the persecution of dissenters. By threats, by vexatious persecutions, by the forfeiture of older charters and the grant of new municipal constitutions on a close oligarchical basis, the later Stuarts made of the whole borough system an offence which stank in the nostrils of whoever was honest in England, and which lingered on, in deserved infamy, till the besom of a reformed Parliament arrived to cleanse the Augean stable.

<small>The Commission of 1833.</small> Then came the great Royal Commission of 1833, a thorough and systematic enquiry into the circumstances of the 246 towns which claimed to exercise municipal privileges. The condemnation pronounced by the Commissioners, after two years of patient investigation, is <small>Inefficiency.</small> complete and sweeping. Inefficiency, anomaly, corruption were everywhere prevalent. As to the first point, the Commissioners say calmly: "It has become customary not to rely on the Municipal Corporations for exercising the powers incident to good municipal government. . . . They have the nominal government of the town; but the efficient duties, and the responsibility, have

PARLIAMENTARY AND MUNICIPAL BOROUGH 197

passed to other hands."[1] Upon the second point, the truth of the Commissioners' accusation may be illustrated by the fact that there were, in one borough and another, no less than twenty-two different ways by which admission to municipal privileges could be acquired, eleven different ways of appointing a Recorder, thirteen of appointing a Town Clerk, and at least seven different kinds of governing bodies. As to the last charge, we may simply refer to the facts that in a large number of cases vacancies in the privileged bodies were filled, not by open election, but by co-optation by the surviving members, and that, of 246 corporations, only *twenty-eight* were in the habit of publishing accounts.

*Anomaly.*

*Corruption.*

The great Municipal Reform Act of 1835, which followed upon the Report of the Commission, though it affirmed the general principle of an uniform system of municipal corporations, only included in its scope 178 of the boroughs reported upon, and left the rest for further treatment. Many of these have been since brought within the general plan, and, after a second commission had reported in 1876, a statute of the year 1883 practically put an end to all municipal corporations not falling within the provisions of the general scheme formulated by the new Act of the preceding session. We may, therefore, now say that, virtually speaking, all the 302 municipal boroughs of England and Wales are regulated by the provisions of the Municipal Corporations Act of 1882 and its amendments (for of course the Act has been amended). The great exception is the City of London, which is still governed by its ancient constitution.

*The statute of 1835.*

*Commission of 1876.*

*Statute of 1883.*

*Statute of 1882.*

[1] Report of 1835, p. 17.

## 198 ENGLISH LOCAL GOVERNMENT

Severance of parliamentary and municipal functions.

One of the most important effects of the legislation of the early thirties was to draw a complete line of severance between parliamentary and municipal functions in the boroughs. Not only were the boundaries of the borough for parliamentary and municipal purposes often made entirely different, but all connection between the parliamentary and the municipal franchise was taken away. The mere fact of burghership no longer gave even a *primâ facie* claim to the parliamentary franchise. Though, doubtless, in the vast majority of cases the man who was a parliamentary voter for a borough was also a burgess, he claimed the two rights by totally different titles. And the converse did not by any means hold. This distinction has since been strictly maintained, and we have therefore to deal now with two totally different kinds of borough, the parliamentary and the municipal. With regard to the first, only a few words will be necessary; for it belongs rather to central than to local government.

### A.—*The Parliamentary Borough.*

The parliamentary borough is now simply a definitely prescribed area for the registration of parliamentary electors and the election of members of parliament. Of these areas there appear to be at present 143 (including the City of London).[1]

No identity of area or name with municipal boroughs.

Many of them, no doubt, coincide in name, and not a few also in area, with municipal boroughs; but, for all that, the Parliamentary and the municipal borough are certainly distinct in idea, the former being a mere electoral area, while the latter is a self-governing unit. And, in many cases, there is no

[1] Census Returns, 1891.

## PARLIAMENTARY AND MUNICIPAL BOROUGH 199

identity at all. The parliamentary boroughs of Clapham and Battersea, Finsbury, Paddington, and Woolwich, for example, have no namesakes among the municipal boroughs; while the parliamentary boroughs of Liverpool, Manchester, Birmingham, Newcastle-under-Lyme, and Reading, though they assume the names, yet have not the areas of their municipal synonyms. If we wish to ascertain the boundaries of a Parliamentary borough, we must dig them out of one of the three great Parliamentary Distribution or Boundaries Acts of 1832, 1867, or 1885, according to the date of its creation. There is no general authority on the subject. If we wish to know the boundaries of a municipal borough, we have merely to look at its charter.

A parliamentary borough has, however, certain resemblances to, as well as differences from, a municipal borough. If it returns more than one member it is nearly always split up into "single member" divisions, which are a good deal like municipal wards, except that the latter generally have three members instead of one. Still more important, the preparation of the lists of voters, both for parliamentary and for municipal elections, goes on concurrently in places which are within the limits both of parliamentary and municipal boroughs; and, by a curious freak of history, the parliamentary and municipal franchises, so violently separated in 1832, have since tended once more to uniformity. Finally, the mayor, who is primarily a municipal official, is, generally speaking, returning-officer for any Parliamentary election which takes place within the limits of his municipal borough.

*Electoral divisions and municipal wards.*

*Polling.*

*Franchise.*

*Returning officer.*

B.—*The Municipal Borough.*

All municipal boroughs existing at the passing of the Municipal Corporations Act, 1882, which were then subject to the provisions of the Act of 1835, are now governed by the provisions of the Act of 1882 ; all boroughs since incorporated have been put on the same footing; all boroughs which, though existing in 1882, were not subject to the general law, have, as we have seen, since been deprived of their municipal character. We may say, therefore, that the Municipal Corporations Act of 1882 virtually lays down the law on the subject of municipal corporations generally. Indeed, the official definition of a municipal borough is now "any place for the time being subject to the Municipal Corporations Act, 1882"; and if any unincorporated town wishes to get itself made into a borough, it must petition Her Majesty for a charter of incorporation under that Act, first giving notice to the County Council of its County, and to the Local Government Board. After due time has elapsed, and upon approval of the petition by a Committee of the Privy Council, Her Majesty may grant a charter of incorporation, which may prescribe the boundaries of the borough[1] and the wards (if any), and fix the number of councillors to be elected for borough and wards. But, with the exception of making provision for temporary arrangements, the charter can do no more ; it merely extends to the town the provisions of the Municipal Corporation Acts.

In every municipal borough the **corporation** or legal personality of the borough consists of mayor, aldermen, and

[1] The Act does not expressly say so; but a power to fix the boundaries of wards implies a power to fix the boundaries of the borough.

## PARLIAMENTARY AND MUNICIPAL BOROUGH 201

burgesses.[1] But all powers belonging to the corporation may be exercised by the **council** of the borough, which, curiously enough, may contain persons who are not burgesses. We shall therefore have to speak of mayor, aldermen, councillors, and burgesses. Taking these in order of dignity, and beginning with the lowest rank, we take first the

(1) **Burgess**, who may be defined as any person who, being duly qualified,[2] is registered on the burgess roll of the borough. Every person (male or female) who has during the twelve months preceding the 15th July in any year occupied any building within the borough rated to the relief of the poor, has resided in the borough or within seven miles thereof during such twelve months, and has paid all rates which have been assessed in respect of such property up to the 20th July immediately following, is qualified to be enrolled as a burgess, unless he is under age, is an alien, has been within the preceding twelve months in receipt of poor relief, or is disqualified by any specific Act of Parliament.[3]

*Burgess qualification.*

The burgesses form the primary body of the corporation, but a burgess takes no direct share in the administration of borough affairs other than in the election of councillors, School Board, and auditors. Occasionally town meetings

---

[1] A certain complimentary distinction exists between the "city" or the "citizen," and the "borough" or the "burgess," and much historical learning has been expended in stating the etiquette of the point. For practical purposes there is no shadow of difference in English law, which knows nothing of "citizens." All are "burgesses."

[2] An unqualified person who gets himself enrolled as a burgess may be entitled to vote as a burgess, or rather, it may be impossible to prevent him so voting. But, for all that, he is not a burgess.

[3] *e.g.*, The Corrupt Practices Act of 1883, which disqualifies for certain periods all borough electors who have been found guilty of corrupt or illegal practice at a Parliamentary election. A similar rule prevails in the case of municipal elections.

are held for the furtherance of public objects, and a burgess has, *primâ facie*, a right to use any of the public buildings or conveniences provided by the council; but there is no direct provision, as there is in the case of parishes, for the actual participation of the primary body in the duties of administration.[1] The electoral duties of the burgess will appear when we speak of—

(2) The **Council**, which consists of a number of councillors fixed by the charter of incorporation, or by subsequent Order in Council or Act of Parliament, and distributed amongst the divisions or *wards* into which the borough is divided for electoral purposes, in the proportion of three councillors, or some multiple of three, to each ward. No person can be elected a councillor unless he is either (1) a burgess, or, (2) a person who is disqualified for enrolment as a burgess solely by the fact of non-residence within the seven-mile limit, *and* who possesses certain property qualification in the borough, whilst he resides not more than fifteen miles from the municipal boundary.[2] But no woman, no one who is an elective auditor or assessor of the borough, or who holds any paid office in the gift of the council (other than that of mayor or sheriff), or who is in Holy Orders, or is the regular minister of a dissenting congregation, or who is directly or indirectly interested in any contract with the council,

[Qualification of ordinary councillors.]

[Disqualifications.]

[1] Every burgess has, however, the right to *criticize* the administration of the council, and, if need be, to compel it to perform its legal duties and to abstain from illegal acts.

[2] This appears to be the effect of the 11th section of the Municipal Corporations Act, 1882; but as a champion specimen of puzzling draughtsmanship, the section may be commended to the study of those who believe in Parliamentary legislation. The section first declares that every councillor requires a property qualification, and then that he does not.

## PARLIAMENTARY AND MUNICIPAL BOROUGH 203

no one who is a bankrupt, or who has been found guilty of corrupt practices at a parliamentary or municipal election, can occupy a seat on the council; and if a burgess ceases to reside for six months within the borough, he loses his qualification as councillor (unless otherwise qualified), even though his name remains on the burgess roll. Councillors hold their seats for three years, the senior third of the members for each ward (or for the whole borough in the case of a borough not divided into wards) retiring every 1st November. Any one who refuses corporate office is liable to a fine. Casual vacancies in the council, caused by death, refusal to accept office, disqualification, or retirement, are filled up in precisely the same way as ordinary vacancies, by the electors who, but for the vacancy, would be the constituents of the holder of the seat; but the person elected to fill a casual vacancy only holds office till the expiry of the term for which the original member was elected. The election of councillors proceeds by ballot, and each elector has as many votes as there are vacancies to be filled; but no elector may give more than one vote to one candidate, and no elector may vote in more than one ward.[1]

*Councillors' term of office.*

*Office compulsory.*

*Casual vacancies.*

*Election by ballot.*

(3) **The Aldermen**, one-third in number of the councillors, are elected by the latter from their own number, or from persons qualified to be of their number. The aldermen are elected for six years, but the senior half retire triennially. The aldermen continue to be members of the council, but the seats which they occupy at the time of their election as aldermen are thereby vacated, and new

*Qualification.*

*Term of office of aldermen.*

---

[1] A ward may be divided by the council into *polling districts*, but the elected councillors represent the whole ward, not any particular district.

councillors are elected to fill them. The election of aldermen takes place on the 9th November in the triennial year, at the quarterly meeting of the council, and is conducted by open voting papers handed in to the chairman of the meeting. Each councillor may give as many votes as there are vacancies, but he may not give more than one vote to any candidate. An outgoing alderman may not vote in the first instance, but if he happens to be chairman of the meeting, he has a casting vote in case of equality. According to the general rule in municipal elections, a retiring alderman, if otherwise qualified, is eligible for re-election.

*Election.*

*Position of alderman.* The only special function performed by the aldermen as such appears to be that of acting as returning officers in ward elections. An alderman, however, is not elected for a ward, but for the whole borough, and must, therefore, as returning officer, take the ward assigned to him by the council. The aldermen are supposed to constitute the experienced or permanent section of the council, but as the council itself is, by reason of the fact that its ordinary members only retire by thirds, virtually a permanent body, the existence of a special section, virtually co-opted by elective councillors, hardly seems necessary. In social matters the alderman takes precedence of the ordinary councillor; but his legal qualifications and disqualifications are the same as those of the ordinary councillor.

(4) **The Mayor** is the chairman and president of the council, annually chosen by the council, either from among its own members or from among persons qualified to be such. The mayor is a member of the council, and his acceptance of office does not vacate his ordinary seat. The qualifications and disqualifications of the ordinary

## PARLIAMENTARY AND MUNICIPAL BOROUGH 205

councillor apply to him, except that on the one hand he may receive remuneration for the performance of his duties, and, on the other, two months' absence from the borough is sufficient to disqualify him for holding his office. He acts as president and chairman of all meetings of the council or any of its committees at which he is present, he represents the borough on all official and ceremonial occa- Mayor and sions, he is *ex-officio* a Justice of the Peace for the borough ex-mayor. both during his year of office and that which succeeds Justices. it,[1] and when engaged in the business of the borough, he takes precedence of all ordinary Justices but not of a stipendiary magistrate. If the borough is not divided into wards, he also acts as returning officer at municipal elections. The mayor may appoint in writing, from among the aldermen or councillors, a deputy to act for him on any occasion at which he may not be present.

The mayor, aldermen, and ordinary councillors constitute, as we have said, the council of the borough, the body through which alone the corporation of the borough is, as a general rule, capable of acting. But there are, or may be, two other groups of office holders who are neither members nor officers of the council. These are the *auditors* and the *revising assessors*.

(5) **The Auditors** of a borough, three in number, are annual officers, one appointed by the mayor from among the members of council, the other two elected by the whole of the electors of the borough acting together, from among those who are qualified to be, but are not, actually members of council.[2] It is the duty of the auditors to audit half-yearly the accounts of the borough

[1] Unless, during the second year, he becomes disqualified to be mayor.
[2] Neither town clerk nor treasurer is eligible as auditor.

treasurer before they are submitted to the Local Government Board.

(6) **Revising Assessors** are only elected in those municipal boroughs which do not wholly or partially coincide with parliamentary boroughs. They are two in number, and are elected annually by ballot, in the same way as, and, where possible, with the elective auditors. Like the elective auditors, the assessors must be qualified as, but must not actually be members of the council; and neither treasurer nor town clerk can be an assessor. The function of the assessor is, in conjunction with the mayor, to revise the parish burgess lists which have been made out by the overseers and transmitted to the town clerk. For this purpose a court is held in the first half of October every year, and objections are stated and discussed. The lists allowed by the court become the burgess-roll of the borough. Where the municipal borough is wholly or partially coincident with a parliamentary borough, the revising barrister takes the place of the assessors, the municipal wards are made to coincide so far as possible with the parliamentary divisions of the borough, and the preparation of parliamentary and municipal lists of voters proceed together in manner provided by the Registration Act of 1878.

We have now to consider, first, the duties which fall to the lot of a borough council, and, second, the machinery by which those duties are performed.

*Functions of council.*

*As sanitary authority. See ante, p. 100.*

But, with regard to the duties of a borough council, much of our work has already been done. For many of the most important municipal functions arise from the fact that almost every borough is (as we said) an *urban sanitary district*, and that its sanitary authority is the borough council. The borough council will therefore have all those

*Revision of burgess lists.*

## PARLIAMENTARY AND MUNICIPAL BOROUGH 207

powers and duties in the matters of drainage, gas and water supply, prevention of the spread of disease, registration of lodging-houses, management and maintenance of streets, provision of markets and public recreation grounds, and housing of the working classes, which, as we said, belong to every urban sanitary authority. Beyond this, every borough council is now entrusted with many of the powers contained in the Town Police Clauses Act of 1847, an Act which formerly only applied in places which had specially adopted it, but whose powers have now been largely conferred, by the terms of the Public Health Act, on every urban sanitary authority, though they are naturally of more importance in boroughs than in extra municipal districts. These powers include the management and direction of public traffic, especially on occasions of public ceremonial, the prevention of fires, the oversight of places of public resort, the licensing and control of hackney carriages, and the regulation of public bathing. It is as urban sanitary authority, too, that a borough council adopts (after due preliminaries) the provisions of the Public Libraries Act of 1892, the Baths and Wash-houses Acts, the Burial Acts, and other optional statutes, and distributes the technical education grant made by the county council. In fact, we may say that, whenever any statute or scheme has been passed or imposed for the benefit of the inhabitants of a borough, the borough council will be the authority to put the statute or scheme into operation and to enforce its provisions. The one great exception to this rule is in the case of the elementary education of the borough, which is not managed by the council, but, as we have seen, by a separately elected School Board. But even here, should there be no School Board, the School Attendance Committee will be appointed by the borough council.

*As police authority.*

*See ante, p. 51.*

*Not as School Board. See ante, p. 55. But as School Attendance Committee.*

This identity of function renders it here only necessary to speak about two very important branches of the council's duty,—its administration of the borough property, and its control of the borough police.

**Property.**—Generally speaking, all property which is destined for the general use and advantage of the inhabitants of a borough, unless it is specially vested in some other body or persons, or unless it is to be used for charitable purposes, is in the legal ownership of the corporation, and is administered by the council. And where the burgesses of a borough or some of them were in their corporate capacity, before the passing of the Municipal Corporations Act of 1835, trustees jointly with any other persons or bodies, and their continuance as trustees is not forbidden by the Act of 1835, or the later Act of 1882 (as, for example, in the case of charities), the power of appointing new trustees on the occurrence of vacancies will belong to the council. Furthermore, a municipal corporation, even where it has not otherwise power to hold land "in mortmain,"[1] may buy five acres of land for public purposes without special permission; and any other land which it may require it may buy with the approval of the Local Government Board. But it may not sell or mortgage any corporate land without the approval of the Local Government Board,

Trust property.

Power to acquire land.

[1] It is an anciently established rule of English law that no corporation (ecclesiastical or secular) may hold land without a permission from the Crown (called a "licence in mortmain"). The reason for the rule originally lay in the fact that as a corporation, having perpetual succession, may never come to an end, the ordinary incident of "escheat," by which, on failure of heirs, a man's land went back to his lord, might never occur with a corporation, and thereby the lord be defrauded. But the rule of mortmain is much older than corporations. The *mortua manus* was often that of a saint to whose service land was given. The rule has been lately relaxed in favour of various public objects.

and its power to grant leases without a similar approval is restricted within very definite limits, to prevent the borough anticipating its future revenue.¹ The council may borrow Loans. from the Public Works Loan Commissioners, apparently without the approval of the Local Government Board, any sums which it may require for building or rebuilding its public buildings, and may mortgage the borough rate to secure repayment. Even where existing works are being Taking administered in the borough by bodies acting under special works. provisions, the borough council may, if it thinks fit, agree to take over the assets and liabilities of such bodies. On Ecclesi-astical the other hand, it is expressly provided by the Municipal patronage. Corporations Act that any ecclesiastical patronage belonging to the corporation, either in connection with land owned by it, or in any other way, shall be sold as soon as possible, under the directions of the Ecclesiastical Commissioners, and, until such sale, shall be exercised by the bishop of the diocese in which it is situated. There are special Improper use of provisions which prevent, or are aimed at preventing the borough use of corporate funds for the purposes of parliamentary funds. elections, but in its legitimate capacity as trustee of the Parlia-interests of the borough, the council may support or oppose, mentary proceed-at the expense of the corporate property, parliamentary ings. proceedings in connection with measures which it may deem for the advantage or disadvantage of the borough. But such support or opposition cannot be undertaken without the sanction of an absolute majority of the whole

¹ The rule is that a lease without fine may be made for thirty-one years, or, with or without fine, of land used or to be used for building purposes, for a term not exceeding seventy-five years. But there are savings for cases in which other rules prevailed before 1835. One result of the restrictions is that municipal property is often let much under its real value.

O

council given at a meeting the object of which has been specially advertised, nor without certain other necessary preliminaries.

**Police.**—As we have said, the extra-metropolitan police forces of the country are virtually now either county or borough forces, the parochial constable being only used to *Ante*, p. 48. supply deficiencies. We have already dealt with the county police. We have now to deal with the borough force.

Some boroughs without separate police forces.

But, in the first place, it must be noticed that it is not every borough which has its own separate police force. The general idea of the first modern police statute, the Lighting and Watching Act of 1833, was that boroughs with less than a population of 5000, if they chose to maintain a separate police force, should do so entirely at their own expense. The Municipal Corporations Act of 1882 prohibits the establishment of any *new* police force in a borough having less than 20,000 inhabitants. And the Local Government Act of 1888 has now provided that all boroughs which, according to the census of 1881, had a population of less than 10,000, shall for the future be considered for police purposes as part of the administrative counties in which they are situated. It remains, therefore, that no borough can maintain its own separate police force, unless in 1881 it had at least 10,000 inhabitants; and, as a matter of fact, less than one-half of the existing municipal boroughs maintain their own separate police.

Where, however, a borough has its own separate force, this force is under the special control of a **Watch Committee**, from time to time appointed by the council from amongst its own members, but not containing more than one-third of the whole number of councillors, exclusive of the mayor, who is *ex-officio* a member. The watch committee, which may act by a quorum of three, appoints, suspends, and discharges the Chief Constable and the ordinary borough constables, passes regulations for the conduct of the force (which regulations must be sent quarterly to the Secretary of State), and generally controls the working of the borough police. A borough constable, when appointed, has the powers and duties by common law and statute of an ordinary constable, and may act not only within the borough itself, but within any county of which the borough forms part, or which lies within seven miles of the borough limits. Within this radius he must obey the lawful commands of any Justice of the Peace, but he has a general power to arrest any idle and disorderly person whom he finds disturbing the public peace, or whom he justly suspects of intention to commit a felony, and to take him to the nearest watch-house, where, however, he may be bailed by the constable in charge, if he cannot immediately be brought before a magistrate. Any person who resists, or incites any one else to resist, a borough constable in the execution of his duty, is liable (in addition to other legal penalties) to a fine of £5, recoverable on summary conviction. On the other hand, a constable who is guilty of neglect or disobedience may be suspended by any two Justices of the borough or by the Watch Committee, or may be sentenced to imprisonment for ten days or to a fine of 40s. by a court of summary jurisdiction, or may, finally, be dismissed by the Watch Committee or the convicting court. {Powers and duties of the borough constable. Resisting a borough constable. Punishment of borough constables for improper conduct.}

With regard to the expense of maintaining a borough police force, we find that it may be provided for from {Cost of police force.}

## 212  ENGLISH LOCAL GOVERNMENT

Treasury subvention.

several sources. In the first place, if the Secretary of State shall have certified that during the preceding year the force has been maintained in a state of efficiency, both as regards numbers and discipline, the county council will, out of its "Exchequer Contribution Account," pay to the borough council a sum equal to one-half of the costs of the pay and clothing of the force during that year, and this sum may even be augmented if the County Council is very rich in Government funds.

Watch rate.

Furthermore, if, at the passing of the Municipal Corporations Act of 1882, the borough council was entitled to levy a *watch rate* upon the borough or any part of it, they may still continue to do so, and the proceeds, although they will be payable into the general borough fund, will be primarily devoted to the payment of police expenses. The watch rate is levied upon the occupiers of the hereditaments liable, not on the valuation for poor rate, but upon a special valuation based upon the net annual worth of the premises to a tenant on repairing lease; and where a part only of any parish within the borough is liable to watch rate, the overseers must make a "separate rate" on the premises liable, and this rate must be allowed by two Justices in the same way as a poor rate. Any person aggrieved thereby may appeal to the Recorder of the borough, if there be one, if not, to the next Quarter Sessions for the county. But no watch rate may exceed eightpence in the pound in any one year; and no separate rate may exceed twopence in the pound beyond the watch rate. If the county council grant, and the watch and separate rates are not sufficient to provide for the expenses of the police, the remainder must be met out of the general funds of the borough; but the salaries, wages, and allowances of the force, though fixed by the watch committee, are subject to the approbation of the Council, though a court of quarter or petty sessions may, of its own discretion, order special rewards or compensation to be paid to a borough constable for special diligence, or for injuries received in the discharge of his duty.

Before leaving the subject of borough police we may notice that, in addition to the borough force, where it exists, *every* borough must have in reserve a force of "special constables" to act if occasion should require. Those special constables are appointed every October by two Justices having jurisdiction in the borough, and may consist of as many inhabitants of the borough, not legally exempt from serving the office of constable, as the justices may think fit. These constables are regulated, not by the County and Borough Police Act, but by the Special Constables Act of 1831. They can only act when ordered to do so by a warrant of a Justice having jurisdiction in the borough, and this warrant must state that, in the opinion of the Justice, the ordinary police force is insufficient to maintain the peace. Each special constable is entitled to the sum of 3s. 6d. for every day during which he actually serves. {Special constables.}

We now come to the constitutional machinery by means of which the borough council performs its various functions. This machinery may be considered under the four heads of by-laws, committees, officials, and finance.

(1) *By-laws.*—In addition to its power, as urban sanitary authority, to make by-laws and regulations under the Public Health Act, 1875, a borough council has a general power to make by-laws "for the good rule and government of the borough, and for prevention and suppression {See *ante*, p. 117.}

of nuisances not already punishable in a summary manner by any Act in force throughout the borough." This very sweeping authority, however, is considerably modified by the manner in which by-laws must be made, and their scope when made. In the first place, no ordinary by-law can be passed at any meeting of the council, unless at least two-thirds of the council are present. And no such by-law comes into operation until forty days after a copy of it has been fixed on the town hall,[1] and another copy sent to the Secretary of State. In the meantime, Her Majesty may, by Order in Council, disallow the by-law or any part of it, which thereupon becomes of no effect. But by-laws made by the council as urban sanitary authority under the Public Health Act require the confirmation of the Local Government Board, not the allowance of the Secretary of State; and it appears from the wording of the Acts that, if a contemplated by-law can be made under the provisions of the Public Health Act, it must not be made under the general power conferred by the Municipal Corporations Act. In the second place, the amount of penalty which can be inflicted by an ordinary by-law of a municipal corporation is limited to £5. Thirdly, the superior courts of law possess the right, upon any case coming before them which involves reliance on a municipal by-law, to declare the by-law invalid, either because it plainly transcends the limits of the powers conferred by the Municipal Corporations Act, or because it is an unreasonable exercise of such powers. Many of us will remember the case of the Croydon magistrates, whose by-law prohibiting Sunday music was

---

[1] The Act does not say that the copy is to remain fixed up during the whole forty days; but, presumably, such is the intention.

PARLIAMENTARY AND MUNICIPAL BOROUGH 215

uncompromisingly set aside by the Queen's Bench Division. Where a by-law is valid it can be enforced by summary conviction of offenders before a court of Petty Sessions.

(2) *Committees.*—It would be impossible, even if the members of the council gave their whole time to the performance of their public duties, for a borough council to perform all the duties which fall to its lot in full meeting. As a matter of fact, the council divides its duties into departments, and confides the discretionary or administrative side of each department to a committee selected from its own body, the executive or ministerial side to various officials, reserving only to itself the power to confirm or disallow the proceedings of committees and officials.

Every borough council has a discretionary power to appoint any number of committees, of a general or special character, which it may deem necessary. And in some cases the appointment of a committee is compulsory,—*e.g.*, if the borough maintains its own police, a Watch Committee must (as we have seen) be appointed, and, if there is no School Board, a School Attendance Committee. But the proceedings of every committee, whether compulsory or not, require confirmation by the council. The minutes of a committee meeting, duly confirmed and signed by the chairman, are evidence of what took place at the meeting, at least until the contrary is proved. A committee meets when summoned by its convener. The council itself must meet quarterly, on the 9th November, and such other days as the meeting on the 9th November decides. But a meeting may at any time be summoned by the mayor, or on the motion of five members.

(3) *Officials.*—In its municipal character every borough council must appoint a town clerk and a treasurer, and in its character as urban sanitary authority, it must appoint a medical officer of health, a surveyor, and an inspector of nuisances, as well as such assistants, collectors, and other officials as are necessary to enable it to perform its duties. As a matter of fact, the council of a great borough has a most elaborate staff of officials, consisting of engineers, accountants, clerks, messengers, porters, and so on. Of these it is only necessary to speak in detail of the town clerk and treasurer, the sanitary officials having been already described in another chapter.

**The Town Clerk** is the head of the permanent borough staff, and his office is essential to the due performance of the council's duties, since no order for the payment of money out of the borough fund is valid unless countersigned by him or his deputy. Consequently it is specially provided that his office shall not be left vacant more than twenty-one days. The Town Clerk holds office at the pleasure of the council, and receives the salary agreed on between him and them. The council may appoint a deputy to act during his absence or illness. The Town Clerk is the Registrar and Secretary of the council, and virtually acts as its legal adviser, except where it is deemed expedient to have professional advice. All documents belonging to the borough are in his custody, and a copy of a borough by-law certified by him is *primâ facie* evidence of its existence. He plays a most important part in the preparation and custody of the burgess rolls, and directs the prosecution of offenders against municipal by-laws.

Tenure of office.

Deputy.
Records.

Documents.
By-laws.
Registration.
Prosecution.

**The Treasurer,** who must be a distinct person from the

## PARLIAMENTARY AND MUNICIPAL BOROUGH 217

town clerk, is, like him, appointed by the council to act during its pleasure, at the salary and upon the other terms agreed upon between them. No payment from the borough fund can be made by any one but the treasurer, and he, as we have seen, can, as a rule, only pay money upon receipt of an order signed by three members of the council and countersigned by the town clerk. The treasurer also prepares the accounts of the borough, and is generally responsible for the due execution of the financial duties of the council. Like all other borough officials, but to a greater extent than most of them, he must give security for the due performance of his office, and, if he is guilty of defalcation, he can be proceeded against in a summary manner.  *Security.*

This brings us to the consideration of municipal

(4) *Finance*, which we may consider under the two aspects of income and expenditure. Besides its income from subventions, from its property, from fines and penalties for offences against its by-laws, of which nothing further need be said, the main sources of a borough council's income are **loans** and **rates**.  *Income.*

The general power of borrowing possessed by a borough council appears to be strictly limited to loans for the purpose of enabling it to acquire land, or to erect any building which it is authorised to build. But it will be remembered, that, as urban sanitary authority, it has very extensive powers of borrowing for sanitary purposes, and this combination of powers often results in a large permanent indebtedness by a borough council. Generally speaking, the council cannot buy land for any but strictly public or sanitary purposes, but a recent statute has given it the power, upon the request of a volunteer corps, to acquire  *Loans.*

land for the military necessities of the corps, and it may borrow money to enable it to fulfil such purpose. But a loan raised by a borough council always requires the sanction of the Local Government Board, which, as a condition of its consent, may stipulate for repayment either by instalments or by a sinking fund. The loan may be secured either upon the land proposed to be purchased, or upon any other land belonging to the corporation, or upon the borough fund or the borough rate, and either by way of mortgage, or by debentures or annuity certificates under the Local Loans Act of 1875.

*Instalments. Sinking fund.*

*Borough rate.*

Finally, any deficiency in the borough fund must be made good by the imposition of a borough rate, which may be ordered by the council to be made and levied by the overseers of the parishes within it. Generally speaking, the council adopts the valuation for the time being in force for poor rate purposes, and it has a right to inspect all assessment books in the hands of the overseers; but, if it pleases, it may order an independent valuation to be made. The council divides the total amount required for borough rate among the parishes or parts of parishes comprised in the borough, according to their respective ratable values; and where the whole of a parish is within the borough, the overseers simply add the amount which they are ordered by the council to pay for borough rate to the poor rate collected by them in the parish. But when only part of a parish is in a borough, they must make a separate assessment on the part within the borough. The overseers of any parish, or, in the case of separate assessment in a divided parish, any individual affected may appeal against the rate to the Recorder of the borough at the next Quarter Sessions, or if the borough have no Quarter Sessions, to the

*Valuation.*

*Separate rate.*

## PARLIAMENTARY AND MUNICIPAL BOROUGH 219

next Quarter Sessions for the county. But (probably) the appeal cannot question the total amount of the rate, only the incidence or distribution of it. All payments on account of borough rates go to the borough fund, *i.e.*, to the fund applicable to the general purposes of the borough, which includes all rents and profits of land, all proceeds of securities belonging to the corporation, and all penalties for offences against by-laws except those parts which are payable to informers. Borough fund.

The outgoings from the borough fund may be classed into two great divisions,—those which are payable as of course, without special order or authority, and those which require special sanction. The first class includes the salaries and allowances of the mayor, recorder, stipendiary magistrate, town clerk, treasurer, clerk to the justices, and other officials of the council, and any sums certified by the Treasury as payable in respect of a municipal election petition. The second comprises registration expenses, the expenses of corporate buildings, coroners' fees and fees payable to a clerk of the peace, the wages, salaries, and allowances of the borough constables, the expenses of prosecutions, and all other expenses properly incurred by the council, or any other authority on behalf of the borough. Payments on account of this latter division require either an order of the council, signed by three members, and counter-signed by the Town Clerk, or (in the case of rewards to constables) of a court of Quarter or Petty Sessions, or the express direction of an Act of Parliament. Where the borough possessed its own court of Quarter Sessions before the passing of the Local Government Act of 1888, it will not be liable to be assessed to the county rate, unless at the census of 1881 its Expenditure.<br><br>Items payable without special sanction.<br><br><br><br><br>Items which require special sanction.<br><br><br><br><br><br><br><br>Costs of prosecution at assizes.

population had fallen below 10,000; but it will be liable to pay to the county treasurer the costs of the prosecution and maintenance of all offenders committed by the borough magistrates for trial at the county assizes.

General county expenses.

And, where the borough was not before 1832 exempt from contributing to general county expenses, it continues liable to contribute to such expenses, though it is not

County rates.

assessed to the county rate. But when the grant of a court of Quarter Sessions is made after the passing of the Local Government Act of 1888, the grant will not interfere with the power of the county council to assess the borough for the purposes of the county rate. And where there is no court of Quarter Sessions the borough is, of course, part of the county for rating purposes.

# CHAPTER XIII

### SPECIAL TYPES OF BOROUGH

IN the last chapter we considered the normal type of municipal borough, the type to which all places claiming to be boroughs must conform. The one exception to this uniformity was, as we saw, the existence of the borough police force ; some boroughs maintaining their own police, others being, for police purposes, part of the county in which they are situated.

But now we must deal, in conclusion, with certain special types of borough, which possess one or more special features, in addition to those already dealt with. The special features may be enumerated as (1) a separate Commission of the Peace ; (2) a separate Court of Quarter Sessions ; (3) a stipendiary magistracy ; (4) a borough civil court ; (5) the organisation of a judicial county ; (6) the organisation of an administrative county. Of these features in their order ; but it must be remembered that the existence of one neither, as a rule, implies nor excludes the possession of others. The distribution is arbitrary, and often the result of historical accident. Whether a borough does or does not possess such and such a feature is a question of fact.

(1) **Separate Commission of the Peace.**—It has long been the practice for the Crown to issue a separate Commission of the Peace for certain boroughs, and its right to

do so on petition of a borough council is expressly reserved by the Municipal Corporations Act. It will be remembered that in its mayor and ex-mayor a borough has always one, sometimes two, *ex-officio* magistrates, but many boroughs (some 120 in all) have also Justices specially appointed by Commission on the recommendation of the Lord Lieutenant of the county to the Lord Chancellor. But it must be carefully remembered that where a borough has only a separate Commission of the Peace, without a separate Court of Quarter Sessions, the jurisdiction of the county justices is not excluded from the borough. In such a case the county Justice can act within the borough in the same way as in the rest of the county.

Concurrent jurisdiction of county Justices.

Although a borough Justice is appointed in the same way as a county Justice, he does not need the special property qualifications of the latter. If he occupies any rated premises in the borough or resides within seven miles of it, that will be sufficient. He need not even possess burgess qualification. He will have the same powers within the borough as the county Justice within the county. The borough council must provide a suitable Justices' room; and every public court held by two borough magistrates will be a court of Petty Sessions for the borough. The Justices of a borough appoint their own clerk, who must not be a member of the borough council nor clerk of the peace for the county.

Qualifications of borough Justice.

(2) **Separate Quarter Sessions.**—The grant to a borough of a separate court of Quarter Sessions is likewise in the discretion of the Crown; but, inasmuch as the grant of Quarter Sessions to a borough will, even now, seriously affect the jurisdiction of its county, a sealed copy of the grant must be sent, within ten days after its receipt, to the

SPECIAL TYPES OF BOROUGH 223

clerk of the peace for the county in which the borough is situated.

The grant of a court of Quarter Sessions puts the borough almost on the footing of a county so far as local *judicial* business is concerned, and the county Justices will have no jurisdiction in the borough, though, by arrangement with the borough council, they may occupy a Sessions House jointly with the borough magistrates. A Quarter Sessions borough will require the following additional officers :—

(*a*) *A Recorder*, appointed by the Crown, but paid by the borough council such salary as Her Majesty directs, within the limits named by the council in their petition for a Quarter Sessions. The Recorder must be a barrister of five years' standing; he becomes *ex-officio* a Justice for the borough, and he takes precedence in the borough next after the mayor. He may not, during his term of office, represent the borough in Parliament, nor be a member of the borough council, nor be stipendiary magistrate for the borough. But he may be appointed revising barrister for the borough, and he may represent any other constituency in Parliament. The Recorder acts as sole judge of the court of Quarter Sessions in all *judicial* business, and sits either with or without a jury, as the chairman of a county Quarter Sessions would do. But he does not, as Recorder, undertake the administrative business of Quarter Sessions; he does not allow or make rates (though, as we have seen, he may hear certain rating appeals), or grant liquor licences. But, in his capacity of Justice of the borough, he may take part in any Quarter Sessions having jurisdiction in such matters. The

<sub>Qualifications.</sub>

<sub>Duties.</sub>

Recorder may appoint a deputy to act for him in case of unavoidable absence or sickness, and, upon request of the borough council, he may appoint an assistant Recorder to preside over a second court when there is a pressure of business. But the assistant Recorder must have been previously approved as a suitable person by a Secretary of State.

(*b*) *A Clerk of the Peace*, appointed by the council, who will have the same powers within the borough as the corresponding official in a county. But the borough clerk of the peace holds office during good behaviour, and he may not be the same person as the clerk to the borough justices. He may be paid either by fees or by salary; but any table of fees drawn up by the council must be confirmed by a Secretary of State.

(*c*) *A Coroner*, also appointed by the council, to act in the borough as a county coroner does for the county. But it is expressly provided by the Local Government Act of 1888, that in the case of boroughs with a population of less than 10,000 at the census of 1881, the powers formerly belonging to the borough council in respect of coroners shall be transferred to the county council of the county in which the borough is situated.

Formerly, too, the grant of a court of Quarter Sessions to a borough practically made it a county for administrative, as well as for judicial purposes. But substantial exceptions to this rule have been introduced by the Local Government Act of 1888. In the first place, as we have seen, a grant of Quarter Sessions to a borough after the coming into operation of that Act will not in the least interfere with the rights of the county council, which will be able, as

## SPECIAL TYPES OF BOROUGH 225

before, to levy the county rates in the borough, and will exercise the administrative control formerly exercised in the borough by the Quarter Sessions of the county, except in those matters which, by the Act, are specially reserved to the Justices at Quarter Sessions. But even in the case of Quarter Sessions boroughs created such before the Local Government Act of 1888, if at the census of 1881 they had less than 10,000 inhabitants, all the former powers of borough *Justices and council* in respect of pauper lunatic asylums, public analysts, reformatory and industrial schools, fish conservancy, explosives, and main roads will now be exerciseable by the county council, and the borough area will now be assessable to county rates. In such a case Her Majesty may, on the petition of the borough council, revoke the grant of Quarter Sessions, and even the Commission of the Peace, so that the borough will become part of the county for all but purely municipal purposes. Further than this, in the case of *all* boroughs with a population by the census of 1881 of less than 10,000, the former powers of the borough *council* in respect of police, analysts, contagious diseases of animals, destructive insects, gas meters, weights and measures, and explosives, will be exerciseable only by the county council.

(3) **A Stipendiary Magistrate** may, by virtue of certain Acts of Parliament, be appointed in any urban district with a population of 25,000, or in any municipal borough. In a borough, the stipendiary magistrate is appointed by the Crown on the petition of the council, which petition states the amount of the salary which the council is willing to pay. The stipendiary magistrate must be a barrister of seven years' standing, he holds

P

office at the pleasure of the Crown, receives from the borough council the salary assigned by the Crown (not exceeding the amount named in the petition of the council), is *ex-officio* a Justice for the borough, and, in the execution of his office, takes precedence of all other borough justices, including the mayor. Generally speaking, he has the powers of two ordinary Justices, and, when sitting in his judicial capacity in a borough which has its own Commission of the Peace, he constitutes a Petty Sessional Court with powers of summary jurisdiction. But he has not the administrative powers of Petty Sessions, though he may act as a licensing Justice for any district wholly or partly within his jurisdiction. In the year 1892 there were twenty-one provincial stipendiary magistrates for boroughs; thirteen acting under the Municipal Corporations Act, and eight under local Acts.

(4) **A Borough Civil Court.**—In a few cases (about twenty in all) a borough possesses its own local court of civil jurisdiction, whose powers have not been superseded by the County Courts Acts. These courts are always survivals of ancient institutions, and are not looked upon with much favour by the legislature. Examples may be seen in the Liverpool Court of Passage, the Tolzey Court of Bristol, the Provost's Court of Exeter. If there is a Recorder in the borough to which such a court belongs, he will act as its judge, unless the appointment of judge is regulated by local Act of Parliament, or unless a barrister of five years' standing acted at the passing of the Municipal Corporations Act of 1835. If there is no Recorder in the borough, the official named in the charter, or the customary official, appointed by the

[margin note: Recorder to be judge, except in certain cases.]

## SPECIAL TYPES OF BOROUGH 227

borough council, acts as judge. The Town Clerk acts as Registrar, unless the council appoints some one specially to the office. The court must be held for trials of law and fact at least four times a year, and there must be no greater interval than four months between any two sessions. *Town Clerk as Registrar. Sessions of Court.*

Where a borough has its own Quarter Sessions or its own civil court, the burgesses are liable to serve as jurors, unless specially exempt, in both courts. The clerk of the peace summons jurors for the Quarter Sessions, the Registrar for the civil court. But the burgesses of a Quarter Sessions borough are not liable to serve as jurors at the county Quarter Sessions. *Borough juries.*

(5) **Counties of Cities or Towns.**—A county of a city or town may be defined as a borough which obtained the full organisation of a county before the passing of the Municipal Corporations Act of 1835. The institution is an anomaly, and only tolerated from that veneration for tradition which is one of the most persistent features of English politics. In fact, it has been considerably trenched upon by the provisions of the Local Government Act of 1888.

The great features of the old county of a city or town were that it possessed its own sheriff, and that assizes were specially held in and for it. The former feature it still retains; for by the Municipal Corporations Act of 1882, every borough which is a county of itself must appoint a sheriff on the 9th November in each year. Generally speaking, city and town sheriffs are governed by the same law as county sheriffs; but the property qualification of the city or town sheriff may be in personalty, and he can only be called upon to perform the customary duties. He is *Sheriff.*

entitled to the customary fees of his office. As to the holding of assizes, however, it has long been the practice, in certain cases, to direct that offences arising in these privileged boroughs shall be tried in the adjoining counties; and this practice has been confirmed in the case of six boroughs by the Local Government Act of 1888. There are altogether eighteen counties of cities or towns.

(6) **County Boroughs.**—Finally, the Local Government Act of 1888 constituted a special class of some sixty large boroughs which, at the passing of the Act, were either counties of themselves or had populations of not less than 50,000. A borough in this class, which is to be known by the name of "county boroughs," is practically exempted from the jurisdiction of the county council of its county, and its borough council has most of the powers which were conferred by the Local Government Act of 1888 upon county councils, except the powers conferred in connection with parliamentary elections. But the constitution of the borough council is unchanged by its new position, and for most purposes the Act merely operates to confer new powers on the councils of the specified boroughs. An equitable adjustment of the financial relations between the county borough and its county in respect of local taxation licences and probate duties must be come to, and may be revised by order of the Local Government Board after every five years. And if assizes are not held in the borough, the latter must contribute a proper share of the costs of the county assizes; while if it has no separate court of Quarter Sessions, the borough must contribute to the expense of Quarter and Petty Sessions for the county, and to the expenses of the county coroners. It must be carefully remembered that there is

# SPECIAL TYPES OF BOROUGH

no *necessary* connection between a county of a city or town and a county borough, though the same place may be both. For there are many county boroughs which are not counties of towns, and, on the other hand, a few counties of cities or towns, such as Lichfield and Poole, which are not county boroughs.

# INDEX

## A

ACCOUNTS, 28, 40, 175, 197.
Administration, defined, 13.
Adoptive Acts, 47.
Adulteration, 111, 112.
Aldermen, Borough, 203, 204.
County, 166.
Gild, 193.
Allotments, 43, 44, 45, 169.
Annuity Certificates, 172.
Appeals, 31, 32, 33, 73, 75, 122, 128 n., 158, 175, 212, 218, 219.
Apprenticeship, 95.
Assessment Committee (of the Guardians). *See* Union Assessment Committee.
(of the County Council), 174.
Assessors (Borough), 206.
Assistant-Overseers, 30, 46.
Assizes, 71, 156, 227, 228.
Attendance Officers, 57.
Audit, 128, 146, 175.
Auditors (Borough), 205.

## B

BABY FARMS, 116, 148.
Bail, 149, 160, 161, 184, 211.
Barons of the Exchequer, 143.
Beadle, 19, 36.
Billeting, 161.
Bills of Mortality, 35.
Board of Guardians. *See* Guardians.
Board of Trade, 118.

Borough (generally), 11, 100, 187-198.
Parliamentary, 198, 199.
Municipal, 200-220.
Fund, 70, 219.
creation of, 200.
council, 201, 202, 203, 206-215.
corporation, 200.
aldermen, 203, 204.
property, 208-210.
Rate, 209, 218, 219.
Commission of the Peace, 221, 222.
Quarter Sessions, 222-225, 227.
Civil Court, 226-227.
Boundaries, 170.
Burgesses, generally, 165, 188-195, 227.
Qualification of, 201.
Powers of, 201, 202.
Burials, 51.
Burial Boards, 51, 52.
By-laws (Sanitary), 117-118.
(County), 176.
(Borough), 213.

## C

CAMBRIDGE, 142.
Chairman, of Parish Council, 42.
of Petty Sessions, 70, 73.
of School Board, 57.
of Sanitary Authority, 119.

# INDEX

Chairman of Quarter Sessions, 156.
  of County Council, 166.
Charities, 45, 169.
Charters, 190, 191, 192, 195, 200.
Chester, 188, 190.
Churchwardens, 27, 28.
Circuits (County Court), 78, 79.
Clerk, of the Peace, 32, 162-163, 176, 222, 223, 224, 227.
  of Parish Council, 46.
  of Petty Sessions, 67, 70, 222.
  of Sanitary Authority, 120.
  of County Council, 176.
  of Borough. *See* Town Clerk.
Collectors, 46.
Commissioners, Library, 52.
Committal for trial, 71.
Committees of Borough Council, 215.
Compound householder, 34.
Conscience, courts of, 77.
Constable, Parish, 48, 179.
  Paid, 48.
  High, 66, 67.
  Chief, 67, 180.
  Special, 183, 213.
  Police. *See* Police.
Contagious diseases of animals, 168, 225.
Coroner, 147-149, 224, 228.
Corporation (municipal), 194.
County (and *see* Shire).
  Council, 37, 40, 41, 108, 112 *n*., 113, 123, 137.
  Constitution of, 164-167.
  Functions of, 167-177.
  Districts, 165.
  Divisions, 164 *n*., 165.
  Boroughs, 166.
  Aldermen, 166.
  Court, 68, 76-86.
  Stock, 172.
  Rate, 70, 174.
  Buildings, 179.
  Boroughs, 228.
County of City or Town, 227-228, 228.
Crown Debts, 145

## D

DEBENTURES, 172.
Deputy-lieutenant, 138.
  sheriff, 147.
  coroner, 148.
Destructive insects, 168, 225.
Diseases. *See* Infectious Diseases.
Disqualifications, for office of overseer, 30 *n*.
  for office of parish councillor 41.
  for membership of School Board, 56 *n*.
  for local government franchise, 166.
  for membership of County Council, 167.
  of county officials, 177.
Dorsetshire, 134.
Drains. *See* Sewers.
Durham, 134.

## E

ECCLESIASTICAL patronage, 209.
Education Department, 55.
Emigrant runners, 116.
Essex, 134.
Exchequer, 140, 143.
Exchequer Contribution Account, 173, 174, 181, 212.
Execution, defined, 13.
Exemptions, from parish office, 27 *n*.
Explosives, 225.
Extra-parochial, 21.

## F

FEE GRANT, 58.
Ferm of the shire, 145.
Finance, sanitary, 122-128.
  county, 171-176.
  committee, 172.
Firma burgi, 189.
Fish conservancy, 168, 225.
Footpaths, 40, 45.
Franchises, 147.
Frankpledge, view of, 139.

# INDEX

## G

GAOLS and Gaol Sessions, 155.
Game dealers, 116.
Gangmasters, 116.
Gas meters, 225.
General rates, 127, 128.
General District Rate, 125, 126.
Gilds, 193.
Guardians of the Poor, general, 15, 56, 60, 61, 89.
  how appointed, 89-91.
  functions, 91-98.

## H

HANSE. *See* Gild.
High Bailiff (County Court), 79, 80.
Highways. *See* Roads.
Highway Boards, 51, 106-108.
Holy Orders, 167.
Housing of the working classes, 112-115.
Hundred, 11, 20, 33, 65-67, 68, 139.
Huntingdon, 142.

## I

IMPRESSMENT, 161.
Imprisonment for debt, 84.
Improvement Act District, 101, 102.
Indictable offences, 70, 71.
Indoor relief, 91.
Infectious diseases, 110-112.
Inquest (Coroner's), 148.
Inspector of Nuisances, 120.

## J

Joint-Committee, 179-184.
Juries, liability to serve on, 157 *n*., 227.
Jurisdiction, of County Court, 80-85.
Jury Lists, 74.
Justices of the Peace, general, 13, 14, 15, 29, 33, 66, 69, 75, 89, 93, 119, 122, 135, 142, 179, 181, 184, 205, 211, 213, 222, 223, 226.
Justice of the Peace, history of, 149-152.
  appointment of, 152-153, 222.
  powers of, 154-162.

## K

Knights of the shire, 135.

## L

LABOURERS, statutes of, 150.
Lathes, 11 *n*.
Leases, by borough council, 209.
Leet, the, 21,
Leet constable, 36.
Leet jury, 47, 66.
Legislation, defined, 13 (and *see* By-laws).
Libraries. *See* Public Libraries.
Licensing Committees, 159.
Lincoln, 190.
Liquor licences, 74.
Loans, to School Boards, 59.
  to Guardians, 97.
  to sanitary authorities, 124.
  to County Councils, 172.
  to Borough Councils, 217.
Loan Societies, rules of, 169.
Local Board District, 102.
Local Government Board, 15, 88, 102, 114, 118, 119 *n*., 123, 124, 127, 164, 172, 176, 208, 218, 228.
Local Loans Act, 1875, 173, 218.
Local Taxation Grant, 123, 173, 228.
London, 188, 193, 197.
(Lord) Lieutenant, 138-139.
Lunatic Asylums, 148, 159, 169, 225.

## M

MAYOR, 193, 199, 204, 205.
Medical Officer of Health, 120, 174, 176.
Militia, 137, 138.

Monasteries, dissolution of the, 23.
Municipal Commission of 1835, 196, 197.
Municipal Corporations Act, 165, 197, 200, 209, 210, 214, 222, 226, 227.
Municipal Council, 59, 60.
Museums. *See* Public Museums.
Music and dancing licences, 170.

### N

NEW boroughs, creation of, 170, 200.

### O

OCCASIONAL Court-house, 74.
Officials, of parish, 27-36, 46.
  of School Board, 57.
  of Hundred, 66.
  of Petty Sessions, 70.
  of County Court, 79-80.
  of Poor Law Union, 97-98.
  of Sanitary District, 119-122.
Outdoor Relief, 91, 95, 96.
Overseers of the Poor, 28-35, 46, 59, 96.

### P

PARISH, generally, 19-24, 87, 89, 90.
  Urban, 25-36.
  Rural, 36-47.
  Clerk, 35, 36, 46.
  Meeting, 38-40.
  Council, 40-47.
Parliamentary Grants, 59.
Parochial Electors, 38.
Part (of a county) 11 *n.*
Passage brokers, 116.
Pawnbrokers' Certificates, 116.
Penalties, 118, 124.
Pension Fund (Police), 182.
Petroleum, 116.
Petty Sessions, 32, 68-75, 78, 180, 181, 215, 222, 226, 228.
Pindar, 19.

Places of worship, registration of, 169.
Plague, The Great, 23, 150.
Police, County, 179-184.
  Borough, 210-213, 225.
Police Fund, 182.
Police Rate, 182.
Poor Law, generally, 151.
  Board, 88.
  Commissioners, 88, 119.
  Union, 37, 68, 87-98, 105.
Posse (Sheriff's), 147.
Prisons Visiting Committee, 159.
Private Improvement Rate, 125, 127.
Public analysts, 177, 225.
Public Health. *See* Sanitary District.
  Board of, 100.
Public Libraries, 52
  Museums, 52.
Public Works Loan Commissioners, 124, 209.

### Q

QUARTER SESSIONS, 32, 68, 69, 71, 154-159, 175, 181, 212, 219, 220, 222, 223, 224, 225, 228.
Quorum, 154.

### R

RACE-COURSES, licences for, 170.
Rapes, 11 *n.*, 68.
Rates, Poor, 31-34, 94.
  Private Improvement, 125, 127.
  Separate, 128, 212, 218.
  County, 32, 174, 219, 220.
  Parish, 40, 46.
  Highway, 50.
  School, 59.
  Sanitary, 125-128.
  Police, 182.
  Borough, 209, 218, 219.
  Watch, 212.
Rate in Aid, 33.

# INDEX

Recorder, 212, 218, 223, 226.
Recreation, 45, 115.
Reeve, 19, 20.
Reformatory and Industrial Schools, 168, 225.
Registrar, County Court, 79, 80.
 Births, Deaths, and Marriages, 98, 111.
Regulations (Sanitary), 118.
Remand, 71.
Removal, 93, 95.
Requests, Courts of, 77, 78.
Revising Assessors. *See* Assessors (Borough).
Riding 11 *n.*
Right of Way, 40.
Riot, 67, 161.
Rivers, Pollution of, 112, 168.
Roads, parish, 48-51, 106.
 high, 123.
 main, 167, 225.
Roads and bridges, 67.
Roses, Wars of the, 23.
Rotten boroughs, 195.

## S

SANITARY DISTRICT, 53, 68.
 Urban, 37, 49, 60, 100-104, 112.
 Rural, 37, 47, 104-105, 107, 112.
 Port, 100, 128-129.
Sanitary legislation, 117-119.
 offences, 121.
School Attendance Committee, 57, 60, 61.
School Board, how created, 55, 56.
 Constitution of, 56.
 Elections for, 56.
 Officials of, 57.
 Compulsory attendance, 57.
 Income of, 58, 59.
School District, 54-61.
School Fund, 59.
Scientific societies, registration of, 169.
Select Vestry. *See* Vestry

Separate rate, 128, 212, 218.
Settlement, 92-95.
Sewers, 108-110.
Sheriff, 67, 76, 134, 135, 136, 139- 147, 153, 194, 227.
Shire, 11, 20, 133-136 (and *see* County).
Somersetshire, 134.
Special rates, 128.
Specific performance, 82.
Standing Joint-Committee. *See* Joint-Committee.
Staple courts, 77.
Statute sessions, 67.
Stipendiary magistrate, 70, 225, 226.
Subsidies, 123.
Summary conviction, 70, 71, 72.
Superannuation Fund (Police), 179.
Surveyor of highways, 50.
 Sanitary, 120.
 County, 177.
Sussex, 134.

## T

TALLAGE, 189-191.
Taxation, 191.
Technical instruction, 168, 169.
Ten pound occupiers, 38, 165.
Tort, definition of, 81 *n.*
 claim on, 80, 81.
Tourn (Sheriff's), 67, 139.
Town Clerk, 120, 206, 216, 219, 226.
Town Police Clauses Act, 1847, 207.
Township, 11, 19, 20, 21, 23, 29.
Treasurer, of parish council, 46.
 of county council, 172, 176.
 of borough, 216.
Turnpikes, 49.

## U

UNDER-SHERIFF, 146.
Union Assessment Committee, 31.
Union Chargeability Act, 1865, 88.

## V

VACCINATION, 98.
Vestry, 22, 25-27, 34, 36.
  select, 26, 27.
Vice-Lieutenant, 139.
Volunteer corps, land for, 218.

## W

WAGES, assessment of by Justices, 150.
Wapontake, 11 *n.*, (and *see* Hundred).
Ward, of a county, 11 *n.*
  of a parish, 41.
  of a borough, 165, 200, 202
  of an urban district, 170.
Warrant, 161, 183.
Watch Committee, 210, 211.
Water supply, 45, 112.
Waywardens, 107.
Weights and measures, 170, 225.
Westmoreland, 142.
Wild birds, protection of, 168.
Wiltshire, 134.

## Y

YORK, 188.

# A CATALOGUE OF BOOKS PUBLISHED BY METHUEN AND COMPANY: LONDON 36 ESSEX STREET W.C.

## CONTENTS

| | PAGE | | PAGE |
|---|---|---|---|
| GENERAL LITERATURE, | 2-24 | LITTLE GALLERIES, | 29 |
| ANTIQUARY'S BOOKS, | 25 | LITTLE GUIDES, | 29 |
| BUSINESS BOOKS, | 25 | LITTLE LIBRARY, | 29 |
| BYZANTINE TEXTS, | 25 | METHUEN'S MINIATURE LIBRARY, | 30 |
| CHURCHMAN'S BIBLE, | 25 | RARIORA, | 30 |
| CHURCHMAN'S LIBRARY, | 25 | SCHOOL EXAMINATION SERIES, | 30 |
| CLASSICAL TRANSLATIONS, | 25 | SOCIAL QUESTIONS OF TO-DAY, | 31 |
| COMMERCIAL SERIES, | 26 | TEXTBOOKS OF TECHNOLOGY, | 31 |
| CONNOISSEURS LIBRARY, | 26 | HANDBOOKS OF THEOLOGY, | 31 |
| LIBRARY OF DEVOTION, | 26 | UNIVERSITY EXTENSION SERIES, | 31 |
| ILLUSTRATED POCKET LIBRARY OF PLAIN AND COLOURED BOOKS, | 26 | WESTMINSTER COMMENTARIES, | 32 |
| JUNIOR EXAMINATION SERIES | 28 | FICTION, | 32-39 |
| METHUEN'S JUNIOR SCHOOL-BOOKS, | 28 | BOOKS FOR BOYS AND GIRLS, | 39 |
| LEADERS OF RELIGION, | 28 | NOVELS OF ALEXANDRE DUMAS, | 39 |
| LITTLE BIOGRAPHIES, | 28 | METHUEN'S ONE SHILLING NOVELS, | 39 |
| LITTLE BLUE BOOKS, | 28 | THE NOVELIST, | 40 |
| LITTLE BOOKS ON ART, | 29 | SIXPENNY LIBRARY, | 40 |

SEPTEMBER 1904

A CATALOGUE OF

# MESSRS. METHUEN'S PUBLICATIONS

Colonial Editions are published of all Messrs. METHUEN'S Novels issued at a price above 2s. 6d., and similar editions are published of some works of General Literature. These are marked in the Catalogue. Colonial editions are only for circulation in the British Colonies and India.

## PART I.—GENERAL LITERATURE

**Abbot (Jacob).** THE BEECHNUT BOOK. Edited by E. V. LUCAS. Illustrated. *Demy 16mo.* 2s. 6d. [Little Blue Books.
**Acatos (M. J.).** See L. A. Sornet.
**Adams (Frank).** JACK SPRATT. With 24 Coloured Pictures. *Pott 4to.* 2s.
**Adeney (W. F.),** M.A. See Bennett and Adeney.
**Æschylus.** AGAMEMNON, CHOEPHOROE, EUMENIDES. Translated by LEWIS CAMPBELL, LL.D., late Professor of Greek at St. Andrews. 5s.
[Classical Translations.
**Æsop.** FABLES. With 380 Woodcuts by THOMAS BEWICK. *Fcap. 8vo.* 3s. 6d. net.
[Illustrated Pocket Library.
**Ainsworth (W. Harrison).** WINDSOR CASTLE. With 22 Plates and 87 Woodcuts in the Text by GEORGE CRUIKSHANK. *Fcap. 8vo.* 3s. 6d. net.
[Illustrated Pocket Library.
THE TOWER OF LONDON. With 40 Plates and 58 Woodcuts in the Text by GEORGE CRUIKSHANK. *Fcap. 8vo.* 3s. 6d. net.
[Illustrated Pocket Library.
**Alexander (William),** D.D., Archbishop of Armagh. THOUGHTS AND COUNSELS OF MANY YEARS. Selected by J. H. BURN, B.D. *Demy 16mo.* 2s. 6d.
**Aiken (Henry).** THE ANALYSIS OF THE HUNTING FIELD. With 7 Coloured Plates and 43 Illustrations on wood. *Fcap. 8vo.* 3s. 6d. net.
[Illustrated Pocket Library.
THE NATIONAL SPORTS OF GREAT BRITAIN. With descriptions in English and French. With 51 Coloured Plates. *Royal Folio. Five Guineas net.*
THE NATIONAL SPORTS OF GREAT BRITAIN. With Descriptions and Coloured Plates by HENRY ALKEN. 4s. 6d. net.
Also a limited edition on large Japanese paper, 30s. net.

This book is completely different from the large folio edition of 'National Sports' by the same artist, and none of the plates are similar. [Illustrated Pocket Library.
See also **Nimrod** and **Egan.**
**Allen (Jessie).** DURER. With many Illustrations. *Demy 16mo.* 2s. 6d. net.
[Little Books on Art.
**Allen (J. Romilly),** F.S.A. CELTIC ART. With numerous Illustrations and Plans. *Demy 8vo.* 7s. 6d. net.
[Antiquary's Books.
**Almack (E.).** BOOKPLATES. With many Illustrations. *Demy 16mo.* 2s. 6d. net.
[Little Books on Art.
**Amherst (Lady).** A SKETCH OF EGYPTIAN HISTORY FROM THE EARLIEST TIMES TO THE PRESENT DAY. With many Illustrations, some of which are in Colour. *Demy 8vo.* 10s. 6d net.
**Anderson (F. M.).** THE STORY OF THE BRITISH EMPIRE FOR CHILDREN. With many Illustrations. *Crown 8vo.* 2s.
**Andrewes (Bishop).** PRECES PRIVATAE. Edited, with Notes, by F. E. BRIGHTMAN, M.A., of Pusey House, Oxford. *Crown 8vo.* 6s.
**Aristophanes.** THE FROGS. Translated into English by E. W. HUNTINGFORD, M.A., Professor of Classics in Trinity College, Toronto. *Crown 8vo.* 2s. 6d.
**Aristotle.** THE NICOMACHEAN ETHICS. Edited, with an Introduction and Notes, by JOHN BURNET, M.A., Professor of Greek at St. Andrews. *Demy 8vo.* 15s. net.
**Ashton. (R.).** THE PEELES AT THE CAPITAL. Illustrated. *Demy 16mo.* 2s. 6d. [Little Blue Books.
MRS. BARBERRY'S GENERAL SHOP. Illustrated. *Demy 16mo.* 2s. 6d.
[The Little Blue Books.

## General Literature

**Asquith (H. H.)**, The Right Hon., M.P. TRADE AND THE EMPIRE. An Examination of Mr. Chamberlain's Proposals. *Demy 8vo.* 6d. net.

**Atkins (H. G.)**. GOETHE. With 12 Illustrations. *Fcap. 8vo.* 3s. 6d.; leather, 4s. net. [Little Biographies. Nearly Ready.

**Atkinson (T. D.)**. A SHORT HISTORY OF ENGLISH ARCHITECTURE. With over 200 Illustrations by the Author and others. *Fcap. 8vo.* 3s. 6d. net.

**Austen (Jane)**. PRIDE AND PREJUDICE. Edited by E. V. Lucas. *Two Volumes. Small Pott 8vo.* Each volume, cloth, 1s. 6d. net.; leather, 2s. 6d. net.
[Little Library.

NORTHANGER ABBEY. Edited by E. V. Lucas. *Small Pott 8vo. Cloth*, 1s. 6d. net.; leather, 2s. net. [Little Library.

**Bacon (Francis)**. THE ESSAYS OF. Edited by Edward Wright. *Small Pott 8vo.* 1s. 6d. net; leather, 2s. 6d. net.
[Little Library.

**Baden-Powell (R. S. S.)**, Major-General. THE DOWNFALL OF PREMPEH. A Diary of Life in Ashanti, 1895. With 21 Illustrations and a Map. *Third Edition. Large Crown 8vo.* 6s.
A Colonial Edition is also published.

THE MATABELE CAMPAIGN, 1896. With nearly 100 Illustrations. *Fourth and Cheaper Edition. Large Crown 8vo.* 6s.
A Colonial Edition is also published.

**Baker (W. G.)**, M.A. JUNIOR GEOGRAPHY EXAMINATION PAPERS. *Fcap. 8vo.* 1s. [Junior Exam. Series.

**Baker (Julian L.)**, F.I.C., F.C.S. THE BREWING INDUSTRY. *Crown 8vo.* 2s. 6d. net. [Books on Business.

**Balfour (Graham)**. THE LIFE OF ROBERT LOUIS STEVENSON. *Second Edition. Two Volumes. Demy 8vo.* 25s. net.
A Colonial Edition is also published.

**Bally (S. E.)**. A FRENCH COMMERCIAL READER. With Vocabulary. *Second Edition. Crown 8vo.* 2s.
[Commercial Series.

FRENCH COMMERCIAL CORRESPONDENCE. With Vocabulary. *Third Edition. Crown 8vo.* 2s.
[Commercial Series.

A GERMAN COMMERCIAL READER. With Vocabulary. *Crown 8vo.* 2s.
[Commercial Series.

GERMAN COMMERCIAL CORRESPONDENCE. With Vocabulary. *Crown 8vo.* 2s. 6d. [Commercial Series.

**Banks (Elizabeth L.)**. THE AUTOBIOGRAPHY OF A 'NEWSPAPER GIRL.' With Portrait of the Author and her Dog. *Second Edition. Crown 8vo.* 6s.
A Colonial Edition is also published.

**Barham (R. H.)**. THE INGOLDSBY LEGENDS. Edited by J. B. Atlay. *Two Volumes. Small Pott 8vo.* Each volume, cloth, 1s. 6d. net; leather, 2s. 6d. net.
[Little Library.

**Baring-Gould (S.)**. Author of 'Mehalah,' etc. THE LIFE OF NAPOLEON BONAPARTE. With over 450 Illustrations in the Text, and 12 Photogravure Plates. *Gilt top. Large quarto.* 36s.

THE TRAGEDY OF THE CÆSARS. With numerous Illustrations from Busts, Gems, Cameos, etc. *Fifth Edition. Royal 8vo.* 15s.

A BOOK OF FAIRY TALES. With numerous Illustrations and Initial Letters by Arthur J. Gaskin. *Second Edition. Crown 8vo. Buckram.* 6s.

A BOOK OF BRITTANY. With numerous Illustrations. *Crown 8vo.* 6s.
Uniform in scope and size with Mr. Baring-Gould's well-known books on Devon, Cornwall, and Dartmoor.

OLD ENGLISH FAIRY TALES. With numerous Illustrations by F. D. Bedford. *Second Edition. Cr. 8vo. Buckram.* 6s.
A Colonial Edition is also published.

THE VICAR OF MORWENSTOW: A Biography. A new and Revised Edition. With Portrait. *Crown 8vo.* 3s. 6d.
A completely new edition of the well-known biography of R. S. Hawker.

DARTMOOR: A Descriptive and Historical Sketch. With Plans and numerous Illustrations. *Crown 8vo.* 6s.

THE BOOK OF THE WEST. With numerous Illustrations. *Two volumes.* Vol. I. Devon. *Second Edition.* Vol. II. Cornwall. *Second Edition. Crown 8vo.* 6s. each.

A BOOK OF NORTH WALES. With numerous Illustrations. *Crown 8vo.* 6s.
This book is uniform with Mr. Baring-Gould's books on Devon, Dartmoor, and Brittany.

A BOOK OF SOUTH WALES. With many Illustrations. *Cr. 8vo.* 6s.

A BOOK OF GHOSTS. With many Illustrations. *Cr. 8vo.* 6s. net.
A Colonial Edition is also published.

BRITTANY. Illustrated by J. A. Wylie. *Pott 8vo. Cloth*, 3s.; leather, 3s. 6d. net.
[Little Guides.

OLD COUNTRY LIFE. With 67 Illustrations. *Fifth Edition. Large Cr. 8vo.* 6s.

AN OLD ENGLISH HOME. With numerous Plans and Illustrations. *Cr. 8vo.* 6s.

YORKSHIRE ODDITIES AND STRANGE EVENTS. *Fifth Edition. Crown 8vo.* 6s.

STRANGE SURVIVALS AND SUPERSTITIONS. *Second Edition. Cr. 8vo.* 6s.
A Colonial Edition is also published.

A GARLAND OF COUNTRY SONG: English Folk Songs with their Traditional Melodies. Collected and arranged by S. Baring-Gould and H. F. Sheppard. *Demy 4to.* 6s.

SONGS OF THE WEST: Traditional Ballads and Songs of the West of England, with their Melodies. Collected by S. BARING-GOULD, M.A., and H. F. SHEPPARD, M.A. In 4 Parts. *Parts I., II., III.*, 2s. 6d. each. *Part IV.*, 4s. In One Volume, French Morocco, 10s. net.

Barker (Aldred F.), Author of 'Pattern Analysis,' etc. AN INTRODUCTION TO THE STUDY OF TEXTILE DESIGN. With numerous Diagrams and Illustrations. *Demy 8vo.* 7s. 6d.

Barnes (W. E.), D.D. ISAIAH. With an Introduction and Notes. *Two Vols. Fcap. 8vo.* 2s. net each. With Map. [Churchman's Bible.

Barnett (Mrs. P. A.). A LITTLE BOOK OF ENGLISH PROSE. *Small Pott 8vo. Cloth*, 1s. 6d. net; *leather*, 2s. 6d. net.
[Little Library.

Baron (R. R. N.), M.A. FRENCH PROSE COMPOSITION. *Crown 8vo.* 2s. 6d. *Key*, 3s. net.

Barron (H. M.), M.A., Wadham College, Oxford. TEXTS FOR SERMONS. With a Preface by Canon SCOTT HOLLAND. *Crown 8vo.* 3s. 6d.

Bastable (C. F.), M.A., Professor of Economics at Trinity College, Dublin. THE COMMERCE OF NATIONS. *Second Edition. Crown 8vo.* 2s. 6d.
[Social Questions Series.

Batson (Mrs. Stephen). A BOOK OF THE COUNTRY AND THE GARDEN. Illustrated by F. CARRUTHERS GOULD and A. C. GOULD. *Demy 8vo.* 10s. 6d. A CONCISE HANDBOOK OF GARDEN FLOWERS. *Fcap. 8vo.* 3s. 6d.

Beaman (A. Hulme). PONS ASINORUM; OR, A GUIDE TO BRIDGE. *Second Edition. Fcap. 8vo.* 2s.

Beard (W. S.). JUNIOR ARITHMETIC EXAMINATION PAPERS. *Second Edition. Fcap. 8vo.* 1s. With or without Answers. [Junior Examination Series. JUNIOR GENERAL INFORMATION EXAMINATION PAPERS. *Fcap. 8vo.* 1s. [Junior Examination Series. EASY EXERCISES IN ARITHMETIC. Arranged by. *Cr. 8vo.* Without Answers, 1s. With Answers, 1s. 3d.

Beckford (Peter). THOUGHTS ON HUNTING. Edited by J. OTHO PAGET, and Illustrated by G. H. JALLAND. *Second and Cheaper Edition. Demy 8vo.* 6s.

Beckford (William). THE HISTORY OF THE CALIPH VATHEK. Edited by E. DENISON ROSS. *Pott 8vo. Cloth*, 1s. 6d. net; *leather*, 2s. 6d. net. [Little Library.

Beeching (H. C.), M.A., Canon of Westminster. LYRA SACRA: A Book of Sacred Verse. With an Introduction and Notes. *Pott 8vo. Cl.*, 2s.; *leather*, 2s. 6d. [Library of Devotion.

Behmen (Jacob). THE SUPERSENSUAL LIFE. Edited by BERNARD HOLLAND. *Fcap. 8vo.* 3s. 6d.

Belloc (Hilaire). PARIS. With Maps and Illustrations. *Crown 8vo.* 6s.

Bellot (H. H. L.), M.A. THE INNER AND MIDDLE TEMPLE. With numerous Illustrations. *Crown 8vo.* 6s. net.
See also L. A. A. Jones.

Bennett (W. H.), M.A. A PRIMER OF THE BIBLE. *Second Edition. Crown 8vo.* 2s. 6d.

Bennett (W. H.) and Adeney (W. F.). A BIBLICAL INTRODUCTION. *Second Edition. Crown 8vo.* 7s. 6d.

Benson (Archbishop). GOD'S BOARD: Communion Addresses. With Introductory Note by Mrs. Benson. *Fcap. 8vo.* 3s. 6d. net.

Benson (A. C.), M.A. TENNYSON. With 8 Illustrations. *Fcap. 8vo. Cloth*, 3s. 6d.; *Leather*, 4s. net. [Little Biographies.

Benson (R. M.). THE WAY OF HOLINESS: a Devotional Commentary on the 119th Psalm. *Crown 8vo.* 5s.

Bernard (E. R.), M.A., Canon of Salisbury. THE ENGLISH SUNDAY. *Fcap. 8vo.* 1s. 6d.

Bertouche (Baroness de). THE LIFE OF FATHER IGNATIUS. With Illustrations. *Demy 8vo.* 10s. 6d. net.
A Colonial Edition is also published.

Bethune-Baker (J. F.), M.A., Fellow of Pembroke College, Cambridge. A HISTORY OF EARLY CHRISTIAN DOCTRINE. *Demy 8vo.* 10s. 6d. net.
[Handbooks of Theology.

Bidez (M.). See Parmentier.

Biggs (C. R. D.), D.D. THE EPISTLE TO THE PHILIPPIANS. With an Introduction and Notes *Fcap. 8vo.* 1s. 6d. net.
[Churchman's Bible.

Bindley (T. Herbert), B.D. THE OECUMENICAL DOCUMENTS OF THE FAITH. With Introductions and Notes. *Crown 8vo.* 6s.
A historical account of the Creeds.

Binyon (Laurence). THE DEATH OF ADAM, AND OTHER POEMS. *Second Edition. Crown 8vo.* 3s. 6d. net.

Blair (Robert). THE GRAVE: a Poem. Illustrated by 12 Etchings executed by LOUIS SCHIAVONETTI, from the original inventions of WILLIAM BLAKE. With an Engraved Title-Page and a Portrait of Blake by T. PHILLIPS, R.A. *Fcap. 8vo.* 3s. 6d. net.
Also a limited edition on large Japanese paper with India Proofs and a duplicate set of plates. 15s. net. [Illustrated Pocket Library.

Blake (William). ILLUSTRATIONS OF THE BOOK OF JOB. Invented and Engraved by. *Fcap. 8vo.* 3s. 6d. net.
Also a limited edition on large Japanese paper with India proofs and a duplicate set of plates. 15s. net. [Illustrated Pocket Library. SELECTIONS. Edited by M. PERUGINI. *Small Pott 8vo.* 1s. 6d. net; *leather*, 2s. 6d. net. [Little Library.

## General Literature 5

**Blaxland (B.)** M.A. THE SONG OF SONGS. Being Selections from ST. BERNARD. *Small Pott 8vo. Cloth, 2s.; leather, 2s. 6d. net.* [Library of Devotion.

**Bloom (T. Harvey),** M.A. SHAKESPEARE'S GARDEN. With Illustrations. *Fcap. 8vo. 2s. 6d.; leather, 3s. 6d. net.*

**Boardman (J. H.).** See W. French.

**Bodley (J. E. C.).** Author of 'France.' THE CORONATION OF EDWARD VII. *Demy 8vo. 21s. net.* By Command of the King.

**Body (George),** D.D. THE SOUL'S PILGRIMAGE: Devotional Readings from his published and unpublished writings. Selected and arranged by J. H. BURN, B.D., F.R.S.E. *Pott 8vo. 2s. 6d.*

**Bona (Cardinal).** A GUIDE TO ETERNITY. Edited with an Introduction and Notes, by J. W. STANBRIDGE, B.D. *Pott 8vo. Cloth, 2s.; leather, 2s. 6d. net.* [Library of Devotion.

**Borrow (George).** LAVENGRO. Edited by F. HINDES GROOME. *Two Volumes. Small Pott 8vo. Each volume, cloth, 1s. 6d. net; leather, 2s. 6d. net.* [Little Library.
THE ROMANY RYE. Edited by JOHN SAMPSON. *Small Pott 8vo. Cloth, 1s. 6d. net; leather, 2s. 6d. net.* [Little Library.

**Bos (J. Ritzema).** AGRICULTURAL ZOOLOGY. Translated by J. R. AINSWORTH DAVIS, M.A. With an Introduction by ELEANOR A. ORMEROD, F.E.S. With 155 Illustrations. *Crown 8vo. Third Edition. 3s. 6d.*

**Botting (C. G.),** B.A. JUNIOR LATIN EXAMINATION PAPERS. *Fcap. 8vo. Second Ed. 1s.* [Junior Examination Series.
EASY GREEK EXERCISES. *Cr. 8vo. 2s.*

**Boulton (E. S.).** GEOMETRY ON MODERN LINES. *Crown 8vo. 2s.*

**Bowden (E. M.).** THE IMITATION OF BUDDHA: Being Quotations from Buddhist Literature for each Day in the Year. *Fourth Edition. Crown 16mo. 2s. 6d.*

**Bowmaker (E.).** THE HOUSING OF THE WORKING CLASSES. *Crown 8vo. 2s. 6d.* [Social Questions Series.

**Boyle (W.).** CHRISTMAS AT THE ZOO. With Verses by W. BOYLE and 24 Coloured Pictures by H. B. NEILSON. *Pott 4to. 6s.*

**Brabant (F. G.),** M.A. SUSSEX. Illustrated by E. H. NEW. *Small Pott 8vo. Cloth, 3s.; leather, 3s. 6d. net.* [Little Guides.
THE ENGLISH LAKES. Illustrated by E. H. NEW. *Small Pott 8vo. Cloth, 4s.; leather, 4s. 6d. net.* [Little Guides.

**Brodrick (Mary) and Morton (Anderson).** A CONCISE HANDBOOK OF EGYPTIAN ARCHÆOLOGY. With many Illustrations. *Crown 8vo. 3s. 6d.*

**Brooke (A. S.),** M.A. SLINGSBY AND SLINGSBY CASTLE. With many Illustrations. *Cr. 8vo. 7s. 6d.*

**Brooks (E. W.).** See F. J. Hamilton.

**Brown (P. H.),** Fraser Professor of Ancient (Scottish) History at the University of Edinburgh. SCOTLAND IN THE TIME OF QUEEN MARY. *Demy 8vo. 7s. 6d. net.*

**Brownell (C. L.).** THE HEART OF JAPAN. Illustrated. *Third Edition. Crown 8vo. 6s.*
A Colonial Edition is also published.

**Browning (Robert).** SELECTIONS FROM THE EARLY POEMS OF. With Introduction and Notes by W. HALL GRIFFIN. *Small Pott 8vo. 1s. 6d. net.; leather, 2s. 6d. net.* [Little Library.

**Buckland (Francis T.).** CURIOSITIES OF NATURAL HISTORY. With Illustrations by HARRY B. NEILSON. *Crown 8vo. 3s. 6d.*

**Buckton (A. M.).** THE BURDEN OF ENGELA: a Ballad-Epic. *Second Edition. Crown 8vo. 3s. 6d. net.*
EAGER HEART: A Mystery Play. *Crown 8vo. 1s. net.*

**Budge (E. A. Wallis).** THE GODS OF THE EGYPTIANS. With over 100 Coloured Plates and many Illustrations. *Two Volumes. Royal 8vo. £3, 3s. net.*

**Bull (Paul),** Army Chaplain. GOD AND OUR SOLDIERS. *Crown 8vo. 6s.*
A Colonial Edition is also published.

**Bulley (Miss).** See Lady Dilke.

**Bunyan (John).** THE PILGRIM'S PROGRESS. Edited, with an Introduction, by C. H. FIRTH, M.A. With 39 Illustrations by R. ANNING BELL. *Cr. 8vo. 6s.*
GRACE ABOUNDING. Edited by C. S. FREER, M.A. *Small Pott 8vo. Cloth, 2s.; leather, 2s. 6d. net.* [Library of Devotion.

**Burch (G. J.),** M.A., F.R.S. A MANUAL OF ELECTRICAL SCIENCE. With numerous Illustrations. *Crown 8vo. 3s.*
[University Extension Series.

**Burgess (Gelett).** GOOPS AND HOW TO BE THEM. With numerous Illustrations. *Small 4to. 6s.*

**Burn (A. E.),** D.D., Prebendary of Lichfield. AN INTRODUCTION TO THE HISTORY OF THE CREEDS. *Demy 8vo. 10s. 6d.* [Handbooks of Theology.

**Burn (J. H.),** B.D., A MANUAL OF CONSOLATION FROM THE SAINTS AND FATHERS. *Small Pott 8vo. Cloth, 2s.; leather, 2s. 6d. net.* [Library of Devotion.

**Burn (J. H.),** B.D. A DAY BOOK FROM THE SAINTS AND FATHERS. With an Introduction and Notes. *Small Pott 8vo. Cloth, 2s.; leather, 2s. 6d. net.*
[Library of Devotion.

**Burnand (Sir F. C.).** RECORDS AND REMINISCENCES, PERSONAL AND GENERAL. With many Illustrations. *Demy 8vo. Two Volumes. Third Edition. 25s.*
A Colonial Edition is also published.

**Burns (Robert),** THE POEMS OF. Edited by ANDREW LANG and W. A. CRAIGIE. With Portrait. *Third Edition. Demy 8vo, gilt top.* 6s.

**Burnside (W. F.),** M.A. OLD TESTAMENT HISTORY FOR USE IN SCHOOLS. *Crown 8vo.* 3s. 6d.

**Burton (Alfred).** THE MILITARY ADVENTURES OF JOHNNY NEWCOME. With 15 Coloured Plates by T. ROWLANDSON. *Fcap. 8vo.* 3s. 6d. *net.* [Illustrated Pocket Library.

THE ADVENTURES OF JOHNNY NEWCOME IN THE NAVY. With 16 Coloured Plates by T. ROWLANDSON. *Fcap.* 8vo. 3s. 6d. *net.* [Illus. Pocket Library

**Caldecott (Alfred),** D.D. THE PHILOSOPHY OF RELIGION IN ENGLAND AND AMERICA. *Demy 8vo.* 10s. 6d. [Handbooks of Theology.

**Calderwood (D. S.),** Headmaster of the Normal School, Edinburgh. TEST CARDS IN EUCLID AND ALGEBRA. In three packets of 40, with Answers. 1s. each. Or in three Books, price 2d., 2d., and 3d.

**Cambridge (Ada) [Mrs. Cross].** THIRTY YEARS IN AUSTRALIA. *Demy 8vo.* 7s. 6d A Colonial Edition is also published.

**Canning (George).** SELECTIONS FROM THE ANTI-JACOBIN; with additional Poems. Edited by LLOYD SANDERS. *Small Pott 8vo, cloth,* 1s. 6d. *net.; leather,* 2s. 6d. *net.* [Little Library.

**Capey (E. F. H.).** ERASMUS. With 12 Illustrations. *Fcap. 8vo. Cloth,* 3s. 6d. *net; leather,* 4s. *net.* [Little Biographies.

**Carlyle (Thomas).** THE FRENCH REVOLUTION. Edited by C. R. L. FLETCHER, Fellow of Magdalen College, Oxford. *Three Volumes. Crown 8vo.* 18s. THE LIFE AND LETTERS OF OLIVER CROMWELL. With an Introduction by C. H. FIRTH, M.A., and Notes and Appendices by Mrs. S. C. LOMAS. *Three Volumes. Demy 8vo.* 18s. *net.*

**Carlyle (R. M. and A. J.),** M.A. BISHOP LATIMER. With Portrait. *Crown 8vo.* 3s. 6d. [Leaders of Religion.

**Chamberlin (Wilbur B.).** ORDERED TO CHINA. *Crown 8vo.* 6s. A Colonial Edition is also published.

**Channer (C. C.) and Roberts (M. E.).** LACE-MAKING IN THE MIDLANDS, PAST AND PRESENT. With 16 fullpage Illustrations. *Crown 8vo.* 2s. 6d.

**Chesterfield (Lord),** THE LETTERS OF, TO HIS SON. Edited, with an Introduction, by C. STRACHEY, and Notes by A. CALTHROP. *Two Volumes. Cr. 8vo.* 12s.

**Christian (F W.).** THE CAROLINE ISLANDS. With many Illustrations and Maps. *Demy 8vo.* 12s. 6d. *net.*

**Cicero.** DE ORATORE I. Translated by E. N. P. MOOR, M.A. *Crown 8vo.* 3s. 6d. [Classical Translations.

SELECT ORATIONS (Pro Milone, Pro Murena, Philippic II., In Catilinam). Translated by H. E. D. BLAKISTON, M.A., Fellow and Tutor of Trinity College, Oxford. *Crown 8vo.* 5s. [Classical Translations.

DE NATURA DEORUM. Translated by F. BROOKS, M.A., late Scholar of Balliol College, Oxford. *Crown 8vo.* 3s. 6d. [Classical Translations.

DE OFFICIIS. Translated by G. B. GARDINER, M.A. *Crown 8vo.* 2s. 6d. [Classical Translations.

**Clarke (F. A.),** M.A. BISHOP KEN. With Portrait. *Crown 8vo.* 3s. 6d. [Leaders of Religion.

**Cleather (A. L.) and Crump (B.).** RICHARD WAGNER'S MUSIC DRAMAS: Interpretations, embodying Wagner's own explanations. *In Four Volumes Fcap 8vo.* 2s. 6d. *each.* VOL. I.—THE RING OF THE NIBELUNG. VOL. II.—PARSIFAL, etc.

**Clinch (G.).** KENT. Illustrated by F. D. BEDFORD. *Small Pott 8vo. Cloth,* 3s.; *leather,* 3s. 6d. *net.* [Little Guides. THE ISLE OF WIGHT. Illustrated by F. D. BEDFORD. *Small Pott 8vo. Cloth,* 3s.; *leather,* 3s. 6d. *net.* [Little Guides.

**Clough (W. T.) and Dunstan (A. E.).** ELEMENTARY EXPERIMENTAL SCIENCE. PHYSICS by W. T. CLOUGH, A.R.C.S. CHEMISTRY by A. E. DUNSTAN, B.Sc. With 2 Plates and 154 Diagrams. *Crown 8vo.* 2s. [Junior School Books.

**Coast (W. G),** B.A. EXAMINATION PAPERS IN VERGIL *Crown 8vo.* 2s.

**Cobb (T.).** THE CASTAWAYS OF MEADOWBANK. Illustrated. *Demy* 16mo. 2s. 6d. [Little Blue Books. THE TREASURY OF PRINCEGATE PRIORY. Illustrated. *Demy* 16mo. 2s. 6d. [Little Blue Books. THE LOST BALL. Illustrated. *Demy* 16mo. 2s. 6d. [Little Blue Books.

**Collingwood (W. G.),** M.A. THE LIFE OF JOHN RUSKIN. With Portraits. *Second and Cheap Edition. Cr. 8vo.* 6s. Also a Popular Edition. *Cr. 8vo.* 2s. 6d. *net.*

**Collins (W. E.),** M.A. THE BEGINNINGS OF ENGLISH CHRISTIANITY. With Map. *Cr. 8vo.* 3s. 6d. [Churchman's Library

**Colonna.** HYPNEROTOMACHIA POLIPHILI UBI HUMANA OMNIA NON NISI SOMNIUM ESSE DOCET ATQUE OBITER PLURIMA SCITU SANE QUAM DIGNA COMMEMORAT. An edition limited to 350 copies on handmade paper. *Folio. Three Guineas net.*

**Combe (William).** THE TOUR OF DR. SYNTAX IN SEARCH OF THE PICTURESQUE. With 30 Coloured Plates by T. ROWLANDSON. *Fcap. 8vo.* 3s. 6d. *net.* Also a limited edition on large Japanese paper. 30s. *net.* [Illustrated Pocket Library.

## GENERAL LITERATURE 7

THE TOUR OF DR. SYNTAX IN SEARCH OF CONSOLATION. With 24 Coloured Plates by T. ROWLANDSON. 3s. 6d. net.
Also a limited edition on large Japanese paper. 30s. net. [Illustrated Pocket Library.
THE THIRD TOUR OF DR. SYNTAX IN SEARCH OF A WIFE. With 24 Coloured Plates by T. ROWLANDSON. 3s. 6d. net
Also a limited edition on large Japansee paper. 30s. net.
[Illustrated Pocket Library.
THE HISTORY OF JOHNNY QUAE GENUS: The Little Foundling of the late Dr. Syntax. With 24 Coloured Plates by ROWLANDSON. Fcap. 8vo. 3s. 6d. net.
Also a limited edition on large Japanese paper. 30s. net.
[Illustrated Pocket Library.
THE ENGLISH DANCE OF DEATH, from the Designs of THOMAS ROWLANDSON, with Metrical Illustrations by the Author of 'Doctor Syntax.' With 74 Coloured Plates. Two Volumes. Fcap. 8vo. 9s. net.
Also a limited edition on large Japanese paper. 30s. net.
[Illustrated Pocket Library.
THE DANCE OF LIFE: a Poem. Illustrated with 26 Coloured Engravings by THOMAS ROWLANDSON. Fcap. 8vo. 3s. 6d. net.
Also a limited edition on large Japanese paper. 30s. net.
[Illustrated Pocket Library.
Cook (A. M.), M.A. See E. C. Marchant.
Cooke-Taylor (R. W.). THE FACTORY SYSTEM. Crown 8vo. 2s. 6d.
[Social Questions Series.
Corelli (Marie). THE PASSING OF THE GREAT QUEEN : A Tribute to the Noble Life of Victoria Regina. Small 4to. 1s.
A CHRISTMAS GREETING. Sm. 4to. 1s.
Corkran (Alice). LEIGHTON. With many Illustrations. Demy 16mo. 2s. 6d. net.
[Little Books on Art.
Cotes (Rosemary). DANTE'S GARDEN. With a Frontispiece. Second Edition. Fcap. 8vo. cloth 2s. 6d.; leather, 3s. 6d. net.
BIBLE FLOWERS. With a Frontispiece and Plan. Fcap. 8vo. 2s. 6d. net.
Cowley (Abraham) THE ESSAYS OF. Edited by H. C. MINCHIN. Small. Pott 8vo. Cloth, 1s. 6d. net; leather, 2s. 6d. net.
[Little Library.
Cox (J. Charles), LL.D., F.S.A. DERBYSHIRE. Illustrated by J. C. WALL Small Pott 8vo. Cloth, 3s.; leather, 3s. 6d. net.
[Little Guides.
HAMPSHIRE. Illustrated by M. E. PURSER. Small Pott 8vo. Cloth, 3s. : Leather, 3s. 6d. net. [Little Guides.
Cox (Harold), B.A. LAND NATIONALIZATION. Crown 8vo. 2s. 6d.
[Social Questions Series.

Crabbe (George), SELECTIONS FROM THE POEMS OF. Edited by A. C. DEANE. Small Pott 8vo. Cloth, 1s. 6d. net; leather, 2s. 6d. net. [Little Library.
Craigie (W. A.). A PRIMER OF BURNS. Crown 8vo. 2s. 6d.
Craik (Mrs.). JOHN HALIFAX, GENTLEMAN. Edited by ANNIE MATHESON. Two Volumes. Small Pott 8vo. Each Volume, Cloth, 1s. 6d. net; leather, 2s. 6d. net. [Little Library.
Crashaw (Richard), THE ENGLISH POEMS OF. Edited by EDWARD HUTTON. Small Pott 8vo. Cloth, 1s. 6d. net; leather, 2s. 6d. net. [Little Library.
Crawford (F. G.). See Mary C. Danson.
Crouch (W.). BRYAN KING. With a Portrait. Crown 8vo. 3s. 6d. net.
Cruikshank (G.) THE LOVING BALLAD OF LORD BATEMAN. With 11 Plates. Crown 16mo. 1s. 6d. net.
From the edition published by C. Tilt, 1811.
Crump (B.). See A. L. Cleather.
Cunliffe (F. H. E.), Fellow of All Souls' College, Oxford. THE HISTORY OF THE BOER WAR. With many Illustrations, Plans, and Portraits. In 2 vols. Vol. I., 15s.
Cutts (E. L.), D.D. AUGUSTINE OF CANTERBURY. With Portrait. Crown 8vo. 3s. 6d. [Leaders of Religion.
Daniell (G. W.), M.A. BISHOP WILBERFORCE. With Portrait. Crown 8vo. 3s. 6d. [Leaders of Religion.
Danson (Mary C.) and Crawford (F. G.). FATHERS IN THE FAITH. Small 8vo. 1s. 6d.
Dante. LA COMMEDIA DI DANTE. The Italian Text edited by PAGET TOYNBEE, M.A., D.Litt. Crown 8vo. 6s.
THE INFERNO OF DANTE. Translated by H. F. CARY. Edited by PAGET TOYNBEE, M.A., D.Litt. Small Pott 8vo. Cloth, 1s. 6d. net; leather, 2s. 6d. net.
[Little Library.
THE PURGATORIO OF DANTE. Translated by H. F. CARY. Edited by PAGET TOYNBEE, M.A., D.Litt. Small Pott 8vo. Cloth, 1s. 6d. net; leather, 2s. 6d. net.
[Little Library.
THE PARADISO OF DANTE. Translated by H. F. CARY. Edited by PAGET TOYNBEE, M.A., D.Litt. Small Pott 8vo. Cloth, 1s. 6d. net; leather, 2s. 6d. net.
[Little Library.
See also Paget Toynbee.
Darley (George), SELECTIONS FROM THE POEMS OF. Edited by R. A. STREATFEILD. Small Pott 8vo. Cloth, 1s. 6d. net; leather, 2s. 6d. net.
[Little Library.
Davenport (Cyril). MEZZOTINTS. With 40 Plates in Photogravure. Wide Royal 8vo. 25s. net.
[Connoisseurs Library.

**JEWELLERY.** With numerous Illustrations. *Demy 16mo. 2s. 6d. net.*
[Little Books on Art.
**Dawson (A. J.).** MOROCCO. Being a bundle of jottings, notes, impressions, tales, and tributes. With many Illustrations. *Demy 8vo. 10s. 6d. net.*

**Deane (A. C.).** A LITTLE BOOK OF LIGHT VERSE. With an Introduction and Notes. *Small Pott 8vo. Cloth, 1s. 6d. net; leather, 2s. 6d. net.* [Little Library.

**Delbos (Leon).** THE METRIC SYSTEM. *Crown 8vo. 2s.*

**Demosthenes:** THE OLYNTHIACS AND PHILIPPICS. Translated upon a new principle by OTHO HOLLAND. *Crown 8vo. 2s. 6d.*

**Demosthenes.** AGAINST CONON AND CALLICLES. Edited with Notes and Vocabulary, by F. DARWIN SWIFT, M.A. *Fcap. 8vo. 2s.*

**Dickens (Charles).**
THE PICKWICK PAPERS. With the 43 Illustrations by SEYMOUR and PHIZ, the two Buss Plates and the 32 Contemporary Onwhyn Plates. *3s. 6d. net.*
This is a particularly interesting volume, containing, as it does, reproductions of very rare plates. [Illustrated Pocket Library.

**Dickinson (Emily).** POEMS. First Series. *Crown 8vo. 4s. 6d. net.*

**Dickinson (G. L.),** M.A., Fellow of King's College, Cambridge. THE GREEK VIEW OF LIFE. *Third Edition. Crown 8vo. 2s. 6d.* [University Extension Series.

**Dickson (H. N.),** F.R.S.E., F.R.Met. Soc. METEOROLOGY. Illustrated. *Crown 8vo. 2s. 6d.* [University Extension Series.

**Dilke (Lady), Bulley (Miss),** and **Whitley (Miss).** WOMEN'S WORK. *Crown 8vo. 2s. 6d.* [Social Questions Series.

**Dillon (Edward).** PORCELAIN. With many Plates in Colour and Photogravure. *Wide Royal 8vo. 25s. net.*
[Connoisseurs Library.

**Ditchfield (P. H.),** M.A., F.S.A. ENGLISH VILLAGES. Illustrated. *Crown 8vo. 6s.*
THE STORY OF OUR ENGLISH TOWNS. With Introduction by AUGUSTUS JESSOPP, D.D. *Second Edition. Crown 8vo. 6s.*
OLD ENGLISH CUSTOMS: Extant at the Present Time. An Account of Local Observances, Festival Customs, and Ancient Ceremonies yet Surviving in Great Britain. *Crown 8vo. 6s.*

**Dixon (W. M.),** M.A. A PRIMER OF TENNYSON. *Second Edition. Crown 8vo. 2s. 6d.*
ENGLISH POETRY FROM BLAKE TO BROWNING. *Second Edition. Crown 8vo. 2s. 6d.* [University Extension Series.

**Dole (N. H.)** FAMOUS COMPOSERS. With Portraits. *Two Volumes. Demy 8vo. 12s. net.*

**Dowden (J.),** D.D., Lord Bishop of Edinburgh. THE WORKMANSHIP OF THE PRAYER BOOK: Its Literary and Liturgical Aspects. *Second Edition. Crown 8vo. 3s. 6d.* [Churchman's Library.

**Driver (S. R.),** D.D., Canon of Christ Church, Regius Professor of Hebrew in the University of Oxford. SERMONS ON SUBJECTS CONNECTED WITH THE OLD TESTAMENT. *Crown 8vo. 6s.*
THE BOOK OF GENESIS. With Notes and Introduction. *Second Edition. Demy 8vo. 10s. 6d.* [Westminster Commentaries.

**Duguid (Charles),** City Editor of the *Morning Post,* author of the 'Story of the Stock Exchange,' etc. THE STOCK EXCHANGE. *Second Edition. Crown 8vo. 2s. 6d. net.* [Books on Business.

**Duncan (S. J.)** (Mrs. COTES), Author of 'A Voyage of Consolation.' ON THE OTHER SIDE OF THE LATCH. *Second Edition. Crown 8vo. 6s.*

**Dunn (J. T.),** D.Sc., and **Mundella (V. A.).** GENERAL ELEMENTARY SCIENCE. With 114 Illustrations. *Crown 8vo. 3s. 6d.*

**Dunstan (A. E.),** B.Sc. See W. T. CLOUGH.

**Durham (The Earl of).** A REPORT ON CANADA. With an Introductory Note. *Demy 8vo. 7s. 6d. net.*

**Dutt (W. A.)** NORFOLK. Illustrated by B. C. BOULTER. *Small Pott 8vo. Cloth, 3s.; leather, 3s. 6d.* [Little Guides.
A POPULAR GUIDE TO NORFOLK. *Medium 8vo. 6d. net.*
SUFFOLK. Illustrated by J. WYLIE. *Small Pott 8vo. Cloth, 3s.; leather, 3s. 6d. net.* [Little Guides.
THE NORFOLK BROADS. With coloured and other Illustrations by FRANK SOUTHGATE. *Large Demy 8vo. 21s. net.*

**Earle (John),** Bishop of Salisbury. MICROCOSMOGRAPHIE, OR A PIECE OF THE WORLD DISCOVERED; IN ESSAYS AND CHARACTERS. *Post 16mo. 2s. net.* [Rariora.
Reprinted from the Sixth Edition published by Robert Allot in 1633.

**Edwards (Clement).** RAILWAY NATIONALIZATION. *Crown 8vo. 2s. 6d.* [Social Questions Series.

**Edwards (W. Douglas).** COMMERCIAL LAW. *Crown 8vo. 2s.*
[Commercial Series.

**Egan (Pierce).** LIFE IN LONDON, OR THE DAY AND NIGHT SCENES OF JERRY HAWTHORN, ESQ., AND HIS ELEGANT FRIEND, CORINTHIAN TOM. With 36 Coloured Plates by I. R. and G. CRUIKSHANK. With numerous designs on wood. *Fcap. 8vo. 4s. 6d. net.*
Also a limited edition on large Japanese paper. *30s. net.* [Illustrated Pocket Library.

## GENERAL LITERATURE 9

REAL LIFE IN LONDON, OR THE RAMBLES AND ADVENTURES OF BOB TALLYHO, ESQ., AND HIS COUSIN, the Hon. TOM DASHALL. With 31 Coloured Plates by ALKEN and ROWLANDSON, etc. *Two Volumes. Fcap. 8vo. 9s. net.*
[Illustrated Pocket Library.
THE LIFE OF AN ACTOR. With 27 Coloured Plates by THEODORE LANE, and several designs on wood. *Fcap. 8vo. 4s. 6d. net.* [Illustrated Pocket Library.

**Egerton (H. E.)**, M.A. A HISTORY OF BRITISH COLONIAL POLICY. *Demy 8vo. 12s. 6d.*
A Colonial Edition is also published.

**Ellaby (C. G.).** ROME. Illustrated by B. C. BOULTER. *Small Pott 8vo. Cloth, 3s.; leather, 3s. 6d. net.* [Little Guides.

**Ellerton (F. G.).** See S. J. Stone.

**Ellwood (Thomas)**, THE HISTORY OF THE LIFE OF. Edited by C. G. CRUMP, M.A. *Crown 8vo. 6s.*

**Engel (E.).** A HISTORY OF ENGLISH LITERATURE: From its Beginning to Tennyson. Translated from the German. *Demy 8vo. 7s. 6d. net.*

**Fairbrother (W. H.)**, M.A. THE PHILOSOPHY OF T. H. GREEN. *Second Edition. Crown 8vo. 3s. 6d.*

FELISSA; OR, THE LIFE AND OPINIONS OF A KITTEN OF SENTIMENT. With 12 Coloured Plates. *Post 16mo. 2s. 6d. net. (5¼×3¼).*
From the edition published by J. Harris, 1811.

**Farrer (Reginald).** THE GARDEN OF ASIA. *Crown 8vo. 6s.*
A Colonial Edition is also published.

**Ferrier (Susan).** MARRIAGE. Edited by Miss GOODRICH FREER and Lord IDDESLEIGH. *Two Volumes. Small Pott 8vo. Each volume, cloth, 1s. 6d. net; leather, 2s. 6d. net.* [Little Library.
THE INHERITANCE. *Two Volumes. Small Pott 8vo. Each Volume, cloth, 1s. 6d. net.; leather, 2s. 6d. net.* [Little Library.

**Finn (S. W.)**, M.A. JUNIOR ALGEBRA EXAMINATION PAPERS. *Fcap. 8vo.* With or Without Answers, 1s.
[Junior Examination Series.

**Firth (C. H.)**, M.A. CROMWELL'S ARMY: A History of the English Soldier during the Civil Wars, the Commonwealth, and the Potectorate. *Crown 8vo. 7s. 6d.*

**Fisher (G. W.)**, M.A. ANNALS OF SHREWSBURY SCHOOL. With numerous Illustrations. *Demy 8vo. 10s. 6d.*

**FitzGerald (Edward).** THE RUB'AIYÁT OF OMAR KHAYYÁM. From the First Edition of 1859. *Second Edition. Leather, 1s. net.* [Miniature Library.
THE RUB'AIYÁT OF OMAR KHAYYÁM. Printed from the Fifth and last Edition. With a Commentary by Mrs. STEPHEN BATSON, and a Biography of Omar by E. D. ROSS. *Crown 8vo. 6s.*
EUPHRANOR: a Dialogue on Youth. *Demy 32mo. Leather, 2s. net.*
[Miniature Library.
POLONIUS: or Wise Saws and Modern Instances. *Demy 32mo. Leather, 2s. net.*
[Miniature Library.
**FitzGerald (E. A.).** THE HIGHEST ANDES. With 2 Maps, 51 Illustrations, 13 of which are in Photogravure, and a Panorama. *Royal 8vo. 30s. net.*

**Flecker (W. H.)**, M.A., D.C.L., Headmaster of the Dean Close School, Cheltenham. THE STUDENTS' PRAYER BOOK. Part I. MORNING AND EVENING PRAYER AND LITANY. With an Introduction and Notes. *Crown 8vo. 2s. 6d.*

**Flux (A. W.)**, M.A., William Dow Professor of Political Economy in M'Gill University, Montreal: sometime Fellow of St. John's College, Cambridge, and formerly Stanley-Jevons Professor of Political Economy in the Owens Coll., Manchester. ECONOMIC PRINCIPLES. *Demy 8vo. 7s. 6d. net.*

**Fortescue (Mrs. G.)** HOLBEIN. With 30 Illustrations. *Demy 16mo. 2s. 6d. net.*
[Little Books on Art.

**Fraser (J. F.).** ROUND THE WORLD ON A WHEEL. With 100 Illustrations. *Third Edition. Crown 8vo. 6s.*
A Colonial Edition is also published.

**French (W.),** M.A., Principal of the Storey Institute, Lancaster. PRACTICAL CHEMISTRY. *Part I.* With numerous Diagrams. *Crown 8vo. 1s. 6d.*
[Textbooks of Technology.

**French (W.),** M.A., and **Boardman (T. H.)**, M.A. PRACTICAL CHEMISTRY. *Part II.* With numerous Diagrams. *Crown 8vo. 1s. 6d.* [Textbooks of Technology.

**Freudenreich (Ed. von).** DAIRY BACTERIOLOGY. A Short Manual for the Use of Students. Translated by J. R. AINSWORTH DAVIS, M.A. *Second Edition. Revised. Crown 8vo. 2s. 6d.*

**Fulford (H. W.)**, M.A. THE EPISTLE OF ST. JAMES. With Notes and Introduction. *Fcap. 8vo. 1s. 6d. net.*
[Churchman's Bible.

C. G., and F. C. G. JOHN BULL'S ADVENTURES IN THE FISCAL WONDERLAND. By CHARLES GEAKE. With 46 Illustrations by F. CARRUTHERS GOULD. *Second Ed. Crown 8vo. 2s. 6d. net.*

**Gambado (Geoffrey, Esq.).** AN ACADEMY FOR GROWN HORSEMEN: Containing the completest Instructions for Walking, Trotting, Cantering, Galloping, Stumbling, and Tumbling. Illustrated with 27 Coloured Plates, and adorned with a Portrait of the Author. *Fcap. 8vo. 3s. 6d. net.*
[Illustrated Pocket Library.

A 2

**Gaskell (Mrs.).** CRANFORD. Edited by E. V. LUCAS. *Small Pott 8vo. Cloth*, 1s. 6d. *net; leather,* 2s. 6d. *net.* [Little Library.

**Gasquet,** the Right Rev. Abbot, O.S.B. ENGLISH MONASTIC LIFE. With Coloured and other Illustrations. *Demy 8vo.* 7s. 6d. *net.* [Antiquary's Books.

**George (H. B.),** M.A., Fellow of New College, Oxford. BATTLES OF ENGLISH HISTORY. With numerous Plans. *Fourth Edition. Crown 8vo.* 6s.
A HISTORICAL GEOGRAPHY OF THE BRITISH EMPIRE. *Cr. 8vo.* 3s. 6d *net.*

**Gibbins (H. de B.),** Litt.D., M.A. INDUSTRY IN ENGLAND: HISTORICAL OUTLINES. With 5 Maps. *Third Edition. Demy 8vo.* 10s. 6d.
A COMPANION GERMAN GRAMMAR. *Crown 8vo.* 1s. 6d.
THE INDUSTRIAL HISTORY OF ENGLAND. *Tenth Edition.* Revised. With Maps and Plans. *Crown 8vo.* 3s.
[University Extension Series.
THE ECONOMICS OF COMMERCE. *Crown 8vo.* 1s. 6d. [Commercial Series.
COMMERCIAL EXAMINATION PAPERS. *Crown 8vo.* 1s. 6d.
[Commercial Series.
BRITISH COMMERCE AND COLONIES FROM ELIZABETH TO VICTORIA. *Third Edition. Crown 8vo.* 2s.
[Commercial Series.
ENGLISH SOCIAL REFORMERS. *Second Edition. Crown 8vo.* 2s. 6d.
[University Extension Series.

**Gibbins (H. de B.),** Litt.D., M.A., and **Hadfield (R. A.),** of the Hecla Works, Sheffield. A SHORTER WORKING DAY. *Crown 8vo.* 2s. 6d.
[Social Questions Series.

**Gibbon (Edward).** THE DECLINE AND FALL OF THE ROMAN EMPIRE. A New Edition, edited with Notes, Appendices, and Maps, by J. B. BURY, M.A., Litt.D., Fellow of Trinity College, Dublin. *In Seven Volumes. Demy 8vo. Gilt top,* 8s. 6d. *each. Also, Crown 8vo.* 6s. *each.*
MEMOIRS OF MY LIFE AND WRITINGS. Edited, with an Introduction and Notes, by G. BIRKBECK HILL, LL.D. *Crown 8vo.* 6s.

**Gibson (E. C. S.),** D.D., Vicar of Leeds. THE BOOK OF JOB. With Introduction and Notes. *Demy 8vo.* 6s.
[Westminster Commentaries.
THE XXXIX. ARTICLES OF THE CHURCH OF ENGLAND. With an Introduction. *Fourth Edition in One Vol. Demy 8vo.* 12s. 6d. [Handbooks of Theology.
JOHN HOWARD. With 12 Illustrations. *Fcap 8vo. Cloth,* 3s. 6d.; *leather,* 4s. *net.*
[Little Biographies.

**Gilbert (A. R.).** See W. Wilberforce.

**Godfrey (Elizabeth).** A BOOK OF REMEMBRANCE. *Demy 16mo.* 2s. 6d. *net.*

**Godley (A. D.),** M.A., Fellow of Magdalen College, Oxford. LYRA FRIVOLA. *Third Edition. Fcap. 8vo.* 2s. 6d.
VERSES TO ORDER. *Second Edition. Crown 8vo.* 2s. 6d.
SECOND STRINGS. *Fcap. 8vo.* 2s. 6d.
A new volume of humorous verse uniform with *Lyra Frivola.*

**Goldsmith (Oliver).** THE VICAR OF WAKEFIELD. With 24 Coloured Plates by T. ROWLANDSON. *Royal 8vo. One Guinea net.*
Reprinted from the edition of 1817.
[Burlington Library.
Also *Fcap. 8vo.* 3s. 6d. *net.* Also a limited edition on large Japanese paper. 30s. *net.* [Illustrated Pocket Library.
Also *Fcap.* 32mo. With 10 Plates in Photogravure by Tony Johannot. *Leather,* 2s. 6d. *net.*

**Goudge (H. L.),** M.A., Principal of Wells Theological College. THE FIRST EPISTLE TO THE CORINTHIANS. With Introduction and Notes. *Demy 8vo.* 6s. [Westminster Commentaries.

**Graham (P. Anderson).** THE RURAL EXODUS. *Crown 8vo.* 2s. 6d.
[Social Questions Series.

**Granger (F. S.),** M.A., Litt.D. PSYCHOLOGY. *Second Edition. Crown 8vo.* 2s. 6d. [University Extension Series.
THE SOUL OF A CHRISTIAN. *Crown 8vo.* 6s.

**Gray (E. M'Queen).** GERMAN PASSAGES FOR UNSEEN TRANSLATION. *Crown 8vo.* 2s. 6d.

**Gray (P. L.),** B.Sc., formerly Lecturer in Physics in Mason University College, Birmingham. THE PRINCIPLES OF MAGNETISM AND ELECTRICITY: an Elementary Text-Book. With 181 Diagrams. *Crown 8vo.* 3s. 6d.

**Green (G. Buckland),** M.A., Assistant Master at Edinburgh Academy, late Fellow of St. John's College, Oxon. NOTES ON GREEK AND LATIN SYNTAX. *Crown 8vo.* 3s. 6d.

**Green (E. T.),** M.A. THE CHURCH OF CHRIST. *Crown 8vo.* 6s.
[Churchman's Library.

**Greenidge (A. H. J.),** M.A. A HISTORY OF ROME: During the Later Republic and the Early Principate. *In Six Volumes. Demy 8vo.* Vol. I. (133-104 B.C.) 12s. 6d. *net.*

**Greenwell (Dora),** THE POEMS OF. From the edition of 1848. *Leather,* 2s. *net.*
[Miniature Library.

**Gregory (R. A.)** THE VAULT OF HEAVEN. A Popular Introduction to Astronomy. With numerous Illustrations. *Crown 8vo.* 2s. 6d.
[University Extension Series.

## GENERAL LITERATURE

Gregory (Miss E. C.) HEAVENLY WISDOM. Selections from the English Mystics. *Pott 8vo. Cloth* 2s.; *leather,* 2s. 6d. *net.*
[Library of Devotion. Nearly Ready.
Greville Minor. A MODERN JOURNAL. Edited by J. A. SPENDER. *Crown 8vo.* 3s. 6d. *net.*
Grinling (C. H.). A HISTORY OF THE GREAT NORTHERN RAILWAY, 1845-95. With Illustrations. Revised, with an additional chapter. *Demy 8vo.* 10s. 6d.
Grubb (H. C.). BUILDERS' QUANTITIES. With many Illustrations. *Crown 8vo.* 4s. 6d. [Textbooks of Technology.
Guiney (L. I.). RICHARD HURRELL FROUDE. Illustrated. *Demy 8vo.* 10s. 6d. *net.*
Gwynn (M. L.). A BIRTHDAY BOOK. *Royal 8vo.* 12s.
Hackett (John), B.D. A HISTORY OF THE ORTHODOX CHURCH OF CYPRUS. With Maps and Illustrations. *Demy 8vo.* 15s. *net.*
Haddon (A. C.), Sc.D., F.R.S. HEADHUNTERS, BLACK, WHITE, AND BROWN. With many Illustrations and a Map. *Demy 8vo.* 15s.
Hadfield (R. A.). See H. de B. Gibbins.
Hall (R. N.) and Neal (W. G.). THE ANCIENT RUINS OF RHODESIA. With numerous Illustrations. *Second Edition, revised. Demy 8vo.* 10s. 6d. *net.*
Hall (R. N.). THE GREAT ZIMBABWE. With numerous Illustrations. *Royal 8vo.* 21s. *net.*
Hamilton (F. J.), D.D., and Brooks (E. W.). ZACHARIAH OF MITYLENE. Translated into English. *Demy 8vo.* 12s. 6d. *net.*
[Byzantine Texts.
Hammond (J. L.). CHARLES JAMES FOX: A Biographical Study. *Demy 8vo.* 10s. 6d.
Hannay (D.). A SHORT HISTORY OF THE ROYAL NAVY, FROM EARLY TIMES TO THE PRESENT DAY. Illustrated. *Two Volumes. Demy 8vo.* 7s. 6d. *each.* Vol. I. 1200-1688.
Hannay (James O.), M.A. THE SPIRIT AND ORIGIN OF CHRISTIAN MONASTICISM. *Crown 8vo.* 6s.
THE WISDOM OF THE DESERT. *Crown 8vo.* 3s. 6d. *net.*
Hare, (A. T.), M.A. THE CONSTRUCTION OF LARGE INDUCTION COILS. With numerous Diagrams. *Demy 8vo.* 6s.
Harrison (Clifford). READING AND READERS. *Fcap. 8vo.* 2s. 6d.
Hawthorne (Nathaniel). THE SCARLET LETTER. Edited by PERCY DEARMER. *Small Pott 8vo. Cloth,* 1s. 6d. *net;* *leather,* 2s. 6d. *net.* [Little Library.
HEALTH, WEALTH AND WISDOM. *Crown 8vo.* 1s. *net.*

Heath (Dudley). MINIATURES. With many Plates in Photogravure. *Wide Royal 8vo.* 25s. *net.* [Connoisseur's Library.
Hedin (Sven), Gold Medallist of the Royal Geographical Society. THROUGH ASIA. With 300 Illustrations from Sketches and Photographs by the Author, and Maps. *Two Volumes. Royal 8vo.* 36s. *net.*
Hello (Ernest). STUDIES IN SAINTSHIP. Translated from the French by V. M. CRAWFORD. *Fcap. 8vo.* 3s. 6d.
Henderson (B. W.), Fellow of Exeter College, Oxford. THE LIFE AND PRINCIPATE OF THE EMPEROR NERO. With Illustrations. *Demy 8vo,* 10s. 6d. *net.*
Henderson (T. P.). A LITTLE BOOK OF SCOTTISH VERSE. *Small Pott 8vo. Cloth,* 1s. 6d. *net;* *leather,* 2s. 6d. *net.*
[Little Library.
ROBERT BURNS. With 12 Illustrations. *Fcap. 8vo. Cloth,* 3s. 6d.; *leather,* 4s. *net.*
[Little Biographies.
Henley (W. E.). ENGLISH LYRICS. *Crown 8vo. Gilt top.* 3s. 6d.
Henley (W. E.) and Whibley (C.). A BOOK OF ENGLISH PROSE. *Crown 8vo. Buckram, gilt top.* 6s.
Henson (H. H.), B.D., Canon of Westminster. APOSTOLIC CHRISTIANITY: As Illustrated by the Epistles of St. Paul to the Corinthians. *Crown 8vo.* 6s.
LIGHT AND LEAVEN: HISTORICAL AND SOCIAL SERMONS. *Crown 8vo.* 6s.
DISCIPLINE AND LAW. *Fcap. 8vo.* 2s. 6d.
THE EDUCATION ACT—AND AFTER. An Appeal addressed with all possible respect to the Nonconformists. *Crown 8vo.* 1s.
Herbert (George). THE TEMPLE. Edited, with an Introduction and Notes, by E. C. S. GIBSON, D.D., Vicar of Leeds. *Small Pott 8vo. Cloth,* 2s.; *leather,* 2s. 6d. *net.*
[Library of Devotion.
Herbert of Cherbury (Lord), THE LIFE OF. Written by himself. *Leather,* 2s. *net.* From the edition printed at Strawberry Hill in the year 1764.
[Miniature Library.
Hewins (W. A. S.), B.A. ENGLISH TRADE AND FINANCE IN THE SEVENTEENTH CENTURY. *Crown 8vo.* 2s. 6d. [University Extension Series.
Heywood (W.). PALIO AND PONTE: A Book of Tuscan Games. Illustrated. *Royal 8vo.* 21s. *net.*
Hilbert (T.). THE AIR GUN: or, How the Mastermans and Dobson Major nearly lost their Holidays. Illustrated. *Demy 16mo.* 2s. 6d. [Little Blue Books.
Hill (Clare), Registered Teacher to the City and Guilds of London Institute. MILLINERY, THEORETICAL, AND PRACTICAL. With numerous Diagrams. *Cr. 8vo.* 2s. [Textbooks of Technology.

**Hill (Henry)**, B.A., Headmaster of the Boy's High School, Worcester, Cape Colony. A SOUTH AFRICAN ARITHMETIC. *Crown 8vo.* 3s. 6d.
This book has been specially written for use in South African schools.

**Hobhouse (Emily)**. THE BRUNT OF THE WAR. With Map and Illustrations. *Crown 8vo.* 6s.
A Colonial Edition is also published.

**Hobhouse (L. T.)**, Fellow of C.C.C., Oxford. THE THEORY OF KNOWLEDGE. *Demy 8vo.* 21s.

**Hobson (J. A.)**, M.A. PROBLEMS OF POVERTY: An Inquiry into the Industrial Condition of the Poor. *Fourth Edition. Crown 8vo.* 2s. 6d.
[Social Questions Series.
THE PROBLEM OF THE UNEMPLOYED. *Crown 8vo.* 2s. 6d.
[Social Questions Series.
INTERNATIONAL TRADE: A Study of Economic Principles. *Crown 8vo.* 2s. 6d. net.

**Hodgkin (T.)**, D.C.L. GEORGE FOX, THE QUAKER. With Portrait. *Crown 8vo.* 3s. 6d. [Leaders of Religion.

**Hogg (Thomas Jefferson)**. SHELLEY AT OXFORD. With an Introduction by R. A. STREATFEILD. *Fcap. 8vo;* 2s. net.

**Holden-Stone (G. de)**. THE AUTOMOBILE INDUSTRY. *Fcap.* 8vo. 2s. 6d. net. [Books on Business.

**Holdich (Sir T. H.)**, K.C.I.E. THE INDIAN BORDERLAND: being a Personal Record of Twenty Years. Illustrated. *Demy 8vo.* 15s. net.

**Holdsworth (W. S.)**, M.A. A HISTORY OF ENGLISH LAW. *In Two Volumes.* Vol. I. *Demy 8vo.* 10s. 6d. net.

**Holyoake (G. J.)**. THE CO-OPERATIVE MOVEMENT TO-DAY. *Third Edition. Crown 8vo.* 2s. 6d.
[Social Questions Series.

**Hoppner**, A LITTLE GALLERY OF. Twenty examples in photogravure of his finest work. *Demy 16mo.* 2s. 6d. net.
[Little Galleries.

**Horace**: THE ODES AND EPODES. Translated by A. D. GODLEY, M.A., Fellow of Magdalen College. Oxford. *Crown 8vo.* 2s. [Classical Translations.

**Horsburgh (E. L. S.)**, M.A. WATERLOO: A Narrative and Criticism. With Plans. *Second Edition. Crown 8vo.* 5s.
SAVONAROLA. With Portraits and Illustrations. *Second Edition. Fcap. 8vo. Cloth,* 3s. 6d.; *leather,* 4s. net.
[Little Biographies.

**Horton (R. F.)**, D.D. JOHN HOWE. With Portrait. *Crown 8vo.* 3s. 6d. [Leaders of Religion.

**Hosie (Alexander)**. MANCHURIA. With Illustrations and a Map. *Second Edition. Demy 8vo.* 10s. 6d. net.

**How (F. D.)**. SIX GREAT SCHOOLMASTERS. With Portraits. *Demy 8vo.* 7s. 6d.

**Howell (G.)**. TRADE UNIONISM—NEW AND OLD. *Third Edition. Crown 8vo.* 2s. 6d. [Social Questions Series.

**Hudson (Robert)**. MEMORIALS OF A WARWICKSHIRE VILLAGE. With many Illustrations. *Demy 8vo.* 10s. 6d. net.

**Hughes (C. E.)**. THE PRAISE OF SHAKESPEARE. An English Anthology. With a Preface by SIDNEY LEE. *Demy 8vo.* 3s. 6d. net.

**Hughes (Thomas)**. TOM BROWN'S SCHOOLDAYS. With an Introduction and Notes by VERNON RENDALL. *Leather. Royal 32mo.* 2s. 6d. net.

**Hutchinson (Horace G.)**. THE NEW FOREST. Described by, Illustrated in colour with 50 Pictures by WALTER TYNDALE and 4 by Miss LUCY KEMP WELCH. *Large Demy 8vo.* 21s. net.

**Hutton (A. W.)**, M.A. CARDINAL MANNING. With Portrait. *Crown 8vo.* 3s. 6d. [Leaders of Religion.

**Hutton (R. H.)**. CARDINAL NEWMAN. With Portrait. *Crown 8vo.* 3s. 6d. [Leaders of Religion.

**Hutton (W. H.)**, M.A. THE LIFE OF SIR THOMAS MORE. With Portraits. *Second Edition. Crown 8vo.* 5s.
WILLIAM LAUD. With Portrait. *Second Edition. Crown 8vo.* 3s. 6d. [Leaders of Religion.

**Hyett (F. A.)**. A SHORT HISTORY OF FLORENCE. *Demy 8vo.* 7s. 6d. net.

HYPNEROTOMACHIA POLIPHILI UBI HUMANA OMNIA NON NISI SOMNIUM ESSE DOCET ATQUE OBITER PLURIMA SCITU SANE QUAM DIGNA COMMEMORAT. An edition limited to 350 copies on handmade paper. *Folio. Three Guineas net.*

**Ibsen (Henrik)**. BRAND. A Drama. Translated by WILLIAM WILSON. *Third Edition. Crown 8vo.* 3s. 6d.

**Inge (W. R.)**, M.A., Fellow and Tutor of Hertford College, Oxford. CHRISTIAN MYSTICISM. The Bampton Lectures for 1899. *Demy 8vo.* 12s. 6d. net.
LIGHT, LIFE, AND LOVE: A Selection from the German Mystics. With an Introduction and Notes. *Small Pott 8vo. Cloth,* 2s.; *leather,* 2s. 6d. net.
[Library of Devotion.

**Innes (A. D.)**, M.A. A HISTORY OF THE BRITISH IN INDIA. With Maps and Plans. *Crown 8vo.* 7s. 6d.

## GENERAL LITERATURE

**Jackson (S.), M.A.** A PRIMER OF BUSINESS. *Third Edition. Crown 8vo. 1s. 6d.* [Commercial Series.

**Jackson (F. Hamilton).** SICILY. With many Illustrations by the Author. *Small Pott 8vo. Cloth, 3s.; Leather, 3s. 6d. net.* [Little Guides.

**Jacob (F.), M.A.** JUNIOR FRENCH EXAMINATION PAPERS. *Fcap. 8vo. 1s.* [Junior Examination Series.

**Jeans (J. Stephen).** TRUSTS, POOLS, AND CORNERS. *Crown 8vo. 2s. 6d.* [Social Questions Series.

**Jeffreys (D. Gwyn).** DOLLY'S THEATRICALS. Described and Illustrated with 24 Coloured Pictures. *Pott 4to. 2s. 6d.*

**Jenks (E.), M.A.**, Reader of Law in the University of Oxford. ENGLISH LOCAL GOVERNMENT. *Crown 8vo. 2s. 6d.* [University Extension Series.

**Jessopp (Augustus), D.D.** JOHN DONNE. With Portrait. *Crown 8vo. 3s. 6d.* [Leaders of Religion.

**Jevons (F. B.), M.A., Litt.D.**, Principal of Hatfield Hall, Durham. EVOLUTION. *Crown 8vo. 3s. 6d.* [Churchman's Library. AN INTRODUCTION TO THE HISTORY OF RELIGION. *Second Edition. Demy 8vo. 10s. 6d.* [Handbooks of Theology.

**Johnston (Sir H. H.), K.C.B.** BRITISH CENTRAL AFRICA. With nearly 200 Illustrations and Six Maps. *Second Edition. Crown 4to. 18s. net.*

**Jones (H.).** A GUIDE TO PROFESSIONS AND BUSINESS. *Crown 8vo. 1s. 6d.* [Commercial Series.

**Jones (L. A. Atherley), K.C., M.P.**, and **Bellot (Hugh H. L.).** THE MINERS' GUIDE TO THE COAL MINES' REGULATION ACTS. *Crown 8vo. 2s. 6d. net.* [Nearly Ready.

**Julian (Lady) of Norwich.** REVELATIONS OF DIVINE LOVE. Edited by GRACE WARRACK. *Crown 8vo. 3s. 6d.*

**Juvenal**, THE SATIRES OF. Translated by S. G. OWEN. *Crown 8vo. 2s. 6d.* [Classical Translations.

**Kaufmann (M.).** SOCIALISM AND MODERN THOUGHT. *Crown 8vo. 2s. 6d.* [Social Questions Series.

**Keating (J. F.), D.D.** THE AGAPE AND THE EUCHARIST. *Crown 8vo. 3s. 6d.*

**Keats (John),** THE POEMS OF. With an Introduction by L. BINYON, and Notes by J. MASEFIELD. *Small Pott 8vo. Cloth, 1s. 6d. net; leather, 2s. 6d. net.* [Little Library.

**Keats.** THE POEMS OF. Edited with Introduction and Notes by E. de Selincourt, M.A. *Demy 8vo. 7s. 6d. net.*

**Keble (John).** THE CHRISTIAN YEAR. With an Introduction and Notes by W. LOCK, D.D., Warden of Keble College. Illustrated by R. ANNING BELL. *Second Edition. Fcap. 8vo. 3s. 6d.; padded morocco, 5s.*

THE CHRISTIAN YEAR. With Introduction and Notes by WALTER LOCK, D.D., Warden of Keble College. *Second Edition. Small Pott 8vo. Cloth, 2s.; leather, 2s. 6d. net.* [Library of Devotion.

LYRA INNOCENTIUM. Edited, with Introduction and Notes, by WALTER LOCK, D.D., Warden of Keble College, Oxford. *Small Pott 8vo. Cloth, 2s.; leather, 2s. 6d. net.* [Library of Devotion.

**Kempis (Thomas à).** THE IMITATION OF CHRIST. With an Introduction by DEAN FARRAR. Illustrated by C. M. GERE. *Second Edition. Fcap. 8vo. 3s. 6d.; padded morocco, 5s.*

THE IMITATION OF CHRIST. A Revised Translation, with an Introduction by C. BIGG, D.D., late Student of Christ Church. *Third Edition. Small Pott 8vo. Cloth, 2s.; leather, 2s. 6d. net.* [Library of Devotion.

A practically new translation of this book which the reader has, almost for the first time, exactly in the shape in which it left the hands of the author.

THE SAME EDITION IN LARGE TYPE. *Crown 8vo. 3s. 6d.*

**Kennedy (James Houghton), D.D.**, Assistant Lecturer in Divinity in the University of Dublin. ST. PAUL'S SECOND AND THIRD EPISTLES TO THE CORINTHIANS. With Introduction, Dissertations and Notes. *Crown 8vo. 6s.*

**Kestell (J. D.).** THROUGH SHOT AND FLAME: Being the Adventures and Experiences of J. D. KESTELL, Chaplain to General Christian de Wet. *Crown 8vo. 6s.*

**Kimmins (C. W.), M.A.** THE CHEMISTRY OF LIFE AND HEALTH. Illustrated. *Crown 8vo. 2s. 6d.* [University Extension Series.

**Kinglake (A. W.).** EOTHEN. With an Introduction and Notes. *Small Pott 8vo. Cloth, 1s. 6d. net; leather, 2s. 6d. net.* [Little Library.

**Kipling (Rudyard).** BARRACK-ROOM BALLADS. *73rd Thousand. Cr. 8vo. Twentieth Edition. 6s.*

A Colonial Edition is also published.

THE SEVEN SEAS. *62nd Thousand. Ninth Edition. Crown 8vo, gilt top, 6s.*

A Colonial Edition is also published.

THE FIVE NATIONS. *41st Thousand. Second Edition. Crown 8vo. 6s.*

A Colonial Edition is also published.

DEPARTMENTAL DITTIES. *Sixteenth Edition. Crown 8vo. Buckram, 6s.*

A Colonial Edition is also published.

**Knowling (R. J.), M.A.,** Professor of New Testament Exegesis at King's College, London. THE EPISTLE OF S. JAMES. With Introduction and Notes. *Demy 8vo.* 6s. [Westminster Commentaries.

**Lamb (Charles and Mary),** THE WORKS OF. Edited by E. V. LUCAS. With Numerous Illustrations. *In Seven Volumes. Demy 8vo.* 7s. 6d. each.
THE ESSAYS OF ELIA. With over 100 Illustrations by A. GARTH JONES, and an Introduction by E. V. LUCAS. *Demy 8vo.* 10s. 6d.
ELIA, AND THE LAST ESSAYS OF ELIA. Edited by E. V. LUCAS. *Small Pott 8vo. Cloth,* 1s. 6d. *net; leather,* 2s. 6d. *net.* [Little Library.
THE KING AND QUEEN OF HEARTS: An 1805 Book for Children. Illustrated by WILLIAM MULREADY. A new edition, in facsimile, edited by E. V. LUCAS. 1s. 6d.

**Lambert (F. A. H.).** SURREY. Illustrated by E. H. NEW. *Small Pott 8vo, cloth,* 3s.; *leather,* 3s. 6d. *net.* [Little Guides.

**Lambros (Professor).** ECTHESIS CHRONICA. Edited by. *Demy 8vo.* 7s. 6d. *net.* [Byzantine Texts.

**Lane-Poole (Stanley).** A HISTORY OF EGYPT IN THE MIDDLE AGES. Fully Illustrated. *Crown 8vo.* 6s.

**Langbridge (F.) M.A.** BALLADS OF THE BRAVE: Poems of Chivalry, Enterprise, Courage, and Constancy. *Second Edition. Crown 8vo.* 2s. 6d.

**Law (William).** A SERIOUS CALL TO A DEVOUT AND HOLY LIFE. Edited, with an Introduction, by C. BIGG, D.D., late Student of Christ Church. *Small Pott 8vo, cloth,* 2s.; *leather,* 2s. 6d. *net.* [Library of Devotion.
This is a reprint, word for word and line for line, of the *Editio Princeps.*

**Leach (Henry).** THE DUKE OF DEVONSHIRE. A Biography. With 12 Illustrations. *Demy 8vo.* 12s. 6d. *net.*
A Colonial Edition is also published.

**Lee (Captain Melville).** A HISTORY OF POLICE IN ENGLAND. *Crown 8vo.* 7s. 6d.

**Leigh (Percival).** THE COMIC ENGLISH GRAMMAR. Embellished with upwards of 50 characteristic Illustrations by JOHN LEECH. *Post 16mo.* 2s. 6d. *net.*

**Lewes (V. B.), M.A.** AIR AND WATER. Illustrated. *Crown 8vo.* 2s. 6d. [University Extension Series.

**Lisle (Miss F. de).** BURNE-JONES. With 30 Illustrations. *Demy 16mo.* 2s. 6d. *net.* [Little Books on Art.

**Littlehales (H.).** See C. Wordsworth.

**Lock (Walter), D.D.,** Warden of Keble College. ST. PAUL, THE MASTER-BUILDER. *Crown 8vo.* 3s. 6d.

JOHN KEBLE. With Portrait. *Crown 8vo.* 3s. 6d. [Leaders of Religion.

**Locker (F.).** LONDON LYRICS. Edited by A. D. GODLEY, M.A. *Small Pott 8vo, cloth,* 1s. 6d. *net; leather,* 2s. 6d. *net.* [Little Library.

**Longfellow,** SELECTIONS FROM. Edited by LILIAN M. FAITHFULL. *Small Pott 8vo, cloth,* 1s. 6d. *net; leather,* 2s. 6d. *net.* [Little Library.

**Lorimer (George Horace).** LETTERS FROM A SELF-MADE MERCHANT TO HIS SON. *Eleventh Edition. Crown 8vo.* 6s.
A Colonial Edition is also published.

**Lover (Samuel).** HANDY ANDY. With 24 Illustrations by the Author. *Fcap. 8vo.* 3s. 6d. *net.* [Illustrated Pocket Library.

**E. V. L.** and **C. L. G.** ENGLAND DAY BY DAY: Or, The Englishman's Handbook to Efficiency. Illustrated by GEORGE MORROW. *Fourth Edition. Fcap. 4to.* 1s. *net.*
A burlesque Year-Book and Almanac.

**Lucian.** SIX DIALOGUES (Nigrinus, Icaro-Menippus, The Cock, The Ship, The Parasite, The Lover of Falsehood). Translated by S. T. IRWIN, M.A., Assistant Master at Clifton; late Scholar of Exeter College, Oxford. *Crown 8vo.* 3s. 6d. [Classical Translations.

**Lyde (L. W.), M.A.** A COMMERCIAL GEOGRAPHY OF THE BRITISH EMPIRE. *Third Edition. Crown 8vo.* 2s. [Commercial Series.

**Lydon (Noel S.).** A JUNIOR GEOMETRY. With numerous diagrams. *Crown 8vo.* 2s. [Junior School Books.

**Lyttelton (Hon. Mrs. A.).** WOMEN AND THEIR WORK. *Crown 8vo.* 2s. 6d.

**M. M.** HOW TO DRESS AND WHAT TO WEAR. *Crown 8vo.* 1s. *net.*

**Macaulay (Lord).** CRITICAL AND HISTORICAL ESSAYS. Edited by F. C. MONTAGUE, M.A. *Three Volumes. Cr. 8vo.* 18s.
The only edition of this book completely annotated.

**M'Allen (J. E. B.), M.A.** THE PRINCIPLES OF BOOKKEEPING BY DOUBLE ENTRY. *Crown 8vo.* 2s. [Commercial Series.

**MacCulloch (J. A.).** COMPARATIVE THEOLOGY. *Crown 8vo.* 6s. [Churchman's Library.

**MacCunn (F.).** JOHN KNOX. With Portrait. *Crown 8vo.* 3s. 6d. [Leaders of Religion.

**McDermott, (E. R.),** Editor of the *Railway News,* City Editor of the *Daily News.* RAILWAYS. *Crown 8vo.* 2s. 6d. *net.* [Books on Business

## GENERAL LITERATURE 15

**M'Dowall (A. S.).** CHATHAM. With 12 Illustrations. *Fcap. 8vo. Cloth, 3s. 6d.*; *leather, 4s. net.* [Little Biographies.

**Mackay (A. M.).** THE CHURCHMAN'S INTRODUCTION TO THE OLD TESTAMENT. *Crown 8vo. 3s. 6d.*
[Churchman's Library.

**Magnus (Laurie),** M.A. A PRIMER OF WORDSWORTH. *Crown 8vo. 2s. 6d.*

**Mahaffy (J. P.),** Litt.D. A HISTORY OF THE EGYPT OF THE PTOLEMIES. Fully Illustrated. *Crown 8vo. 6s.*

**Maitland (F. W.),** LL.D., Downing Professor of the Laws of England in the University of Cambridge. CANON LAW IN ENGLAND. *Royal 8vo. 7s. 6d.*

**Malden (H. E.),** M.A. ENGLISH RECORDS. A Companion to the History of England. *Crown 8vo. 3s. 6d.*
THE ENGLISH CITIZEN: HIS RIGHTS AND DUTIES. *Crown 8vo. 1s. 6d.*

**Marchant (E. C.),** M.A., Fellow of Peterhouse, Cambridge. A GREEK ANTHOLOGY. *Second Edition. Crown 8vo. 3s. 6d.*

**Marchant (E. C.),** M.A., and **Cook (A. M.),** M.A. PASSAGES FOR UNSEEN TRANSLATION. *Second Edition. Crown 8vo. 3s. 6d.*

**Marr (J. E.),** F.R.S., Fellow of St John's College, Cambridge. THE SCIENTIFIC STUDY OF SCENERY. *Second Edition.* Illustrated. *Crown 8vo. 6s.*
AGRICULTURAL GEOLOGY. With numerous Illustrations. *Crown 8vo. 6s.*

**Marvell (Andrew).** THE POEMS OF. Edited by EDWARD WRIGHT. *Small Pott 8vo, cloth, 1s. 6d. net; leather, 2s. 6d. net.*
[Little Library.

**Maskell (A.)** IVORIES. With many plates in Collotype and Photogravure. *Wide Royal 8vo. 25s. net.* [Connoisseurs Library.

**Mason (A. J.),** D.D. THOMAS CRANMER. With Portrait. *Crown 8vo. 3s. 6d.*
[Leaders of Religion.

**Massee (George).** THE EVOLUTION OF PLANT LIFE: Lower Forms. With Illustrations. *Crown 8vo. 2s. 6d.*
[University Extension Series.

**Masterman (C. F. G.),** M.A. TENNYSON AS A RELIGIOUS TEACHER. *Crown 8vo. 6s.*

**May (Phil)** THE PHIL MAY ALBUM. *Second Edition. 4to. 1s. net.*

**Mellows (Emma S.).** A SHORT STORY OF ENGLISH LITERATURE. *Crown 8vo. 3s. 6d.*

**Michell (E. B).** THE ART AND PRACTICE OF HAWKING. With 3 Photogravures by G. E. LODGE, and other Illustrations. *Demy 8vo. 10s. 6d.*

**Millais (J. G.)** THE LIFE AND LETTERS OF SIR JOHN EVERETT MILLAIS, President of the Royal Academy. With 319 Illustrations, of which 9 are in Photogravure. 2 vols. *Royal 8vo. 20s. net.*

**Millais.** A LITTLE GALLERY OF. Twenty examples in Photogravure of his finest work. *Demy 16mo. 2s. 6d. net.*
[Little Galleries.

**Millis (C. T.),** M.I.M.E., Principal of the Borough Polytechnic College. TECHNICAL ARITHMETIC AND GEOMETRY. With Diagrams. *Crown 8vo. 3s. 6d.* [Textbooks of Technology.

**Milne (J. G.),** M.A. A HISTORY OF ROMAN EGYPT. Fully Illustrated. *Crown 8vo. 6s.*

**Milton, John.** THE POEMS OF, BOTH ENGLISH AND LATIN, Compos'd at several times. Printed by his true Copies. The Songs were set in Musick by Mr. HENRY LAWES, Gentleman of the King's Chappel, and one of His Majesties Private Musick.
Printed and publish'd according to Order. Printed by RUTH RAWORTH for HUMPHREY MOSELEY, and are to be sold at the signe of the Princes Armes in Pauls Churchyard, 1645.
THE MINOR POEMS OF JOHN MILTON. Edited by H. C. BEECHING, M.A., Canon of Westminster. *Small Pott 8vo, cloth, 1s. 6d. net; leather, 2s. 6d. net.*
[Little Library.

**Minchin (H. C.),** M.A. A LITTLE GALLERY OF ENGLISH POETS. *Demy 16mo. 2s. 6d. net.* [Little Galleries.

**Mitchell (P. Chalmers),** M.A. OUTLINES OF BIOLOGY. Illustrated. *Second Edition. Crown 8vo. 6s.*
A text-book designed to cover the Schedule issued by the Royal College of Physicians and Surgeons.

**'Moil (A.).'** MINING AND MINING INVESTMENTS. *Crown 8vo. 2s. 6d. net.* [Books on Business.

**Moir (D. M.).** MANSIE WAUCH. Edited by T. F. HENDERSON. *Small Pott 8vo. Cloth, 1s. 6d. net; leather, 2s. 6d. net.*
[Little Library.

**Moore (H. E.).** BACK TO THE LAND: An Inquiry into the cure for Rural Depopulation. *Crown 8vo. 2s. 6d.*
[Social Questions Series.

**Morfill (W. R.),** Oriel College, Oxford. A HISTORY OF RUSSIA FROM PETER THE GREAT TO ALEXANDER II. With Maps and Plans. *Crown 8vo. 7s. 6d.*

**Morich (R. J.),** late of Clifton College. GERMAN EXAMINATION PAPERS IN MISCELLANEOUS GRAMMAR AND IDIOMS. *Sixth Edition. Crown 8vo. 2s. 6d.* [School Examination Series.
A KEY, issued to Tutors and Private Students only, to be had on application to the Publishers. *Second Edition. Crown 8vo. 6s. net.*

**Morris (J. E.).** THE NORTH RIDING OF YORKSHIRE. Illustrated by R. J. S. BERTRAM, *Small Pott 8vo, cloth,* 3s. ; *leather,* 3s. 6d. *net.*
[Little Guides.

**Morton (Miss Anderson).** See Miss Brodrick.

**Moule (H. C. G.),** D.D., Lord Bishop of Durham. CHARLES SIMEON. With Portrait. *Crown 8vo.* 3s. 6d.
[Leaders of Religion.

**Muir (M. M. Pattison),** M.A. THE CHEMISTRY OF FIRE. The Elementary Principles of Chemistry. Illustrated. *Crown 8vo.* 2s. 6d.
[University Extension Series.

**Mundella (V. A.),** M.A. See J. T. Dunn.

**Naval Officer (A).** THE ADVENTURES OF A POST CAPTAIN. With 24 coloured plates by Mr. WILLIAMS. *Fcap. 8vo.* 3s. 6d. *net.*
[Illustrated Pocket Library.

**Neal (W. G.).** See R. N. Hall.

**Newman (J. H.) and others.** LYRA APOSTOLICA. With an Introduction by CANON SCOTT HOLLAND, and Notes by CANON BEECHING, M.A. *Small Pott 8vo. Cloth,* 2s.; *leather,* 2s. 6d. *net.*
[Library of Devotion.

**Nichols (J. B. B.).** A LITTLE BOOK OF ENGLISH SONNETS. *Small Pott 8vo. Cloth,* 1s. 6d. *net; leather,* 2s. 6d. *net.*
[Little Library.

**Nicklin (T.),** M.A. EXAMINATION PAPERS IN THUCYDIDES. *Crown 8vo.* 2s.

**Nimrod.** THE LIFE AND DEATH OF JOHN MYTTON, ESQ. With 18 Coloured Plates by HENRY ALKEN and T. J. RAWLINS. *Third Edition. Fcap. 8vo.* 3s. 6d. *net.*
Also a limited edition on large Japanese paper. 30s. *net.*
[Illustrated Pocket Library.
THE LIFE OF A SPORTSMAN. With 35 Coloured Plates by HENRY ALKEN. *Fcap. 8vo.* 4s. 6d. *net.*
Also a limited edition on large Japanese paper. 30s. *net.*
[Illustrated Pocket Library.

**Norway (A. H.),** Author of 'Highways and Byways in Devon and Cornwall.' NAPLES: PAST AND PRESENT. With many Illustrations. *Crown 8vo.* 6s.

**Novalis.** THE DISCIPLES AT SAÏS AND OTHER FRAGMENTS. Edited by Miss UNA BIRCH. *Fcap. 8vo.* 3s. 6d.

**Oliphant (Mrs.).** THOMAS CHALMERS. With Portrait. *Crown 8vo.* 3s. 6d.
[Leaders of Religion.

**Oman (C. W.),** M.A., Fellow of All Souls', Oxford. A HISTORY OF THE ART OF WAR. Vol. II.: The Middle Ages, from the Fourth to the Fourteenth Century. Illustrated. *Demy 8vo.* 21s.

**Ottley (R. L.),** D.D., Professor of Pastoral Theology at Oxford and Canon of Christ Church. THE DOCTRINE OF THE INCARNATION. *Second and Cheaper Edition. Demy 8vo.* 12s. 6d.
[Handbooks of Theology.
LANCELOT ANDREWES. With Portrait. *Crown 8vo.* 3s. 6d.
[Leaders of Religion.

**Overton (J. H.),** M.A. JOHN WESLEY. With Portrait. *Crown 8vo.* 3s. 6d.
[Leaders of Religion.

**Owen (Douglas),** Barrister-at-Law, Secretary to the Alliance Marine and General Assurance Company. PORTS AND DOCKS. *Crown 8vo.* 2s. 6d. *net.*
[Books on Business.

**Oxford (M. N.),** of Guy's Hospital. A HANDBOOK OF NURSING. *Second Edition. Crown 8vo.* 3s. 6d.

**Pakes (W. C. C.).** THE SCIENCE OF HYGIENE. With numerous Illustrations. *Demy 8vo.* 15s.

**Parkinson (John).** PARADISI IN SOLE PARADISUS TERRISTRIS, OR A GARDEN OF ALL SORTS OF PLEASANT FLOWERS. *Folio.* £2, 2s. *net.*
Also an Edition of 20 copies on Japanese vellum. *Ten Guineas net.*

**Parmenter (John).** HELIO-TROPES, OR NEW POSIES FOR SUNDIALS, 1625. Edited by PERCIVAL LANDON. *Quarto.* 3s. 6d. *net.*

**Parmentier (Prof. Léon) and Bidez (M.).** EVAGRIUS. *Demy 8vo.* 10s. 6d. *net.*
[Byzantine Texts.

**Pascal,** THE THOUGHTS OF. With Introduction and Notes by C. S. JERRAM. *Small Pott 8vo.* 2s.; *leather,* 2s. 6d. *net.*
[Library of Devotion.

**Paston (George).** AUTHORS AND ARTISTS OF ENGLISH COLOURED BOOKS. Illustrated. *Fcap. 8vo.* 2s. 6d. *net.*
ROMNEY. With many Illustrations. *Demy 16mo.* 2s. 6d. *net.* [Little Books on Art.

**Patterson (A. H.).** NOTES OF AN EAST COAST NATURALIST. Illustrated in Colour by F. SOUTHGATE. *Cr. 8vo.* 6s.

**Peacock (Miss).** MILLET. With 30 Illustrations. *Demy 16mo.* 2s. 6d. *net.*

**Pearce (E. H.),** M.A. THE ANNALS OF CHRIST'S HOSPITAL. With many Illustrations. *Demy 8vo.* 7s. 6d.

**Peary (R. E.),** Gold Medallist of the Royal Geographical Society. NORTHWARD OVER THE GREAT ICE. With over 800 Illustrations. *2 vols. Royal 8vo.* 32s. *net.*

# General Literature

**Peel (Sidney)**, late Fellow of Trinity College, Oxford, and Secretary to the Royal Commission on the Licensing Laws. PRACTICAL LICENSING REFORM. *Second Edition. Crown 8vo. 1s. 6d.*

**Peters (J. P.)**, D.D. THE OLD TESTAMENT AND THE NEW SCHOLARSHIP. *Cr. 8vo. 6s.* [Churchman's Library.

**Petrie (W. M. Flinders)**, D.C.L., LL.D., Professor of Egyptology at University College. A HISTORY OF EGYPT, FROM THE EARLIEST TIMES TO THE PRESENT DAY. Fully Illustrated. *In six volumes. Crown 8vo. 6s. each.*
  VOL. I. PREHISTORIC TIMES TO XVITH DYNASTY. *Fifth Edition.*
  VOL. II. THE XVIITH AND XVIIITH DYNASTIES. *Fourth Edition.*
  VOL. IV. THE EGYPT OF THE PTOLEMIES. J. P. MAHAFFY, Litt.D.
  VOL. V. ROMAN EGYPT. J. G. MILNE, M.A.
  VOL. VI. EGYPT IN THE MIDDLE AGES. STANLEY LANE-POOLE, M.A.
RELIGION AND CONSCIENCE IN ANCIENT EGYPT. Fully Illustrated. *Crown 8vo. 2s. 6d.*
SYRIA AND EGYPT, FROM THE TELL EL AMARNA TABLETS. *Crown 8vo. 2s. 6d.*
EGYPTIAN TALES. Illustrated by TRISTRAM ELLIS. *In Two Volumes. Crown 8vo. 3s. 6d. each.*
EGYPTIAN DECORATIVE ART. With 120 Illustrations. *Crown 8vo. 3s. 6d.*

**Phillips (W. A.).** CANNING. With 12 Illustrations *Fcap. 8vo. Cloth, 3s. 6d.; leather, 4s. net.* [Little Biographies.

**Phillpotts (Eden).** MY DEVON YEAR. With 38 Illustrations by J. LEY PETHYBRIDGE. *Large Crown 8vo. 6s.*

**Pienaar (Philip).** WITH STEYN AND DE WET. *Second Edition. Crown 8vo. 3s. 6d.*

**Plautus.** THE CAPTIVI. Edited, with an Introduction, Textual Notes, and a Commentary, by W. M. LINDSAY, Fellow of Jesus College, Oxford. *Demy 8vo. 10s. 6d. net.*

**Plowden-Wardlaw (J. T.)**, B.A., King's Coll. Cam. EXAMINATION PAPERS IN ENGLISH HISTORY. *Crown 8vo. 2s. 6d.* [School Examination Series.

**Pocock (Roger).** A FRONTIERSMAN. *Third Edition. Crown 8vo. 6s.*
A Colonial Edition is also published.

**Podmore (Frank).** MODERN SPIRITUALISM. *Two Volumes. Demy 8vo. 21s. net.*
A History and a Criticism.

**Poer (J. Patrick La).** A MODERN LEGIONARY. *Crown 8vo. 6s.*
A Colonial Edition is also published.

**Pollard (Alice) and Birnstingl (Ethel).** COROT. With 30 Illustrations. *Demy 16mo.* [Little Books on Art.

**Pollard (A. W.).** OLD PICTURE BOOKS. With many Illustrations. *Demy 8vo. 7s. 6d. net.*

**Pollard (Eliza F.).** GREUZE AND HOUCHER. *Demy 16mo. 2s. 6d. net.* [Little Books on Art.

**Pollock (David), M.I.N.A.**, Author of *Modern Shipbuilding and the Men engaged in it*,' etc., etc. THE SHIPBUILDING INDUSTRY. *Crown 8vo. 2s. 6d. net.* [Books on Business.

**Potter (M. C.), M.A., F.L.S.** A TEXTBOOK OF AGRICULTURAL BOTANY. Illustrated. *Second Edition. Crown 8vo. 4s. 6d.* [University Extension Series.

**Potter Boy (An Old).** WHEN I WAS A CHILD. *Crown 8vo. 6s.*

**Pradeau (G.).** A KEY TO THE TIME ALLUSIONS IN THE DIVINE COMEDY. With a Dial. *Small quarto. 3s. 6d.*

**Prance (G.).** See R. Wyon.

**Prescott (O. L.).** ABOUT MUSIC, AND WHAT IT IS MADE OF. *Crown 8vo. 3s. 6d. net.*

**Price (L. L.), M.A.**, Fellow of Oriel College, Oxon. A HISTORY OF ENGLISH POLITICAL ECONOMY. *Fourth Edition. Crown 8vo. 2s. 6d.* [University Extension Series.

**Primrose (Deborah).** A MODERN BŒOTIA. *Cr. 8vo. 6s.* [Nearly Ready. PROTECTION AND INDUSTRY. By various Writers. *Crown 8vo. 1s. 6d. net.*

**Pugin and Rowlandson.** THE MICROCOSM OF LONDON, OR LONDON IN MINIATURE. With 104 Illustrations in colour. *In Three Volumes. Small 4to.*

"Q." THE GOLDEN POMP. A Procession of English Lyrics. Arranged by A. T. QUILLER COUCH. *Crown 8vo. Buckram. 6s.*

QUEVEDO VILLEGAS, THE VISIONS OF DOM FRANCISCO DE, Knight of the Order of St. James. Made English by R. L.
From the edition printed for H. Herringman, 1668. *Leather, 2s. net.* [Miniature Library.

**G. R. and E. S.** THE WOODHOUSE CORRESPONDENCE. *Crown 8vo. 6s.*

**Rackham (R. B.), M.A.** THE ACTS OF THE APOSTLES. With an Introduction and Notes. *Demy 8vo. New and Cheaper Ed. 10s. 6d.* [Westminster Commentaries.

**Randolph (B. W.), D.D.**, Principal of the Theological College, Ely. THE PSALMS OF DAVID. With an Introduction and Notes. *Small Pott 8vo. Cloth, 2s.; leather, 2s. 6d. net.* [Library of Devotion.

**Rannie (D. W.), M.A.** A STUDENT'S HISTORY OF SCOTLAND. *Cr. 8vo. 3s. 6d.*

**Rashdall (Hastings),** M.A., Fellow and Tutor of New College, Oxford. DOCTRINE AND DEVELOPMENT. *Crown 8vo.* 6s.

**Rawstorne (Lawrence, Esq.).** GAMONIA: or, The Art of Preserving Game; and an Improved Method of making plantations and covers, explained and illustrated by. With 15 Coloured Drawings by T. RAWLINS. *Fcap. 8vo.* 3s. 6d. *net.*
[Illustrated Pocket Library.

**A Real Paddy.** REAL LIFE IN IRELAND, or The Day and Night Scenes of Brian Boru, Esq., and his Elegant Friend, Sir Shawn O'Dogherty. With 19 Coloured Plates by HEATH, MARKS, etc. *Fcap. 8vo.* 3s. 6d. *net.* [Illustrated Pocket Library.

**Reason (W.),** M.A. UNIVERSITY AND SOCIAL SETTLEMENTS. *Crown 8vo.* 2s. 6d. [Social Questions Series.

**Redfern (W. B.),** Author of 'Ancient Wood and Iron Work in Cambridge,' etc. ROYAL AND HISTORIC GLOVES AND ANCIENT SHOES. Profusely Illustrated in colour and half-tone. *Quarto,* £2, 2s. *net.*

**Reynolds,** A LITTLE GALLERY OF. Twenty examples in photogravure of his finest work. *Demy 16mo.* 2s. 6d. *net.*
[Little Galleries.

**Roberts (M. E.).** See C. C. Channer.

**Robertson, (A.),** D.D., Lord Bishop of Exeter. REGNUM DEI. The Bampton Lectures of 1901. *Demy 8vo.* 12s. 6d. *net.*

**Robertson (C. Grant),** M.A., Fellow of All Souls' College, Oxford, Examiner in the Honour School of Modern History, Oxford, 1901-1904. SELECT STATUTES, CASES, AND CONSTITUTIONAL DOCUMENTS, 1660-1832. *Demy 8vo.* 10s. 6d. *net.*

**Robertson (Sir G. S.)** K.C.S.I. CHITRAL: The Story of a Minor Siege. With numerous Illustrations, Map and Plans. *Fourth Edition. Crown 8vo.* 6s.

**Robinson (A. W.),** M.A. THE EPISTLE TO THE GALATIANS. With an Introduction and Notes. *Fcap. 8vo.* 1s. 6d. *net.*
[Churchman's Bible.

**Robinson (Cecilia).** THE MINISTRY OF DEACONESSES. With an Introduction by the late Archbishop of Canterbury. *Crown 8vo.* 3s. 6d.

**Rochefoucauld (La),** THE MAXIMS OF. Translated by DEAN STANHOPE. Edited by G. H. POWELL. *Small Pott 8vo, cloth,* 1s. 6d. *net; leather,* 2s. 6d. *net.* [Little Library.

**Rodwell (G.),** B.A. NEW TESTAMENT GREEK. A Course for Beginners. With a Preface by WALTER LOCK, D.D., Warden of Keble College. *Fcap. 8vo.* 3s. 6d.

**Roe (Fred).** ANCIENT COFFERS AND CUPBOARDS: Their History and Description. With many Illustrations. *Quarto,* £3, 3s. *net.*

**Rogers (A. G. L.),** M.A., Editor of the last volume of *The History of Agriculture and Prices in England.* THE AGRICULTURAL INDUSTRY. *Crown 8vo.* 2s. 6d. *net.* [Books on Business.

**Romney.** A LITTLE GALLERY OF. Twenty examples in Photogravure of his finest work. *Demy 16mo.* 2s. 6d. *net.*
[Little Galleries.

**Roscoe (E. S.).** ROBERT HARLEY, EARL OF OXFORD. Illustrated. *Demy 8vo.* 7s. 6d.
This is the only life of Harley in existence.

BUCKINGHAMSHIRE. Illustrated by F. D. BEDFORD. *Small Pott 8vo, cloth* 3s.; *leather,* 3s. 6d. [Little Guides.

**Rose (Edward).** THE ROSE READER. With numerous Illustrations. *Crown 8vo.* 2s. 6d. *Also in 4 Parts. Parts I. and II.* 6d. *each; Part III.* 8d.; *Part IV.* 10d.

**Rubie (A. E.),** M.A., Head Master of College, Eltham. THE GOSPEL ACCORDING TO ST. MARK. With three Maps. *Crown 8vo.* 1s. 6d.
[Junior School Books.
THE ACTS OF THE APOSTLES. *Crown 8vo.* 2s. [Junior School Books.
THE FIRST BOOK OF KINGS. With Notes. *Crown 8vo.* 1s. 6d.
[Junior School Books.

**Russell (W. Clark).** THE LIFE OF ADMIRAL LORD COLLINGWOOD. With Illustrations by F. BRANGWYN. *Fourth Edition. Crown 8vo.* 6s.
A Colonial Edition is also published.

**St. Anselm,** THE DEVOTIONS OF. Edited by C. C. J. WEBB, M.A. *Small Pott 8vo. Cloth,* 2s.; *leather,* 2s. 6d. *net.* [Library of Devotion.

**St. Augustine,** THE CONFESSIONS OF. Newly Translated, with an Introduction and Notes, by C. BIGG, D.D., late Student of Christ Church. *Third Edition. Small Pott 8vo. Cloth,* 2s.; *leather,* 2s. 6d. *net.*
[Library of Devotion.

**'Saki' (Munro H.).** REGINALD. *Fcap.* 2s. 6d. *net.*

**Sales (St. Francis de).** ON THE LOVE OF GOD. Edited by W. J. KNOX-LITTLE, M.A. *Small Pott 8vo. Cloth,* 2s.; *leather,* 2s. 6d. *net.* [Library of Devotion.

**Salmon (A. L.).** CORNWALL. Illustrated by B. C. BOULTER. *Small Pott 8vo. Cloth,* 3s.; *leather,* 3s. 6d. *net.* [Little Guides.
A POPULAR GUIDE TO DEVON. *Medium 8vo.* 6d. *net.*

**Sargeaunt (J.),** M.A. ANNALS OF WESTMINSTER SCHOOL. With numerous Illustrations. *Demy 8vo.* 7s. 6d.

**Sathas (C.).** THE HISTORY OF PSELLUS. *Demy 8vo.* 15s. *net.*
[Byzantine Texts.

GENERAL LITERATURE 19

Schmitt (John). THE CHRONICLE OF MOREA. *Demy 8vo.* 15s. net.
[Byzantine Texts.
Seeley (H.G.) F.R.S. DRAGONS OF THE AIR. With many Illustrations. *Crown 8vo.* 6s.
Sells (V. P.), M.A. THE MECHANICS OF DAILY LIFE. Illustrated. *Crown 8vo.* 2s. 6d. [University Extension Series.
Selous (Edmund). TOMMY SMITH'S ANIMALS. Illustrated by G. W. Ord. *Second Edition. Fcap. 8vo.* 2s. 6d.
Settle (J. H.). ANECDOTES OF BRITISH SOLDIERS. *Crown 8vo.* 3s. 6d. net.
A Colonial Edition is also published.

Shakespeare (William).
THE FOUR FOLIOS, 1623; 1632; 1664; 1685. Each *Four Guineas net*, or a complete set, *Twelve Guineas net*.
The Arden Shakespeare.
*Demy 8vo.* 3s. 6d. each volume. General Editor, W. J. Craig. An Edition of Shakespeare in single Plays. Edited with a full Introduction, Textual Notes, and a Commentary at the foot of the page.
HAMLET. Edited by Edward Dowden, Litt.D.
ROMEO AND JULIET. Edited by Edward Dowden, Litt.D.
KING LEAR. Edited by W. J. Craig.
JULIUS CAESAR. Edited by M. Macmillan, M.A.
THE TEMPEST. Edited by Morton Luce.
OTHELLO. Edited by H. C. Hart.
CYMBELINE. Edited by Edward Dowden.
TITUS ANDRONICUS. Edited by H. B. Baildon.
THE MERRY WIVES OF WINDSOR. Edited by H. C. Hart.
MIDSUMMER NIGHTS DREAM. Edited by H. Cuningham.
KING HENRY V. Edited by H. A. Evans.
TITUS ANDRONICUS. Edited by H. B. Baildon.
ALL'S WELL THAT ENDS WELL. Edited by W. O. Brigstocke.
THE TAMING OF THE SHREW. Edited by R. M. Bond.
The Little Quarto Shakespeare. *Pott 16mo. Leather, price 1s. net each volume.*
TWO GENTLEMEN OF VERONA.
A COMEDY OF ERRORS.
THE TEMPEST.
THE MERRY WIVES OF WINDSOR.
MEASURE FOR MEASURE.
LOVE'S LABOUR'S LOST.
A MIDSUMMER NIGHT'S DREAM.
MUCH ADO ABOUT NOTHING.
AS YOU LIKE IT.
THE MERCHANT OF VENICE.
ALL'S WELL THAT ENDS WELL.

A WINTER'S TALE.
THE TAMING OF THE SHREW.
TWELFTH NIGHT.
KING JOHN.
KING RICHARD II.
KING HENRY IV. Part I.
KING HENRY IV. Part II.
KING HENRY V.
KING HENRY VI. Part I.
KING HENRY VI. Part II.
KING HENRY VI. Part III.
KING RICHARD III.
KING HENRY VIII.
TROILUS AND CRESSIDA.
CORIOLANUS.
TITUS ANDRONICUS.
ROMEO AND JULIET.
TIMON OF ATHENS.
JULIUS CAESAR.

Sharp (A.). VICTORIAN POETS. *Crown 8vo.* 2s. 6d. [University Extension Series.
Sharp (Mrs. E. A.). REMBRANDT. With 30 Illustrations. *Demy 8vo.* 2s. 6d. net.
[Little Books on Art.
Shedlock (J. S.). THE PIANOFORTE SONATA: Its Origin and Development. *Crown 8vo.* 5s.
Shelley (Percy B.). ADONAIS; an Elegy on the death of John Keats, Author of Endymion, etc. Pisa. From the types of Didot, 1821. 2s. net.
Sherwell (Arthur), M.A. LIFE IN WEST LONDON. *Third Edition. Crown 8vo.* 2s. 6d. [Social Questions Series.
Sichel (Walter). DISRAELI: A Study in Personality and Ideas. With 3 Portraits. *Demy 8vo.* 12s. 6d. net.
A Colonial Edition is also published.
BEACONSFIELD. With 12 Illustrations. *Fcap. 8vo, cloth,* 3s. 6d.; *leather,* 4s. net.
[Little Biographies.
Sime (J.). REYNOLDS. With many Illustrations. *Demy 16mo.* 2s. 6d. net.
[Little Books on Art.
Simonsen (G. A.). FRANCESCO GUARDI. With 32 Plates. *Royal folio.* £2, 2s. net.
Sketchley (R. E. D.). WATTS. With many Illustrations. *Demy 16mo.* 2s. 6d. net.
[Little Books on Art.
Skipton (H. P. R.). HOPPNER. With numerous Illustrations. *Demy 16mo.* 2s. 6d. net.
[Little Books on Art.
Sladen (Douglas). SICILY. With over 200 Illustrations. *Crown 8vo.* 5s. net.
Small (Evan), M.A. THE EARTH. An Introduction to Physiography. Illustrated. *Crown 8vo.* 2s. 6d.
[University Extension Series.
Smallwood, (M. G.). VANDYCK. With many Illustrations. *Demy 16mo.* 2s. 6d. net.
[Little Books on Art.

# 20  MESSRS. METHUEN'S CATALOGUE

**Smedley (F. E.).** FRANK FAIRLEGH. With 28 Plates by GEORGE CRUIKSHANK. *Fcap. 8vo.* 3s. 6d. net.
[Illustrated Pocket Library.

**Smith (Adam).** THE WEALTH OF NATIONS. Edited with an Introduction and numerous Notes by EDWIN CANNAN, M.A. *Two volumes. Demy 8vo.* 21s. net.

**Smith (Horace and James).** REJECTED ADDRESSES. Edited by A. D. GODLEY, M.A. *Small Pott 8vo, cloth,* 1s. 6d. net.; *leather,* 2s. 6d. net. [Little Library.

**Snell (F. J.).** A BOOK OF EXMOOR. Illustrated. *Crown 8vo.* 6s.

**Sophocles.** ELECTRA AND AJAX. Translated by E. D. A. MORSHEAD, M.A., Assistant Master at Winchester. 2s. 6d.
[Classical Translations.

**Sornet (L. A.), and Acatos (M. J.),** Modern Language Masters at King Edward's School, Birmingham. A JUNIOR FRENCH GRAMMAR. *Crown 8vo.* 2s.
[Junior School Books.

**South (Wilton E.),** M.A. THE GOSPEL ACCORDING TO ST. MATTHEW. *Crown 8vo,* 1s. 6d. [Junior School Books.

**Southey (R.)** ENGLISH SEAMEN. Vol. I. (Howard, Clifford, Hawkins, Drake, Cavendish). Edited, with an Introduction, by DAVID HANNAY. *Second Edition. Crown 8vo.* 6s.
Vol. II. (Richard Hawkins, Grenville, Essex, and Raleigh). *Crown 8vo.* 6s.

**Spence (C. H.),** M.A., Clifton College. HISTORY AND GEOGRAPHY EXAMINATION PAPERS. *Second Edition. Crown 8vo.* 2s. 6d.
[School Examination Series.

**Spooner (W. A.),** M.A., Warden of New College, Oxford. BISHOP BUTLER. With Portrait. *Crown 8vo.* 3s. 6d.
[Leaders of Religion.

**Stanbridge (J.W.),** B.D., late Canon of York, and sometime Fellow of St. John's College, Oxford. A BOOK OF DEVOTIONS. *Second Edition. Small Pott 8vo. Cloth,* 2s.; *leather,* 2s. 6d. net. [Library of Devotion.

**'Stancliffe.'** GOLF DO'S AND DONT'S. *Second Edition. Fcap. 8vo.* 1s.

**Stedman (A. M. M.),** M.A.
INITIA LATINA: Easy Lessons on Elementary Accidence. *Sixth Edition. Fcap. 8vo.* 1s.
FIRST LATIN LESSONS. *Eighth Edition. Crown 8vo.* 2s.
FIRST LATIN READER. With Notes adapted to the Shorter Latin Primer and Vocabulary. *Sixth Edition revised.* 18mo. 1s. 6d.
EASY SELECTIONS FROM CÆSAR. The Helvetian War. *Second Edition.* 18mo. 1s.

EASY SELECTIONS FROM LIVY. Part 1. The Kings of Rom~. 18mo. *Second Edition.* 1s. 6d.
EASY LATIN PASSAGES FOR UNSEEN TRANSLATION. *Ninth Edition. Fcap. 8vo.* 1s. 6d.
EXEMPLA LATINA. First Exercises in Latin Accidence. With Vocabulary. *Third Edition. Crown 8vo.* 1s.
EASY LATIN EXERCISES ON THE SYNTAX OF THE SHORTER AND REVISED LATIN PRIMER. With Vocabulary. *Ninth and Cheaper Edition, re-written. Crown 8vo.* 1s. 6d. KEY, 3s. net. *Original Edition.* 2s. 6d.
THE LATIN COMPOUND SENTENCE: Rules and Exercises. *Second Edition. Crown 8vo.* 1s. 6d. With Vocabulary. 2s.
NOTANDA QUAEDAM: Miscellaneous Latin Exercises on Common Rules and Idioms. *Fourth Edition. Fcap. 8vo.* 1s. 6d. With Vocabulary. 2s. Key, 2s. net.
LATIN VOCABULARIES FOR REPETITION: Arranged according to Subjects. *Eleventh Edition. Fcap. 8vo.* 1s. 6d.
A VOCABULARY OF LATIN IDIOMS. 18mo. *Second Edition.* 1s.
STEPS TO GREEK. *Second Edition, revised.* 18mo. 1s.
A SHORTER GREEK PRIMER. *Crown 8vo.* 1s. 6d.
EASY GREEK PASSAGES FOR UNSEEN TRANSLATION. *Third Edition, revised. Fcap. 8vo.* 1s. 6d.
GREEK VOCABULARIES FOR REPETITION. Arranged according to Subjects. *Third Edition. Fcap. 8vo.* 1s. 6d.
GREEK TESTAMENT SELECTIONS. For the use of Schools. With Introduction, Notes, and Vocabulary. *Third Edition. Fcap. 8vo.* 2s. 6d.
STEPS TO FRENCH. *Sixth Edition.* 18mo. 8d.
FIRST FRENCH LESSONS. *Sixth Edition, revised. Crown 8vo.* 1s.
EASY FRENCH PASSAGES FOR UNSEEN TRANSLATION. *Fifth Edition, revised. Fcap. 8vo.* 1s. 6d.
EASY FRENCH EXERCISES ON ELEMENTARY SYNTAX. With Vocabulary. *Fourth Edition. Crown 8vo.* 2s. 6d. KEY, 3s. net.
FRENCH VOCABULARIES FOR REPETITION: Arranged according to Subjects. *Twelfth Edition. Fcap. 8vo.* 1s.
FRENCH EXAMINATION PAPERS IN MISCELLANEOUS GRAMMAR AND IDIOMS. *Twelfth Edition. Crown 8vo.* 2s. 6d. [School Examination Series.
A KEY, issued to Tutors and Private Students only, to be had on application to the Publishers. *Fifth Edition. Crown 8vo.* 6s. net.

GENERAL KNOWLEDGE EXAMINATION PAPERS. *Fifth Edition. Crown 8vo.* 2s. 6d. [School Examination Series.
KEY (*Third Edition*) issued as above. 7s. net.

GREEK EXAMINATION PAPERS IN MISCELLANEOUS GRAMMAR AND IDIOMS. *Seventh Edition. Crown 8vo.* 2s. 6d. [School Examination Series.
KEY (*Third Edition*) issued as above. 6s. net.

LATIN EXAMINATION PAPERS IN MISCELLANEOUS GRAMMAR AND IDIOMS. *Twelfth Edition. Crown 8vo.* 2s. 6d. [School Examination Series.
KEY (*Fifth Edition*) issued as above. 6s. net.

**Steel (R. Elliott), M.A., F.C.S.** THE WORLD OF SCIENCE. Including Chemistry, Heat, Light, Sound, Magnetism, Electricity, Botany, Zoology, Physiology, Astronomy, and Geology. 147 Illustrations. *Second Edition. Crown 8vo.* 2s. 6d.
PHYSICS EXAMINATION PAPERS. *Crown 8vo.* 2s. 6d. [School Examination Series.

**Stephenson (C.),** of the Technical College, Bradford, and **Suddards (F.)** of the Yorkshire College, Leeds. ORNAMENTAL DESIGN FOR WOVEN FABRICS. Illustrated. *Demy 8vo. Second Edition.* 7s. 6d.

**Stephenson (J.), M.A.** THE CHIEF TRUTHS OF THE CHRISTIAN FAITH. *Crown 8vo.* 3s. 6d.

**Sterne (Laurence).** A SENTIMENTAL JOURNEY. Edited by H. W. PAUL. *Small Pott 8vo. Cloth,* 1s. 6d. *net; leather,* 2s. 6d. *net.* [Little Library.

**Sterry (W.), M.A.** ANNALS OF ETON COLLEGE. With numerous Illustrations. *Demy 8vo.* 7s. 6d.

**Steuart (Katherine).** BY ALLAN WATER. *Second Edition. Crown 8vo.* 6s.

**Stevenson (R. L.).** THE LETTERS OF ROBERT LOUIS STEVENSON TO HIS FAMILY AND FRIENDS. Selected and Edited, with Notes and Introductions, by SIDNEY COLVIN. *Sixth and Cheaper Edition. Crown 8vo.* 12s.
LIBRARY EDITION. *Demy 8vo.* 2 vols. 25s. *net.*
A Colonial Edition is also published.

VAILIMA LETTERS. With an Etched Portrait by WILLIAM STRANG. *Third Edition. Crown 8vo. Buckram.* 6s.
A Colonial Edition is also published.

THE LIFE OF R. L. STEVENSON. See G. Balfour.

**Stevenson (M. I.).** FROM SARANAC TO THE MARQUESAS. Being Letters written by Mrs. M. I. STEVENSON during 1887-8 to her sister, Miss JANE WHYTE BALFOUR. With an Introduction by George W. Balfour, M.D., LL.D., F.R.S.S. *Crown 8vo.* 6s. *net.*
A Colonial Edition is also published.

**Stoddart (Anna M.)** ST. FRANCIS OF ASSISI. With 16 Illustrations. *Fcap. 8vo. Cloth,* 3s. 6d.; *leather,* 4s. *net.* [Little Biographies.

**Stone (E. D.), M.A.,** late Assistant Master at Eton. SELECTIONS FROM THE ODYSSEY. *Fcap. 8vo.* 1s. 6d.

**Stone (S. J.).** POEMS AND HYMNS. With a Memoir by F. G. ELLERTON, M.A. With Portrait. *Crown 8vo.* 6s.

**Straker (F.),** Assoc. of the Institute of Bankers, and Lecturer to the London Chamber of Commerce. THE MONEY MARKET. *Crown 8vo.* 2s. 6d. *net.* [Books on Business.

**Streane (A. W.), D.D.** ECCLESIASTES. With an Introduction and Notes. *Fcap. 8vo.* 1s. 6d. *net.* [Churchman's Bible.

**Stroud (H.), D.Sc., M.A.,** Professor of Physics in the Durham College of Science, Newcastle-on-Tyne. PRACTICAL PHYSICS. Fully Illustrated. *Crown 8vo.* 3s. 6d. [Textbooks of Technology.

**Strutt (Joseph).** THE SPORTS AND PASTIMES OF THE PEOPLE OF ENGLAND. Illustrated by many engravings. Revised by J. Charles Cox, LL.D., F.S.A. *Quarto.* 21s. *net.*

**Stuart (Capt. Donald).** THE STRUGGLE FOR PERSIA. With a Map. *Crown 8vo.* 6s.

**Suckling (Sir John).** FRAGMENTA AUREA: a Collection of all the Incomparable Peeces, written by. And published by a friend to perpetuate his memory. Printed by his own copies.
Printed for HUMPHREY MOSELEY, and are to be sold at his shop, at the sign of the Princes Arms in St. Paul's Churchyard, 1646.

**Suddards (F.).** See C. Stephenson.

**Surtees (R. S.).** HANDLEY CROSS. With 17 Coloured Plates and 100 Woodcuts in the Text by JOHN LEECH. *Fcap. 8vo.* 4s. 6d. *net.*
Also a limited edition on large Japanese paper. 30s. *net.*
[Illustrated Pocket Library.

MR. SPONGE'S SPORTING TOUR. With 13 Coloured Plates and 90 Woodcuts in the Text by JOHN LEECH. *Fcap. 8vo.* 3s. 6d. *net.*
Also a limited edition on large Japanese paper. 30s. *net.*
[Illustrated Pocket Library.

JORROCKS' JAUNTS AND JOLLITIES. With 15 Coloured Plates by H. ALKEN. *Fcap. 8vo.* 3s. 6d. *net.*
Also a limited edition on large Japanese paper. 30s. *net.*
[Illustrated Pocket Library.

## 22    MESSRS. METHUEN'S CATALOGUE

**ASK MAMMA.** With 13 Coloured Plates and 70 Woodcuts in the Text by JOHN LEECH. *Fcap. 8vo, 3s. 6d. net.*
Also a limited edition on large Japanese paper, 30s. *net.*
[Illustrated Pocket Library. NearlyReady.

**Swift (Jonathan).** THE JOURNAL TO STELLA. Edited by G. A. AITKEN. *Crown 8vo. 6s.*

**Symes (J. E.),** M.A. THE FRENCH REVOLUTION. *Second Edition. Crown 8vo. 2s. 6d.* [University Extension Series.

**Syrett (Netta).** A SCHOOL YEAR. Illustrated. *Demy 16mo. 2s. 6d.*
[Little Blue Books.

**Tacitus.** AGRICOLA. With Introduction, Notes, Map, etc. By R. F. DAVIS, M.A., late Assistant Master at Weymouth College. *Crown 8vo. 2s.*
GERMANIA. By the same Editor. *Crown 8vo. 2s.*
AGRICOLA AND GERMANIA. Translated by R. B. TOWNSHEND, late Scholar of Trinity College, Cambridge. *Crown 8vo. 2s. 6d.* [Classical Translations.

**Tauler (J.).** THE INNER WAY. Being Thirty-six Sermons for Festivals by JOHN TAULER. Edited by A. W. HUTTON, M.A. *Small Pott 8vo. Cloth, 2s.; leather, 2s. 6d. net.* [Library of Devotion.

**Taunton (E. L.).** A HISTORY OF THE JESUITS IN ENGLAND. With Illustrations. *Demy 8vo. 21s. net.*

**Taylor (A. E.).** THE ELEMENTS OF METAPHYSICS. *Demy 8vo. 10s. 6d. net.*

**Taylor (F. G.),** M.A. COMMERCIAL ARITHMETIC. *Third Edition. Crown 8vo. 1s. 6d.* [Commercial Series.

**Taylor (Miss J. A.).** SIR WALTER RALEIGH. With 12 Illustrations. *Fcap. 8vo. Cloth, 3s. 6d.; leather, 4s. net.*
[Little Biographies.

**Taylor (T. M.),** M.A., Fellow of Gonville and Caius College, Cambridge. A CONSTITUTIONAL AND POLITICAL HISTORY OF ROME. *Crown 8vo. 7s. 6d.*

**Tennyson (Alfred, Lord).** THE EARLY POEMS OF. Edited, with Notes and an Introduction, by J. CHURTON COLLINS, M.A. *Crown 8vo. 6s.*
IN MEMORIAM, MAUD, AND THE PRINCESS. Edited by J. CHURTON COLLINS, M.A. *Crown 8vo. 6s.*
MAUD. Edited by ELIZABETH WORDSWORTH. *Small Pott 8vo. Cloth, 1s. 6d. net; leather, 2s. 6d. net.* [Little Library.
IN MEMORIAM. Edited by H. C. BEECHING, M.A. *Small Pott 8vo. Cloth, 1s. 6d. net; leather, 2s. 6d. net.* [Little Library.
THE EARLY POEMS OF. Edited by J. C. COLLINS, M.A. *Small Pott 8vo. Cloth, 1s. 6d. net; leather, 2s. 6d. net.* [Little Library.

**THE PRINCESS.** Edited by ELIZABETH WORDSWORTH. *Small Pott 8vo. Cloth, 1s. 6d. net; leather, 2s. 6d. net.* [Little Library.

**Terry (C. S.).** THE YOUNG PRETENDER. With 12 Illustrations. *Fcap. 8vo. Cloth, 3s. 6d.; leather, 4s. net.*
[Little Biographies.

**Terton (Alice).** LIGHTS AND SHADOWS IN A HOSPITAL. *Crown 8vo. 3s. 6d.*

**Thackeray (W. M.).** VANITY FAIR. Edited by STEPHEN GWYNN. *Three Volumes. Small Pott 8vo. Each volume, cloth, 1s. 6d. net; leather, 2s. 6d. net.*
[Little Library.
PENDENNIS. Edited by STEPHEN GWYNN. *Three Volumes. Small Pott 8vo. Each volume, cloth, 1s. 6d. net; leather, 2s. 6d. net.* [Little Library.
ESMOND. Edited by STEPHEN GWYNN. *Small Pott 8vo. Cloth, 1s. 6d. net; leather, 2s. 6d. net.* [Little Library.
CHRISTMAS BOOKS. Edited by STEPHEN GWYNN. *Small Pott 8vo. Cloth, 1s. 6d. net; leather, 2s. 6d. net.* [Little Library.

**Theobald (F. W.),** M.A. INSECT LIFE. Illustrated. *Crown 8vo. 2s. 6d.*
[University Extension Series.

**Thompson (A. H.).** CAMBRIDGE AND ITS COLLEGES. Illustrated by E. H. NEW. *Small Pott 8vo. Cloth, 3s.; leather, 3s. 6d. net.*
[Little Guides.

**Tileston (Mary W.).** DAILY STRENGTH FOR DAILY NEEDS. *Fcap. 8vo. 3s. 6d.*
Also editions in superior binding 5s. and 6s.

**Tompkins (H. W.),** F.R.H.S. HERTFORDSHIRE. Illustrated by E. H. NEW. *Small Pott 8vo. Cloth, 3s.; leather, 3s. 6d. net.*
[Little Guides.

**Townley (Lady Susan).** MY CHINESE NOTE-BOOK. With 16 Illustrations. *Demy 8vo. 10s. 6d. net.*
A Colonial Edition is also published.

**Toynbee (Paget),** M.A., D.Litt. DANTE STUDIES AND RESEARCHES. *Demy 8vo. 10s. 6d. net.*
DANTE ALIGHIERI. With 12 Illustrations. *Second Edition. Fcap. 8vo. Cloth, 3s. 6d.; leather, 4s. net.*
[Little Biographies.

**Trench (Herbert).** DEIRDRE WED: and Other Poems. *Crown 8vo. 5s.*

**Trevelyan (G. M.),** Fellow of Trinity College, Cambridge. ENGLAND UNDER THE STUARTS. *Demy 8vo. 10s. 6d. net.*

**Troutbeck (G. E.).** WESTMINSTER ABBEY. Illustrated by F. D. BEDFORD. *Small Pott 8vo. Cloth, 3s.; leather, 3s. 6d. net.* [Little Guides.

**Tuckwell (Gertrude).** THE STATE AND ITS CHILDREN. *Crown 8vo. 2s. 6d.*
[Social Questions Series.

**Twining (Louisa).** WORKHOUSES AND PAUPERISM. *Crown 8vo. 2s. 6d.*
[Social Questions Series.

# General Literature 23

**Tyler (E. A.), B.A., F.C.S.** A JUNIOR CHEMISTRY. *Crown 8vo. 2s. 6d.*
[Junior School Books.

**Tyrrell-Gill (Frances).** TURNER. *Demy 16mo. 2s. 6d. net.*
[Little Books on Art.

**Vaughan (Henry),** THE POEMS OF. Edited by Edward Hutton. *Small Pott 8vo. Cloth, 1s. 6d. net; leather, 2s. 6d. net.*
[Little Library.

**Voegelin (A.), M.A.** JUNIOR GERMAN EXAMINATION PAPERS. *Fcap. 8vo. 1s.*
[Junior Examination Series.

**Wade (G. W.), D.D.** OLD TESTAMENT HISTORY. With Maps. *Second Edition. Crown 8vo. 6s.*

This book presents a connected account of the Hebrew people during the period covered by the Old Testament; and has been drawn up from the Scripture records in accordance with the methods of historical criticism.

**Wagner (Richard).** See A. L. Cleather.

**Wall (J. C.)** DEVILS. Illustrated by the Author. *Demy 8vo. 4s. 6d. net.*

**Walters (H. B.).** GREEK ART. With many Illustrations. *Demy 16mo. 2s. 6d. net.*
[Little Books on Art.

**Walton (Izaak) and Cotton (Charles).** THE COMPLEAT ANGLER. With 14 Plates and 77 Woodcuts in the Text. *Fcap 8vo. 3s. 6d. net.*
[Illustrated Pocket Library.

This volume is reproduced from the beautiful edition of John Major of 1824-5.

THE COMPLEAT ANGLER. Edited by J. Buchan. *Small Pott 8vo. Cloth, 1s. 6d. net; leather, 2s. 6d. net.* [Little Library.

**Warmelo (D. S. Van).** ON COMMANDO. With Portrait. *Crown 8vo. 3s. 6d.*

**Waterhouse (Mrs. Alfred).** A LITTLE BOOK OF LIFE AND DEATH. Selected. *Fourth Edition. Small Pott 8vo. Cloth, 1s. 6d. net; leather, 2s. 6d. net.*
[Little Library.

WITH THE SIMPLE-HEARTED: Little Homilies to Women in Country Places. *Fcap. 8vo. 2s. net.*

**Weatherhead (T. C.), M.A.** EXAMINATION PAPERS IN HORACE. *Crown 8vo. 2s.*

JUNIOR GREEK EXAMINATION PAPERS. *Fcap. 8vo. 1s.*
[Junior Examination Series.

**Webb (W. T.).** A BOOK OF BAD CHILDREN. With 50 Illustrations by H. C. Sandy. *Demy 16mo. 2s. 6d.*
[Little Blue Books.

**Webber (F. C.).** CARPENTRY AND JOINERY. With many Illustrations. *Third Edition. Crown 8vo. 3s. 6d.*

**Wells (Sidney H.).** PRACTICAL MECHANICS. With 75 Illustrations and Diagrams. *Second Edition. Crown 8vo. 3s. 6d.*
[Textbooks of Technology.

**Wells (J.), M.A.,** Fellow and Tutor of Wadham College. OXFORD AND OXFORD LIFE. By Members of the University. *Third Edition. Crown 8vo. 3s. 6d.*

A SHORT HISTORY OF ROME. *Fifth Edition.* With 3 Maps. *Cr. 8vo. 3s. 6d.*

This book is intended for the Middle and Upper Forms of Public Schools and for Pass Students at the Universities. It contains copious Tables, etc.

OXFORD AND ITS COLLEGES. Illustrated by E. H. New. *Fifth Edition. Pott 8vo. Cloth, 3s.; leather, 3s. 6d. net.*
[Little Guides.

**Wetmore (Helen C.).** THE LAST OF THE GREAT SCOUTS ('Buffalo Bill'). With Illustrations. *Second Edition. Demy 8vo. 6s.*

**Whibley (C.).** See Henley and Whibley.

**Whibley (L.), M.A.,** Fellow of Pembroke College, Cambridge. GREEK OLIGARCHIES: THEIR ORGANISATION AND CHARACTER. *Crown 8vo. 6s.*

**Whitaker (G. H.), M.A.** THE EPISTLE OF ST. PAUL THE APOSTLE TO THE EPHESIANS. With an Introduction and Notes. *Fcap. 8vo. 1s. 6d. net.*
[Churchman's Bible.

**White (Gilbert).** THE NATURAL HISTORY OF SELBORNE. Edited by L. C. Miall, F.R.S., assisted by W. Warde Fowler, M.A. *Crown 8vo. 6s.*

**Whitfield (E. E.).** PRECIS WRITING AND OFFICE CORRESPONDENCE. *Second Edition. Crown 8vo. 2s.*
[Commercial Series.

COMMERCIAL EDUCATION IN THEORY AND PRACTICE. *Crown 8vo. 5s.*
[Commercial Series.

An introduction to Methuen's Commercial Series treating the question of Commercial Education fully from both the point of view of the teacher and of the parent.

**Whitehead (A. W.).** COLIGNY. With many Illustrations. *Demy 8vo. 12s. 6d. net.*

**Whitley (Miss).** See Lady Dilke.

**Whyte (A. G.),** B.Sc., Editor of *Electrical Investments.* THE ELECTRICAL INDUSTRY. *Crown 8vo. 2s. 6d. net.*
[Books on Business.

**Wilberforce (Wilfrid) and Gilbert (A. R.).** VELASQUEZ. With many Illustrations. *Demy 16mo. 2s. 6d. net.*
[Little Books on Art.

**Wilkins (W. H.), B.A.** THE ALIEN INVASION. *Crown 8vo. 2s. 6d.*
[Social Questions Series.

**Williamson (W.).** THE BRITISH GARDENER. Illustrated. *Demy 8vo. 10s. 6d.*

**Williamson (W.), B.A.** JUNIOR ENGLISH EXAMINATION PAPERS. *Fcap. 8vo. 1s.* [Junior Examination Series.

A JUNIOR ENGLISH GRAMMAR. With numerous passages for parsing and analysis, and a chapter on Essay Writing. *Crown 8vo.* 2s. [Junior School Books.

A CLASS-BOOK OF DICTATION PASSAGES. Eighth Edition. *Crown 8vo.* 1s. 6d. [Junior School Books.

EASY DICTATION AND SPELLING. Third Edition. *Fcap. 8vo.* 1s.

**Wilmot-Buxton (E. M.).** THE MAKERS OF EUROPE. *Crown 8vo.* Second Edition. 3s. 6d.
A Text-book of European History for Middle Forms.

THE STORY OF THE ANCIENT WORLD. With Maps and Illustrations. *Crown 8vo.* 3s. 6d.

**Wilson (Bishop).** SACRA PRIVATA. Edited by A. E. BURN, B.D. *Small Pott 8vo. Cloth*, 2s.; *leather*, 2s. 6d. net.
[Library of Devotion.

**Willson (Beckles).** LORD STRATHCONA: the Story of his Life. Illustrated. *Demy 8vo.* 7s. 6d.
A Colonial Edition is also published.

**Wilson (A. J.),** Editor of the *Investor's Review*, City Editor of the *Daily Chronicle*. THE INSURANCE INDUSTRY. *Crown 8vo.* 2s. 6d. net.
[Books on Business.

**Wilson (H. A.).** LAW IN BUSINESS. *Crown 8vo.* 2s. 6d. net. [Books on Business.

**Wilton (Richard),** M.A. LYRA PASTORALIS: Songs of Nature, Church, and Home. *Pott 8vo.* 2s. 6d.
A volume of devotional poems.

**Winbolt (S. E.),** M.A., Assistant Master in Christ's Hospital. EXERCISES IN LATIN ACCIDENCE. *Crown 8vo.* 1s.6d.
An elementary book adapted for Lower Forms to accompany the Shorter Latin Primer.

LATIN HEXAMETER VERSE: An Aid to Composition. *Crown 8vo.* 3s. 6d. KEY, 5s. net.

**Windle (B. C. A.),** D.Sc., F.R.S. SHAKESPEARE'S COUNTRY. Illustrated by E. H. NEW. Second Edition. *Small Pott 8vo. cloth*, 3s.; *leather*, 3s.6d. net.
[Little Guides.

THE MALVERN COUNTRY. Illustrated by E. H. NEW. *Small Pott 8vo. Cloth*, 3s.; *leather*, 3s. 6d. net. [Little Guides.

REMAINS OF THE PREHISTORIC AGE IN ENGLAND. With numerous Illustrations and Plans. *Demy 8vo.* 7s. 6d. net. [Antiquary's Books.

CHESTER. Illustrated by E. H. New. *Crown 8vo.* 3s. 6d. net. [Ancient Cities.

**Winterbotham (Canon),** M.A., B.Sc., LL.B. THE KINGDOM OF HEAVEN HERE AND HEREAFTER. *Crown 8vo.* 3s. 6d.
[Churchman's Library.

**Wood (J. A. E.).** HOW TO MAKE A DRESS. Illustrated. Third Edition. *Cr. 8vo.* 1s. 6d. [Textbooks of Technology.

**Wordsworth (Christopher),** M.A., and **Littlehales (Henry).** OLD SERVICE BOOKS OF THE ENGLISH CHURCH. With Coloured and other Illustrations. *Demy 8vo.* 7s. 6d. net.
[Antiquary's Books.

**Wordsworth (W.).** SELECTIONS. Edited by NOWELL C. SMITH, M.A. *Small Pott 8vo. Cloth*, 1s. 6d. net; *leather*, 2s. 6d. net. [Little Library.

**Wordsworth (W.) and Coleridge (S. T.).** LYRICAL BALLADS. Edited by GEORGE SAMPSON. *Small Pott 8vo. Cloth*, 1s. 6d. net; *leather*, 2s. 6d. net. [Little Library.

**Wright (Arthur),** M.A., Fellow of Queen's College, Cambridge. SOME NEW TESTAMENT PROBLEMS. *Crown 8vo.* 6s. [Churchman's Library.

**Wright (Sophie).** GERMAN VOCABULARIES FOR REPETITION. *Fcap. 8vo.* 1s. 6d.

**Wylde (A. B.).** MODERN ABYSSINIA. With a Map and a Portrait. *Demy 8vo.* 15s. net.

**Wyndham (G.),** M.P. THE POEMS OF WILLIAM SHAKESPEARE. With an Introduction and Notes. *Demy 8vo.* Buckram, gilt top. 10s. 6d.

**Wyon (R.) and Prance (G.).** THE LAND OF THE BLACK MOUNTAIN. Being a description of Montenegro. With 40 Illustrations. *Crown 8vo.* 6s.
A Colonial Edition is also published.

**Yeats (W. B.).** AN ANTHOLOGY OF IRISH VERSE. Revised and Enlarged Edition. *Crown 8vo.* 3s. 6d.

**Yendis (M.).** THE GREAT RED FROG. A Story told in 40 Coloured Pictures. *Fcap. 8vo.* 1s. net.

**Young (Filson).** THE COMPLETE MOTORIST. With many Illustrations. *Demy 8vo.* 12s. 6d. net.

**Young (T. M.).** THE AMERICAN COTTON INDUSTRY: A Study of Work and Workers. With an Introduction by ELIJAH HELM, Secretary to the Manchester Chamber of Commerce. *Crown 8vo. cloth*, 2s. 6d.; *paper boards*, 1s. 6d.

# General Literature

## Antiquary's Books, The
General Editor, J. CHARLES COX, LL.D., F.S.A.

ENGLISH MONASTIC LIFE. By the Right Rev. Abbot Gasquet, O.S.B. Illustrated. *Demy 8vo.* 7s. 6d. net.
REMAINS OF THE PREHISTORIC AGE IN ENGLAND. By B. C. A. Windle, D.Sc., F.R.S. With numerous Illustrations and Plans. *Demy 8vo.* 7s. 6d. net.
OLD SERVICE BOOKS OF THE ENGLISH CHURCH. By Christopher Wordsworth, M.A., and Henry Littlehales. With Coloured and other Illustrations. *Demy 8vo.* 7s. 6d. net.
CELTIC ART. By J. Romilly Allen, F.S.A. With numerous Illustrations and Plans. *Demy 8vo.* 7s. 6d. net.

## Business, Books on
*Crown 8vo.* 2s. 6d. net.

The first Twelve volumes are—

PORTS AND DOCKS. By Douglas Owen.
RAILWAYS. By E. R. McDermott.
THE STOCK EXCHANGE. By Chas Duguid. *Second Edition.*
THE INSURANCE INDUSTRY. By A. J. Wilson.
THE ELECTRICAL INDUSTRY. By A. G. Whyte, B.Sc.
THE SHIPBUILDING INDUSTRY. By David Pollock, M.I.N.A.
THE MONEY MARKET. By F. Straker.
THE AGRICULTURAL INDUSTRY. By A. G. L. Rogers, M.A.
LAW IN BUSINESS. By H. A. Wilson.
THE BREWING INDUSTRY. By Julian L. Baker, F.I.C., F.C.S.
THE AUTOMOBILE INDUSTRY. By G. de H. Stone.
MINING AND MINING INVESTMENTS. By 'A. Moil.

## Byzantine Texts
Edited by J. B. BURY, M.A., Litt.D.

ZACHARIAH OF MITYLENE. Translated by F. J. Hamilton, D.D., and E. W. Brooks. *Demy 8vo.* 12s. 6d. net.
EVAGRIUS. Edited by Léon Parmentier and M. Bidez. *Demy 8vo.* 10s. 6d. net.
THE HISTORY OF PSELLUS. Edited by C. Sathas. *Demy 8vo.* 15s. net.
ECTHESIS CHRONICA. Edited by Professor Lambros. *Demy 8vo.* 7s. 6d. net.
THE CHRONICLE OF MOREA. Edited by John Schmitt. *Demy 8vo.* 15s. net.

## Churchman's Bible, The
General Editor, J. H. BURN, B.D., F.R.S.E.

The volumes are practical and devotional, and the text of the Authorised Version is explained in sections, which correspond as far as possible with the Church Lectionary.

THE EPISTLE TO THE GALATIANS. Edited by A. W. Robinson, M.A. *Fcap. 8vo.* 1s. 6d. net.
ECCLESIASTES. Edited by A. W. Streane, D.D. *Fcap. 8vo.* 1s. 6d. net.
THE EPISTLE TO THE PHILIPPIANS. Edited by C. R. D. Biggs, D.D. *Fcap. 8vo.* 1s. 6d. net.
THE EPISTLE OF ST. JAMES. Edited by H. W. Fulford, M.A. *Fcap. 8vo.* 1s. 6d. net.
ISAIAH. Edited by W. E. Barnes, D.D., Hulsean Professor of Divinity. *Two Volumes. Fcap. 8vo.* 2s. net each. With Map.
THE EPISTLE OF ST. PAUL THE APOSTLE TO THE EPHESIANS. Edited by G. H. Whitaker, M.A. *Fcap. 8vo.* 1s. 6d. net.

## Churchman's Library, The
General Editor, J. H. BURN, B.D., F.R.S.E.

THE BEGINNINGS OF ENGLISH CHRISTIANITY. By W. E. Collins, M.A. With Map. *Crown 8vo.* 3s. 6d.
SOME NEW TESTAMENT PROBLEMS. By Arthur Wright, M.A. *Crown 8vo.* 6s.
THE KINGDOM OF HEAVEN HERE AND HEREAFTER. By Canon Winterbotham, M.A., B.Sc., LL.B. *Crown 8vo.* 3s. 6d.
THE WORKMANSHIP OF THE PRAYER BOOK: Its Literary and Liturgical Aspects. By J. Dowden, D.D. *Second Edition. Crown 8vo.* 3s. 6d.
EVOLUTION. By F. B. Jevons, M.A., Litt.D. *Crown 8vo.* 3s. 6d.
THE OLD TESTAMENT AND THE NEW SCHOLARSHIP. By J. W. Peters, D.D. *Crown 8vo.* 6s.
THE CHURCHMAN'S INTRODUCTION TO THE OLD TESTAMENT. Edited by A. M. Mackay, B.A. *Crown 8vo.* 3s. 6d.
THE CHURCH OF CHRIST. By E. T. Green, M.A. *Crown 8vo.* 6s.
COMPARATIVE THEOLOGY. By J. A. MacCulloch. *Crown 8vo.* 6s.

## Classical Translations
Edited by H. F. FOX, M.A., Fellow and Tutor of Brasenose College, Oxford.
*Crown 8vo.*

ÆSCHYLUS—Agamemnon, Choephoroe, Eumenides. Translated by Lewis Campbell, LL.D. 5s.
CICERO—De Oratore I. Translated by E. N. P. Moor, M.A. 3s. 6d.
CICERO—Select Orations (Pro Milone, Pro Murena, Philippic II., in Catilinam). Translated by H. E. D. Blakiston, M.A. 5s.
CICERO—De Natura Deorum. Translated by F. Brooks, M.A. 3s. 6d.
CICERO—De Officiis. Translated by G. B. Gardiner, M.A. 2s. 6d.
HORACE—The Odes and Epodes. Translated by A. Godley, M.A. 2s.
LUCIAN—Six Dialogues (Nigrinus, Icaro-Menippus, The Cock, The Ship, The Parasite, The Lover of Falsehood). Translated by S. T. Irwin, M.A. 3s. 6d.
SOPHOCLES—Electra and Ajax. Translated by E. D. A. Morshead, M.A. 2s. 6d.
TACITUS—Agricola and Germania. Translated by R. B. Townshend. 2s. 6d.
THE SATIRES OF JUVENAL. Translated by S. G. Owen. *Crown 8vo.* 2s. 6d.

## MESSRS. METHUEN'S CATALOGUE

### Commercial Series, Methuen's
Edited by H. DE B. GIBBINS, Litt.D., M.A.
*Crown 8vo.*

COMMERCIAL EDUCATION IN THEORY AND PRACTICE. By E. E. Whitfield, M.A. 5s.
An introduction to Methuen's Commercial Series treating the question of Commercial Education fully from both the point of view of the teacher and of the parent.
BRITISH COMMERCE AND COLONIES FROM ELIZABETH TO VICTORIA. By H. de B. Gibbins, Litt.D., M.A. *Third Edition.* 2s.
COMMERCIAL EXAMINATION PAPERS. By H. de B. Gibbins, Litt.D., M.A. 1s. 6d.
THE ECONOMICS OF COMMERCE. By H. de B. Gibbins, Litt.D., M.A. 1s. 6d.
A GERMAN COMMERCIAL READER. By S. E. Bally, With Vocabulary. 2s.
A COMMERCIAL GEOGRAPHY OF THE BRITISH EMPIRE. By L. W. Lyde, M.A. *Third Edition.* 2s.

A PRIMER OF BUSINESS. By S. Jackson, M.A. *Third Edition.* 1s. 6d.
COMMERCIAL ARITHMETIC. By F. G. Taylor, M.A. *Third Edition.* 1s. 6d.
FRENCH COMMERCIAL CORRESPONDENCE. By S. E. Bally. With Vocabulary. *Third Edition.* 2s.
GERMAN COMMERCIAL CORRESPONDENCE. By S. E. Bally. With Vocabulary. 2s. 6d.
A FRENCH COMMERCIAL READER. By S. E. Bally. With Vocabulary. *Second Edition.* 2s.
PRECIS WRITING AND OFFICE CORRESPONDENCE. By E. E. Whitfield, M.A. *Second Edition.* 2s.
A GUIDE TO PROFESSIONS AND BUSINESS. By H. Jones. 1s. 6d.
THE PRINCIPLES OF BOOK-KEEPING BY DOUBLE ENTRY. By J. E. B. M'Allen, M.A. 2s.
COMMERCIAL LAW. By W. Douglas Edwards. 2s.

### Connoisseurs Library, The
*Wide Royal 8vo.* 25s. *net.*

The first volumes are—
MEZZOTINTS. By Cyril Davenport.
MINIATURES. By Dudley Heath.
PORCELAIN. By Edward Dillon.
IVORIES. By A. Maskell.

### Devotion, The Library of
With Introductions and (where necessary) Notes.
*Small Pott 8vo, cloth,* 2s. ; *leather,* 2s. 6d. *net.*

THE CONFESSIONS OF ST. AUGUSTINE. Edited by C. Bigg, D.D. *Third Edition.*
THE CHRISTIAN YEAR. Edited by Walter Lock, D.D. *Second Edition.*
THE IMITATION OF CHRIST. Edited by C. Bigg, D.D. *Second Edition.*
A BOOK OF DEVOTIONS. Edited by J. W. Stanbridge, B.D. *Second Edition.*
LYRA INNOCENTIUM. Edited by Walter Lock, D.D.
A SERIOUS CALL TO A DEVOUT AND HOLY LIFE. Edited by C. Bigg, D.D. *Second Edition.*
THE TEMPLE. Edited by E. C. S. Gibson, D.D.
A GUIDE TO ETERNITY. Edited by J. W. Stanbridge, B.D.
THE PSALMS OF DAVID. Edited by B. W. Randolph, D.D.
LYRA APOSTOLICA. Edited by Canon Scott Holland and Canon H. C. Beeching, M.A.
THE INNER WAY. Edited by A. W. Hutton, M.A.
THE THOUGHTS OF PASCAL. Edited by C. S. Jerram, M.A.

ON THE LOVE OF GOD. By St. Francis de Sales. Edited by W. J. Knox-Little, M.A.
A MANUAL OF CONSOLATION FROM THE SAINTS AND FATHERS. Edited by J. H. Burn, B.D
THE SONG OF SONGS. Edited by B. Blaxland, M.A.
THE DEVOTIONS OF ST. ANSELM. Edited by C. J. Webb, M.A.
GRACE ABOUNDING. By John Bunyan. Edited by S. C. Freer, M.A.
BISHOP WILSON'S SACRA PRIVATA. Edited by A. E. Burn, B.D.
LYRA SACRA: A Book of Sacred Verse. Edited by H. C. Beeching, M.A., Canon of Westminster.
A DAY BOOK FROM THE SAINTS AND FATHERS. Edited by J. H. BURN, B.D.
HEAVENLY WISDOM. A Selection from the English Mystics. Edited by E. C. Gregory.
LIGHT, LIFE, AND LOVE. A Selection from the German Mystics. Edited by W. R. Inge, M.A.

### Illustrated Pocket Library of Plain and Coloured Books, The
*Fcap. 8vo.* 3s. 6d. *net to* 4s. 6d. *net each volume.*

A series, in small form, of some of the famous illustrated books of fiction and general literature. These are faithfully reprinted from the first or best editions without introduction or notes.

#### COLOURED BOOKS

THE LIFE AND DEATH OF JOHN MYTTON, ESQ. By Nimrod. With 18 Coloured Plates by Henry Alken and T. J. Rawlins. *Third Edition.* 3s. 6d. *net.*
Also a limited edition on large Japanese paper. 30s. *net.*

THE LIFE OF A SPORTSMAN. By Nimrod. With 35 Coloured Plates by Henry Alken. 4s. 6d. *net.*
Also a limited edition on large Japanese paper. 30s. *net.*

HANDLEY CROSS. By R. S. Surtees. With 17 Coloured Plates and 100 Woodcuts in the Text by John Leech. 4s. 6d. *net.*
Also a limited edition on large Japanese paper. 30s. *net.*

MR. SPONGE'S SPORTING TOUR. By R. S. Surtees. With 13 Coloured Plates and 90 Woodcuts in the Text by John Leech. 3s. 6d. *net.*
Also a limited edition on large Japanese paper. 30s. *net.*

*[Continued.*

## GENERAL LITERATURE 27

THE ILLUSTRATED POCKET LIBRARY—*continued.*

JORROCKS' JAUNTS AND JOLLITIES. By R. S. Surtees. With 15 Coloured Plates by H. Alken. 3s. 6d. net.
Also a limited edition on large Japanese paper. 30s. net.
This volume is reprinted from the extremely rare and costly edition of 1843, which contains Alken's very fine illustrations instead of the usual ones by Phiz.

ASK MAMMA. By R. S. Surtees. With 13 Coloured Plates and 70 Woodcuts in the Text by John Leech. 3s. 6d. net.
Also a limited edition on large Japanese paper. 30s. net.

THE ANALYSIS OF THE HUNTING FIELD. By R. S. Surtees. With 7 Coloured Plates by Henry Alken, and 43 Illustrations on Wood. 3s. 6d. net.

THE TOUR OF DR. SYNTAX IN SEARCH OF THE PICTURESQUE. By William Combe. With 30 Coloured Plates by T. Rowlandson. 3s. 6d. net.
Also a limited edition on large Japanese paper.

THE TOUR OF DOCTOR SYNTAX IN SEARCH OF CONSOLATION. By William Combe. With 24 Coloured Plates by T. Rowlandson. 3s. 6d. net.
Also a limited edition on large Japanese paper. 30s. net.

THE THIRD TOUR OF DOCTOR SYNTAX IN SEARCH OF A WIFE. By William Combe. With 24 Coloured Plates by T. Rowlandson. 3s. 6d. net.
Also a limited edition on large Japanese paper. 30s. net.

THE HISTORY OF JOHNNY QUAE GENUS: the Little Foundling of the late Dr. Syntax. By the Author of 'The Three Tours.' With 24 Coloured Plates by Rowlandson. 3s. 6d. net. 100 copies on large Japanese paper. 21s. net.
Also a limited edition on large Japanese paper. 30s. net.

THE ENGLISH DANCE OF DEATH, from the Designs of T. Rowlandson, with Metrical Illustrations by the Author of 'Doctor Syntax.' Two Volumes. 9s. net.
This book contains 76 Coloured Plates.
Also a limited edition on large Japanese paper. 30s. net.

THE DANCE OF LIFE: A Poem. By the Author of 'Doctor Syntax.' Illustrated with 26 Coloured Engravings by T. Rowlandson. 3s. 6d. net.
Also a limited edition on large Japanese paper. 30s. net.

LIFE IN LONDON; or, the Day and Night Scenes of Jerry Hawthorn, Esq., and his Elegant Friend, Corinthian Tom. By Pierce Egan. With 36 Coloured Plates by I. R. and G. Cruikshank. With numerous Designs on Wood. 4s. 6d. net.
Also a limited edition on large Japanese paper. 30s. net.

REAL LIFE IN LONDON; or, the Rambles and Adventures of Bob Tallyho, Esq., and his Cousin, The Hon. Tom Dashall. By an Amateur (Pierce Egan). With 31 Coloured Plates by Alken and Rowlandson, etc. Two Volumes. 9s. net.

THE LIFE OF AN ACTOR. By Pierce Egan. With 27 Coloured Plates by Theodore Lane, and several Designs on Wood. 4s. 6d. net.

THE VICAR OF WAKEFIELD. By Oliver Goldsmith. With 24 Coloured Plates by T. Rowlandson. 3s. 6d. net.
Also a limited edition on large Japanese paper. 30s. net.
A reproduction of a very rare book.

THE MILITARY ADVENTURES OF JOHNNY NEWCOME. By an Officer. With 15 Coloured Plates by T. Rowlandson. 3s. 6d. net.

THE NATIONAL SPORTS OF GREAT BRITAIN. With Descriptions and 51 Coloured Plates by Henry Alken. 4s. 6d. net.
Also a limited edition on large Japanese paper. 30s. net.
This book is completely different from the large folio edition of 'National Sports' by the same artist, and none of the plates are similar.

THE ADVENTURES OF A POST CAPTAIN. By A Naval Officer. With 24 Coloured Plates by Mr. Williams. 3s. 6d. net.

GAMONIA: or, the Art of Preserving Game; and an Improved Method of making Plantations and Covers, explained and Illustrated by Lawrence Rawstorne, Esq. With 15 Coloured Plates by T. Rawlins. 3s. 6d. net.

AN ACADEMY FOR GROWN HORSEMEN: Containing the completest Instructions for Walking, Trotting, Cantering, Galloping, Stumbling, and Tumbling. Illustrated with 27 Coloured Plates, and adorned with a Portrait of the Author. By Geoffrey Gambado, Esq. 3s. 6d. net.

REAL LIFE IN IRELAND, or the Day and Night Scenes of Brian Boru, Esq., and his Elegant Friend, Sir Shawn O'Dogherty. By a Real Paddy. With 19 Coloured Plates by Heath, Marks, etc. 3s. 6d. net.

THE ADVENTURES OF JOHNNY NEWCOME IN THE NAVY. By Alfred Burton. With 16 Coloured Plates by T. Rowlandson. 3s. 6d. net.

## PLAIN BOOKS

THE GRAVE: A Poem. By Robert Blair. Illustrated by 12 Etchings executed by Louis Schiavonetti from the Original Inventions of William Blake. With an Engraved Title Page and a Portrait of Blake by T. Phillips, R.A. 3s. 6d. net.
The Illustrations are reproduced in photogravure.
Also a limited edition on large Japanese paper, with India proofs and a duplicate set of the plates. 15s. net.

ILLUSTRATIONS OF THE BOOK OF JOB. Invented and engraved by William Blake. 3s. 6d. net.
These famous Illustrations—21 in number—are reproduced in photogravure. Also a limited edition on large Japanese paper, with India proofs and a duplicate set of the plates. 15s. net.

ÆSOP'S FABLES. With 380 Woodcuts by Thomas Bewick. 3s. 6d. net.

WINDSOR CASTLE. By W. Harrison Ainsworth. With 22 Plates and 87 Woodcuts in the Text by George Cruikshank. 3s. 6d. net.

THE TOWER OF LONDON. By W. Harrison Ainsworth. With 40 Plates and 58 Woodcuts in the Text by George Cruikshank. 3s. 6d. net.

FRANK FAIRLEGH. By F. E. Smedley. With 30 Plates by George Cruikshank. 3s. 6d. net.

HANDY ANDY. By Samuel Lover. With 24 Illustrations by the Author. 3s. 6d. net.

THE COMPLEAT ANGLER. By Izaak Walton and Charles Cotton. With 14 Plates and 77 Woodcuts in the Text. 3s. 6d. net.
This edition is reproduced from the beautiful edition of John Major of 1824.

THE PICKWICK PAPERS. By Charles Dickens. With the 43 Illustrations by Seymour and Phiz, the two Buss Plates, and the 32 Contemporary Onwhyn Plates. 3s. 6d. net.

## Junior Examination Series

Edited by A. M. M. STEDMAN, M.A. *Fcap. 8vo.* 1s.

JUNIOR FRENCH EXAMINATION PAPERS. By F. Jacob, B.A.
JUNIOR LATIN EXAMINATION PAPERS. *Second Edition.* By C. G. Botting, M.A.
JUNIOR ENGLISH EXAMINATION PAPERS. By W. Williamson, B.A.
JUNIOR ARITHMETIC EXAMINATION PAPERS. By W. S. Beard. *Second Edition.*
JUNIOR ALGEBRA EXAMINATION PAPERS. By S. W. Finn, M.A.
JUNIOR GREEK EXAMINATION PAPERS. By T. C. Weatherhead, M.A.
JUNIOR GENERAL INFORMATION EXAMINATION PAPERS. By W. S. Beard.
JUNIOR GEOGRAPHY EXAMINATION PAPERS. By W. G. Baker, M.A.
JUNIOR GERMAN EXAMINATION PAPERS. By A. Voegelin, M.A.

## Junior School-Books, Methuen's

Edited by O. D. INSKIP, LL.D., and W. WILLIAMSON, B.A.

A CLASS-BOOK OF DICTATION PASSAGES. By W. Williamson, B.A. *Eighth Edition. Crown 8vo.* 1s. 6d.
THE GOSPEL ACCORDING TO ST. MATTHEW. Edited by E. Wilton South, M.A. *Crown 8vo.* 1s. 6d.
THE GOSPEL ACCORDING TO ST. MARK. Edited by A. E. Rubie, M.A., Headmaster of College, Eltham. With Three Maps. *Crown 8vo.* 1s. 6d.
A JUNIOR ENGLISH GRAMMAR. By W. Williamson, B.A. With numerous passages for parsing and analysis, and a chapter on Essay Writing. *Crown 8vo.* 2s.
A JUNIOR CHEMISTRY. By E. A. Tyler, B.A., F.C.S., Science Master at Swansea Grammar School. With 73 Illustrations. *Crown 8vo.* 2s. 6d.
THE ACTS OF THE APOSTLES. Edited by A. E. Rubie, M.A., Headmaster of College, Eltham. *Crown 8vo.* 2s.
THE FIRST BOOK OF KINGS. Edited by A. E. Rubie, M.A. *Crown 8vo.* 1s. 6d.
A JUNIOR FRENCH GRAMMAR. By L. A. Sornet and M. J. Acatos. Modern Language Masters at King Edward's School, Birmingham. *Cr. 8vo.* 2s.
ELEMENTARY EXPERIMENTAL SCIENCE. PHYSICS by W. T. Clough, A.R.C.S. CHEMISTRY by A. E. Dunstan, B.Sc. With 2 Plates and 154 Diagrams. *Crown 8vo.* 2s.
A JUNIOR GEOMETRY. By Noel S. Lydon. With 239 Diagrams. *Crown 8vo.* 2s.

## Leaders of Religion

Edited by H. C. BEECHING, M.A., Canon of Westminster. *With Portraits. Crown 8vo.* 3s. 6d.

A series of short biographies of the most prominent leaders of religious life and thought of all ages and countries.

CARDINAL NEWMAN. By R. H. Hutton.
JOHN WESLEY. By J. H. Overton, M.A.
BISHOP WILBERFORCE. By G. W. Daniell, M.A.
CARDINAL MANNING. By A. W. Hutton, M.A.
CHARLES SIMEON. By H. C. G. Moule, D.D.
JOHN KEBLE. By Walter Lock, D.D.
THOMAS CHALMERS. By Mrs. Oliphant.
LANCELOT ANDREWES. By R. L. Ottley, M.A.
AUGUSTINE OF CANTERBURY. By E. L. Cutts, D.D.
WILLIAM LAUD. By W. H. Hutton, M.A.
JOHN KNOX. By F. MacCunn.
JOHN HOWE. By R. F. Horton, D.D.
BISHOP KEN. By F. A. Clarke, M.A.
GEORGE FOX, THE QUAKER. By T. Hodgkin, D.C.L.
JOHN DONNE. By Augustus Jessopp, D.D.
THOMAS CRANMER. By A. J. Mason, D.D.
BISHOP LATIMER. By R. M. Carlyle and A. J. Carlyle, M.A.
BISHOP BUTLER. By W. A. Spooner, M.A.

## Little Biographies

*Fcap. 8vo. Each volume, cloth,* 3s. 6d. ; *leather,* 4s. *net.*

DANTE ALIGHIERI. By Paget Toynbee, M.A., D.Litt. With 12 Illustrations. *Second Edition.*
SAVONAROLA. By E. L. S. Horsburgh, M.A. With 12 Illustrations. *Second Edition.*
JOHN HOWARD. By E. C. S. Gibson, D.D., Vicar of Leeds. With 12 Illustrations.
TENNYSON. By A. C. Benson, M.A. With 9 Illustrations.
WALTER RALEIGH. By J. A. Taylor. With 12 Illustrations.
ERASMUS. By E. F. H. Capey. With 12 Illustrations.
THE YOUNG PRETENDER. By C. S. Terry. With 12 Illustrations.
ROBERT BURNS. By T. F. Henderson. With 12 Illustrations.
CHATHAM. By A. S. M'Dowall. With 12 Illustrations.
ST. FRANCIS OF ASSISI. By Anna M. Stoddart. With 16 Illustrations.
CANNING. By W. A. Phillips. With 12 Illustrations.
BEACONSFIELD. By Walter Sichel. With 12 Illustrations.
GOETHE. By H. G. Atkins. With 12 Illustrations.

## Little Blue Books, The

General Editor, E. V. LUCAS.

*Illustrated. Demy 16mo.* 2s. 6d.

1. THE CASTAWAYS OF MEADOWBANK. By T. Cobb.
2. THE BEECHNUT BOOK. By Jacob Abbott. Edited by E. V. Lucas.
3. THE AIR GUN. By T. Hilbert.
4. A SCHOOL YEAR. By Netta Syrett.
5. THE PEELES AT THE CAPITAL. By Roger Ashton.

*[Continued.*

# GENERAL LITERATURE 29

THE LITTLE BLUE BOOKS—*continued.*
6. THE TREASURE OF PRINCEGATE PRIORY. By T. Cobb.
7. MRS. BARBERRY'S GENERAL SHOP. By Roger Ashton.
8. A BOOK OF BAD CHILDREN. By W. T. Webb.
9. THE LOST BALL. By Thomas Cobb.

## Little Books on Art
*Demy 16mo. 2s. 6d. net.*

GREEK ART. H. B. Walters.
BOOKPLATES. E. Almack.
REYNOLDS. J. Sime.
ROMNEY. George Paston.
WATTS. Miss R. E. D. Sketchley.
LEIGHTON. Alice Corkran.
VELASQUEZ. Wilfrid Wilberforce and A. R. Gilbert.
GREUZE AND BOUCHER. Eliza F. Pollard.
VANDYCK. M. G. Smallwood.
TURNER. F. Tyrell-Gill.
DÜRER. Jessie Allen.
HOPPNER. H. P. K. Skipton.
HOLBEIN. Mrs. G. Fortescue.
MILLET. Miss N. Peacock.
BURNE-JONES. Miss F. de Lisle.
REMBRANDT. Mrs. E. A. Sharp.
COROT. Alice Pollard and Ethel Birnstingl.

## Little Galleries, The
*Demy 16mo. 2s. 6d. net.*

A LITTLE GALLERY OF REYNOLDS.
A LITTLE GALLERY OF ROMNEY.
A LITTLE GALLERY OF HOPPNER.
A LITTLE GALLERY OF MILLAIS.
A LITTLE GALLERY OF ENGLISH POETS.

## Little Guides, The
*Small Pott 8vo, cloth, 3s.; leather, 3s. 6d. net.*

OXFORD AND ITS COLLEGES. By J. Wells, M.A. Illustrated by E. H. New. *Fourth Edition.*
CAMBRIDGE AND ITS COLLEGES. By A. Hamilton Thompson. Illustrated by E. H. New.
THE MALVERN COUNTRY. By B. C. A. Windle, D.Sc., F.R.S. Illustrated by E. H. New.
SHAKESPEARE'S COUNTRY. By B. C. A. Windle, D.Sc., F.R.S. Illustrated by E. H. New. *Second Edition.*
SUSSEX. By F. G. Brabant, M.A. Illustrated by E. H. New.
WESTMINSTER ABBEY. By G. E. Troutbeck. Illustrated by F. D. Bedford.
NORFOLK. By W. A. Dutt. Illustrated by B. C. Boulter.
CORNWALL. By A. L. Salmon. Illustrated by B. C. Boulter.
BRITTANY. By S. Baring-Gould. Illustrated by J. Wylie.
HERTFORDSHIRE. By H. W. Tompkins, F.R.H.S. Illustrated by E. H. New.
THE ENGLISH LAKES. By F. G. Brabant, M.A. Illustrated by E. H. New. 4s.; leather, 4s. 6d. net.
KENT. By G. Clinch. Illustrated by F. D. Bedford.
ROME. By C. G. Ellaby. Illustrated by B. C. Boulter.
THE ISLE OF WIGHT. By G. Clinch. Illustrated by F. D. Bedford.
SURREY. By F. A. H. Lambert. Illustrated by E. H. New.
BUCKINGHAMSHIRE. By E. S. Roscoe. Illustrated by F. D. Bedford.
SUFFOLK. By W. A. Dutt. Illustrated by J. Wylie.
DERBYSHIRE. By J. Charles Cox, LL.D., F.S.A. Illustrated by J. C. Wall.
THE NORTH RIDING OF YORKSHIRE. By J. E. Morris. Illustrated by R. J. S. Bertram.
HAMPSHIRE. By J. C. Cox. Illustrated by M. E. Purser.
SICILY. By F. H. Jackson. With many Illustrations by the Author.

## Little Library, The
With Introductions, Notes, and Photogravure Frontispieces.

*Small Pott 8vo. Each Volume, cloth, 1s. 6d. net; leather, 2s. 6d. net.*

VANITY FAIR. By W. M. Thackeray. Edited by S. Gwynn. *Three Volumes.*
PENDENNIS. By W. M. Thackeray. Edited by S. Gwynn. *Three Volumes.*
ESMOND. By W. M. Thackeray. Edited by S. Gwynn.
CHRISTMAS BOOKS. By W. M. Thackeray. Edited by S. Gwynn.
SELECTIONS FROM GEORGE CRABBE. Edited by A. C. Deane.
JOHN HALIFAX, GENTLEMAN. By Mrs. Craik. Edited by Annie Matheson. *Two Volumes.*
PRIDE AND PREJUDICE. By Jane Austen. Edited by E. V. Lucas. *Two Volumes.*
NORTHANGER ABBEY. By Jane Austen. Edited by E. V. Lucas.
THE PRINCESS. By Alfred, Lord Tennyson. Edited by Elizabeth Wordsworth.
MAUD. By Alfred, Lord Tennyson. Edited by Elizabeth Wordsworth.
IN MEMORIAM. By Alfred, Lord Tennyson. Edited by H. C. Beeching, M.A.
THE EARLY POEMS OF ALFRED, LORD TENNYSON. Edited by J. C. Collins, M.A.
A LITTLE BOOK OF ENGLISH LYRICS. With Notes.
THE INFERNO OF DANTE. Translated by H. F. Cary. Edited by Paget Toynbee, M.A., D.Litt.
THE PURGATORIO OF DANTE. Translated by H. F. Cary. Edited by Paget Toynbee, M.A., D.Litt.
THE PARADISO OF DANTE. Translated by H. F. Cary. Edited by Paget Toynbee, M.A., D.Litt.

*[Continued.*

THE LITTLE LIBRARY—*continued*.

A LITTLE BOOK OF SCOTTISH VERSE. Edited by T. F. Henderson.
A LITTLE BOOK OF LIGHT VERSE. Edited by A. C. Deane.
A LITTLE BOOK OF ENGLISH SONNETS. Edited by J. B. B. Nichols.
POEMS. By John Keats. With an Introduction by L. Binyon, and Notes by J. Masefield. A complete Edition.
THE MINOR POEMS OF JOHN MILTON. Edited by H. C. Beeching, M.A.
THE POEMS OF HENRY VAUGHAN. Edited by Edward Hutton.
SELECTIONS FROM WORDSWORTH. Edited by Nowell C. Smith.
SELECTIONS FROM THE EARLY POEMS OF ROBERT BROWNING. Edited by W. Hall Griffin, M.A.
THE ENGLISH POEMS OF RICHARD CRASHAW. Edited by Edward Hutton.
SELECTIONS FROM WILLIAM BLAKE. Edited by M. Perugini.
SELECTIONS FROM THE POEMS OF GEORGE DARLEY. Edited by R. A. Streatfeild.
LYRICAL BALLADS. By W. Wordsworth and S. T. Coleridge. Edited by George Sampson.
SELECTIONS FROM LONGFELLOW. Edited by Lilian M. Faithfull.
SELECTIONS FROM THE ANTI-JACOBIN; with George Canning's additional Poems. Edited by Lloyd Sanders.
THE POEMS OF ANDREW MARVELL. Edited by Edward Wright.
A LITTLE BOOK OF LIFE AND DEATH. Edited by Mrs. Alfred Waterhouse. *Fourth Edition.*
A LITTLE BOOK OF ENGLISH PROSE. Edited by Mrs. P. A. Barnett.
EOTHEN. By A. W. Kinglake. With an Introduction and Notes.

CRANFORD. By Mrs. Gaskell. Edited by E. V. Lucas.
LAVENGRO. By George Borrow. Edited by F. Hindes Groome. *Two Volumes.*
THE ROMANY RYE. By George Borrow. Edited John Sampson.
THE HISTORY OF THE CALIPH VATHEK. By William Beckford. Edited by E. Denison Ross.
THE COMPLEAT ANGLER. By Izaak Walton. Edited by J. Buchan.
MARRIAGE. By Susan Ferrier. Edited by Miss Goodrich-Freer and Lord Iddesleigh. *Two Volumes.*
THE INHERITANCE. By Susan Ferrier. Edited by Miss Goodrich-Freer and Lord Iddesleigh. *Two Volumes.*
ELIA, AND THE LAST ESSAYS OF ELIA. By Charles Lamb. Edited by E. V. Lucas.
THE ESSAYS OF ABRAHAM COWLEY. Edited by H. C. Minchin.
THE ESSAYS OF FRANCIS BACON. Edited by Edward Wright.
THE MAXIMS OF LA ROCHEFOUCAULD. Translated by Dean Stanhope. Edited by G. H. Powell.
A SENTIMENTAL JOURNEY. By Laurence Sterne. Edited by H. W. Paul.
MANSIE WAUCH. By D. M. Moir. Edited by T. F. Henderson.
THE INGOLDSBY LEGENDS. By R. H. Barham. Edited by J. B. Atlay. *Two Volumes.*
THE SCARLET LETTER. By Nathaniel Hawthorne. Edited by P. Dearmer.
REJECTED ADDRESSES. By Horace and James Smith. Edited by A. D. Godley, M.A.
LONDON LYRICS. By F. Locker. Edited by A. D. Godley, M.A. A reprint of the First Edition.

## Miniature Library, Methuen's

EUPHRANOR: a Dialogue on Youth. By Edward FitzGerald. From the edition published by W. Pickering in 1851. *Demy 32mo. Leather, 2s. net.*
POLONIUS: or Wise Saws and Modern Instances. By Edward FitzGerald. From the edition published by W. Pickering in 1852. *Demy 32mo. Leather, 2s. net.*
THE RUBAIYAT OF OMAR KHAYYAM. By Edward FitzGerald. From the 1st edition of 1859. *Second Edition. Leather, 1s. net.*

THE LIFE OF EDWARD, LORD HERBERT OF CHERBURY. Written by himself. From the edition printed at Strawberry Hill in the year 1764. *Medium 32mo. Leather, 2s. net.*
THE VISIONS OF DON FRANCISCO DE QUEVEDO VILLEGAS, Knight of the Order of St. James. Made English by R. L. From the edition printed for H. Herringman, 1668. *Leather, 2s. net.*
POEMS. By Dora Greenwell. From the edition of 1848. *Leather, 2s. net.*

## School Examination Series

Edited by A. M. M. STEDMAN, M.A. *Crown 8vo. 2s. 6d.*

FRENCH EXAMINATION PAPERS. By A. M. M. Stedman, M.A. *Twelfth Edition.*
A KEY, issued to Tutors and Private Students only, to be had on application to the Publishers. *Fifth Edition. Crown 8vo. 6s. net.*
LATIN EXAMINATION PAPERS. By A. M. M. Stedman, M.A. *Twelfth Edition.*
KEY (*Fourth Edition*) issued as above. *6s. net.*
GREEK EXAMINATION PAPERS. By A. M. M. Stedman, M.A. *Seventh Edition.*
KEY (*Second Edition*) issued as above. *6s. net.*
GERMAN EXAMINATION PAPERS. By R. J. Morich. *Fifth Edition.*
KEY (*Second Edition*) issued as above. *6s. net.*

HISTORY AND GEOGRAPHY EXAMINATION PAPERS. By C. H. Spence, M.A., Clifton College. *Second Edition.*
PHYSICS EXAMINATION PAPERS. By R. E. Steel, M.A., F.C.S.
GENERAL KNOWLEDGE EXAMINATION PAPERS. By A. M. M. Stedman, M.A. *Fourth Edition.*
KEY (*Third Edition*) issued as above. *7s. net.*
EXAMINATION PAPERS IN ENGLISH HISTORY. By J. Tait Plowden-Wardlaw, B.A.

GENERAL LITERATURE 31

## Social Questions of To-day
Edited by H. DE B. GIBBINS, Litt.D., M.A.
*Crown 8vo.* 2s. 6d.

TRADE UNIONISM—NEW AND OLD. By G. Howell. *Third Edition.*
THE CO-OPERATIVE MOVEMENT TO-DAY. By G. J. Holyoake. *Second Edition.*
PROBLEMS OF POVERTY. By J. A. Hobson, M.A. *Fourth Edition.*
THE COMMERCE OF NATIONS. By C. F. Bastable, M.A. *Third Edition.*
THE ALIEN INVASION. By W. H. Wilkins, B.A.
THE RURAL EXODUS. By P. Anderson Graham.
LAND NATIONALIZATION. By Harold Cox, B.A.
A SHORTER WORKING DAY. By H. de B. Gibbins and R. A. Hadfield.
BACK TO THE LAND: An Inquiry into Rural Depopulation. By H. E. Moore.
TRUSTS, POOLS, AND CORNERS. By J. Stephen Jeans.
THE FACTORY SYSTEM. By R. W. Cooke-Taylor.
THE STATE AND ITS CHILDREN. By Gertrude Tuckwell.
WOMEN'S WORK. By Lady Dilke, Miss Bulley, and Miss Whitley.
SOCIALISM AND MODERN THOUGHT. By M. Kauffmann.
THE HOUSING OF THE WORKING CLASSES. By E. Bowmaker.
THE PROBLEM OF THE UNEMPLOYED. By J. A. Hobson, M.A.
LIFE IN WEST LONDON. By Arthur Sherwell, M.A. *Third Edition.*
RAILWAY NATIONALIZATION. By Clement Edwards.
WORKHOUSES AND PAUPERISM. By Louisa Twining.
UNIVERSITY AND SOCIAL SETTLEMENTS. By W. Reason, M.A.

## Technology, Textbooks of
Edited by PROFESSOR J. WERTHEIMER, F.I.C.
*Fully Illustrated.*

HOW TO MAKE A DRESS. By J. A. E. Wood. *Third Edition. Crown 8vo.* 1s. 6d.
CARPENTRY AND JOINERY. By F. C. Webber. *Third Edition. Crown 8vo.* 3s. 6d.
PRACTICAL MECHANICS. By Sidney H. Wells. *Second Edition. Crown 8vo.* 3s. 6d.
PRACTICAL PHYSICS. By H. Stroud, D.Sc., M.A. *Crown 8vo.* 3s. 6d.
MILLINERY, THEORETICAL AND PRACTICAL. By Clare Hill. *Crown 8vo.* 2s.
PRACTICAL CHEMISTRY. By W. French, M.A. *Crown 8vo.* Part I. *Second Edition.* 1s. 6d. Part II.
TECHNICAL ARITHMETIC AND GEOMETRY. By C. T. Millis, M.I.M.E. With Diagrams. *Crown 8vo.* 3s. 6d.
BUILDER'S QUANTITIES. By H. C. Grubb. With many Illustrations. *Crown 8vo.* 4s. 6d.

## Theology, Handbooks of

THE XXXIX. ARTICLES OF THE CHURCH OF ENGLAND. Edited by E. C. S. Gibson, D.D. *Third and Cheaper Edition in One Volume. Demy 8vo.* 12s. 6d.
AN INTRODUCTION TO THE HISTORY OF RELIGION. By F. B. Jevons, M.A., Litt.D. *Second Edition. Demy 8vo.* 10s. 6d.
THE DOCTRINE OF THE INCARNATION. By R. L. Ottley, M.A. *Second and Cheaper Edition. Demy 8vo.* 12s. 6d.
AN INTRODUCTION TO THE HISTORY OF THE CREEDS. By A. E. Burn, B.D. *Demy 8vo.* 10s. 6d.
THE PHILOSOPHY OF RELIGION IN ENGLAND AND AMERICA. By Alfred Caldecott, D.D. *Demy 8vo.* 10s. 6d.
A HISTORY OF EARLY CHRISTIAN DOCTRINE. By J. F. Bethune-Baker, M.A., Fellow of Pembroke College, Cambridge. *Demy 8vo.* 10s. 6d.

## University Extension Series
Edited by J. E. SYMES, M.A.,
Principal of University College, Nottingham.
*Crown 8vo. Price (with some exceptions)* 2s. 6d.

A series of books on historical, literary, and scientific subjects, suitable for extension students and home-reading circles. Each volume is complete in itself, and the subjects are treated by competent writers in a broad and philosophic spirit.

THE INDUSTRIAL HISTORY OF ENGLAND. By H. de B. Gibbins, Litt.D., M.A. *Tenth Edition.* Revised. With Maps and Plans. 3s.
A HISTORY OF ENGLISH POLITICAL ECONOMY. By L. L. Price, M.A. *Third Edition.*
VICTORIAN POETS. By A. Sharp.
THE FRENCH REVOLUTION. By J. E. Symes, M.A.
PSYCHOLOGY. By F. S. Granger, M.A. *Second Edition.*
THE EVOLUTION OF PLANT LIFE: Lower Forms. By G. Massee. Illustrated.
AIR AND WATER. By V. B. Lewes, M.A. Illustrated.
THE CHEMISTRY OF LIFE AND HEALTH. By C. W. Kimmins, M.A. Illustrated.
THE MECHANICS OF DAILY LIFE. By V. P. Sells, M.A. Illustrated.
ENGLISH SOCIAL REFORMERS. By H. de B. Gibbins, Litt.D., M.A. *Second Edition.*
ENGLISH TRADE AND FINANCE IN THE SEVENTEENTH CENTURY. By W. A. S. Hewins, B.A.
THE CHEMISTRY OF FIRE. By M. M. Pattison Muir, M.A. Illustrated.
A TEXT-BOOK OF AGRICULTURAL BOTANY. By M. C. Potter, M.A., F.L.S. Illustrated. *Second Edition.* 4s. 6d.
THE VAULT OF HEAVEN. A Popular Introduction to Astronomy. By R. A. Gregory. With numerous Illustrations.
METEOROLOGY. By H. N. Dickson, F.R.S.E., F.R. Met. Soc. Illustrated.
A MANUAL OF ELECTRICAL SCIENCE. By George J. Burch, M.A., F.R.S. Illustrated. 3s.
THE EARTH. An Introduction to Physiography. By Evan Small, M.A. Illustrated.
INSECT LIFE. By F. W. Theobald, M.A. Illustrated.
ENGLISH POETRY FROM BLAKE TO BROWNING. By W. M. Dixon, M.A. *Second Edition.*
ENGLISH LOCAL GOVERNMENT. By E. Jenks, M.A.
THE GREEK VIEW OF LIFE. By G. L. Dickinson. *Third Edition.*

## Westminster Commentaries The

General Editor, WALTER LOCK, D.D., Warden of Keble College, Dean Ireland's Professor of Exegesis in the University of Oxford.

THE BOOK OF GENESIS. Edited with Introduction and Notes by S. R. Driver, D.D., Canon of Christ Church, and Regius Professor of Hebrew at Oxford. *Second Edition. Demy 8vo.* 10s. 6d.

THE BOOK OF JOB. Edited by E. C. S. Gibson, D.D. *Demy 8vo.* 6s.

THE ACTS OF THE APOSTLES. Edited by R. B. Rackham, M.A. *Demy 8vo. Second and Cheaper Edition.* 10s. 6d.

THE FIRST EPISTLE OF PAUL THE APOSTLE TO THE CORINTHIANS. Edited by H. L. Goudge, M.A. *Demy 8vo.* 6s.

THE EPISTLE OF ST. JAMES. Edited by R. J. Knowling, M.A. *Demy 8vo.* 6s.

# PART II.—FICTION

## Marie Corelli's Novels.
*Crown 8vo   6s. each.*

A ROMANCE OF TWO WORLDS. *Twenty-Fourth Edition.*

VENDETTA. *Twentieth Edition.*

THELMA. *Thirtieth Edition.*

ARDATH: THE STORY OF A DEAD SELF. *Fifteenth Edition.*

THE SOUL OF LILITH. *Twelfth Edit.*

WORMWOOD. *Thirteenth Edition.*

BARABBAS: A DREAM OF THE WORLD'S TRAGEDY. *Thirty-Ninth Edition.*
'The tender reverence of the treatment and the imaginative beauty of the writing have reconciled us to the daring of the conception. This "Dream of the World's Tragedy" is a lofty and not inadequate paraphrase of the supreme climax of the inspired narrative.'—*Dublin Review.*

THE SORROWS OF SATAN. *Forty-Eighth Edition.*
'A very powerful piece of work.... The conception is magnificent, and is likely to win an abiding place within the memory of man.... The author has immense command of language, and a limitless audacity. ... This interesting and remarkable romance will live long after much of the ephemeral literature of the day is forgotten.... A literary phenomenon ... novel, and even sublime.'—W. T. STEAD in the *Review of Reviews.*

THE MASTER CHRISTIAN.
[165th Thousand.
'It cannot be denied that "The Master Christian" is a powerful book ; that it is one likely to raise uncomfortable questions in all but the most self-satisfied readers, and that it strikes at the root of the failure of the Churches—the decay of faith—in a manner which shows the inevitable disaster heaping up.... The good Cardinal Bonpré is a beautiful figure, fit to stand beside the good Bishop in "Les Misérables." It is a book with a serious purpose expressed with absolute unconventionality and passion ... And this is to say it is a book worth reading.'—*Examiner.*

TEMPORAL POWER: A STUDY IN SUPREMACY.   [150th Thousand.
'It is impossible to read such a work as "Temporal Power" without becoming convinced that the story is intended to convey certain criticisms on the ways of the world and certain suggestions for the betterment of humanity.... If the chief intention of the book was to hold the mirror up to shams, injustice, dishonesty, cruelty, and neglect of conscience, nothing but praise can be given to that intention.'—*Morning Post.*

GOD'S GOOD MAN: A SIMPLE LOVE STORY.

## Anthony Hope's Novels.
*Crown 8vo   6s. each.*

THE GOD IN THE CAR. *Ninth Edition.*
'A very remarkable book, deserving of critical analysis impossible within our limit; brilliant, but not superficial; well considered, but not elaborated; constructed with the proverbial art that conceals, but yet allows itself to be enjoyed by readers to whom fine literary method is a keen pleasure.'—*The World.*

A CHANGE OF AIR. *Sixth Edition.*
'A graceful, vivacious comedy, true to human nature. The characters are traced with a masterly hand.'—*Times.*

A MAN OF MARK. *Fifth Edition.*
'Of all Mr. Hope's books, "A Man of Mark" is the one which best compares with "The Prisoner of Zenda."'—*National Observer.*

THE CHRONICLES OF COUNT ANTONIO. *Fifth Edition.*
'It is a perfectly enchanting story of love and chivalry, and pure romance. The Count is the most constant, desperate, and

# FICTION

modest and tender of lovers, a peerless gentleman, an intrepid fighter, a faithful friend, and a magnanimous foe.'—*Guardian.*

PHROSO. Illustrated by H. R. MILLAR. Sixth Edition.
'The tale is thoroughly fresh, quick with vitality, stirring the blood.'—*St. James's Gazette.*

SIMON DALE. Illustrated. *Sixth Edition.*
'There is searching analysis of human nature, with a most ingeniously constructed plot. Mr. Hope has drawn the contrasts

of his women with marvellous subtlety and delicacy.'—*Times.*

THE KING'S MIRROR. *Fourth Edition.*
'In elegance, delicacy, and tact it ranks with the best of his novels, while in the wide range of its portraiture and the subtilty of its analysis it surpasses all his earlier ventures.'—*Spectator.*

QUISANTÉ. *Fourth Edition.*
'The book is notable for a very high literary quality, and an impress of power and mastery on every page.'—*Daily Chronicle.*

THE DOLLY DIALOGUES.

## W. W. Jacobs' Novels
### Crown 8vo     3s. 6d. each.

MANY CARGOES. *Twenty-Seventh Edition.*
SEA URCHINS. *Tenth Edition.*
A MASTER OF CRAFT. Illustrated. Sixth Edition.
'Can be unreservedly recommended to all who have not lost their appetite for wholesome laughter.'—*Spectator.*
'The best humorous book published for many a day.'—*Black and White.*

LIGHT FREIGHTS. Illustrated. *Fourth Edition.*

'His wit and humour are perfectly irresistible. Mr. Jacobs writes of skippers, and mates, and seamen, and his crew are the jolliest lot that ever sailed.'—*Daily News.*
'Laughter in every page.'—*Daily Mail.*

## Lucas Malet's Novels
### Crown 8vo.    6s. each.

COLONEL ENDERBY'S WIFE. *Third Edition.*
A COUNSEL OF PERFECTION. *New Edition.*
LITTLE PETER. *Second Edition.* 3s. 6d.
THE WAGES OF SIN. *Fourteenth Edition.*
THE CARISSIMA. *Fourth Edition.*
THE GATELESS BARRIER. *Fourth Edition.*
'In "The Gateless Barrier" it is at once evident that, whilst Lucas Malet has preserved her birthright of originality, the artistry, the actual writing, is above even the high level of the books that were born before.'—*Westminster Gazette.*

THE HISTORY OF SIR RICHARD CALMADY. *Seventh Edition.* A Limited Edition in Two Volumes. *Crown 8vo.* 12s.
'A picture finely and amply conceived. In the strength and insight in which the story has been conceived, in the wealth of fancy and reflection bestowed upon its execution, and in the moving sincerity of its pathos throughout, "Sir Richard Calmady" must rank as the great novel of a great writer.'—*Literature.*
'The ripest fruit of Lucas Malet's genius. A picture of maternal love by turns tender and terrible.'—*Spectator.*
'A remarkably fine book, with a noble motive and a sound conclusion.'—*Pilot.*

## Gilbert Parker's Novels
### Crown 8vo.    6s. each.

PIERRE AND HIS PEOPLE. *Fifth Edition.*
'Stories happily conceived and finely executed. There is strength and genius in Mr. Parker's style.'—*Daily Telegraph.*
MRS. FALCHION. *Fourth Edition.*
'A splendid study of character.'—*Athenæum.*
THE TRANSLATION OF A SAVAGE. *Second Edition.*
THE TRAIL OF THE SWORD. Illustrated. *Eighth Edition.*

'A rousing and dramatic tale. A book like this is a joy inexpressible.'—*Daily Chronicle.*
WHEN VALMOND CAME TO PONTIAC: The Story of a Lost Napoleon. *Fifth Edition.*
'Here we find romance—real, breathing, living romance. The character of Valmond is drawn unerringly.'—*Pall Mall Gazette.*
AN ADVENTURER OF THE NORTH: The Last Adventures of 'Pretty Pierre.' *Third Edition.*

# 34 MESSRS. METHUEN'S CATALOGUE

'The present book is full of fine and moving stories of the great North.'—*Glasgow Herald.*

THE SEATS OF THE MIGHTY. Illustrated. *Thirteenth Edition.*
'Mr. Parker has produced a really fine historical novel.'—*Athenæum.*
'A great book.'—*Black and White.*

THE BATTLE OF THE STRONG: a Romance of Two Kingdoms. Illustrated. *Fourth Edition.*
'Nothing more vigorous or more human has come from Mr. Gilbert Parker than this novel.'—*Literature.*

THE POMP OF THE LAVILETTES. *Second Edition.* 3s. 6d.
'Unforced pathos, and a deeper knowledge of human nature than he has displayed before.'—*Pall Mall Gazette.*

## Arthur Morrison's Novels

*Crown 8vo. 6s. each.*

TALES OF MEAN STREETS. *Sixth Edition.*
'A great book. The author's method is amazingly effective, and produces a thrilling sense of reality. The writer lays upon us a master hand. The book is simply appalling and irresistible in its interest. It is humorous also; without humour it would not make the mark it is certain to make.'—*World.*

A CHILD OF THE JAGO. *Fourth Edition.*
'The book is a masterpiece.'—*Pall Mall Gazette.*

TO LONDON TOWN. *Second Edition.*
'This is the new Mr. Arthur Morrison, gracious and tender, sympathetic and human.'—*Daily Telegraph.*

CUNNING MURRELL.
'Admirable. . . . Delightful humorous relief . . . a most artistic and satisfactory achievement.'—*Spectator.*

THE HOLE IN THE WALL. *Third Edition.*
'A masterpiece of artistic realism. It has a finality of touch that only a master may command.'—*Daily Chronicle.*
'An absolute masterpiece, which any novelist might be proud to claim.'—*Graphic.*
'"The Hole in the Wall" is a masterly piece of work. His characters are drawn with amazing skill. Extraordinary power.' —*Daily Telegraph.*

## Eden Phillpotts' Novels

*Crown 8vo. 6s. each.*

LYING PROPHETS.
CHILDREN OF THE MIST. *Fifth Edition.*
THE HUMAN BOY. With a Frontispiece. *Fourth Edition.*
'Mr. Phillpotts knows exactly what school-boys do, and can lay bare their inmost thoughts; likewise he shows an all-pervading sense of humour.'—*Academy.*

SONS OF THE MORNING. *Second Edition.*
'A book of strange power and fascination.'—*Morning Post.*

THE STRIKING HOURS. *Second Edition.*
'Tragedy and comedy, pathos and humour, are blended to a nicety in this volume.'—*World.*
'The whole book is redolent of a fresher and ampler air than breathes in the circumscribed life of great towns.'—*Spectator.*

THE RIVER. *Third Edition.*
'"The River" places Mr. Phillpotts in the front rank of living novelists.'—*Punch.*
'Since "Lorna Doone" we have had nothing so picturesque as this new romance.' *Birmingham Gazette.*
'Mr. Phillpotts's new book is a masterpiece which brings him indisputably into the front rank of English novelists.'—*Pall Mall Gazette.*
'This great romance of the River Dart. The finest book Mr. Eden Phillpotts has written.'—*Morning Post.*

THE AMERICAN PRISONER. *Third Edition.*

## S. Baring-Gould's Novels

*Crown 8vo. 6s. each.*

ARMINELL. *Fifth Edition.*
URITH. *Fifth Edition.*
IN THE ROAR OF THE SEA. *Seventh Edition.*
CHEAP JACK ZITA. *Fourth Edition.*
MARGERY OF QUETHER. *Third Edition.*

THE QUEEN OF LOVE. *Fifth Edition.*
JACQUETTA. *Third Edition.*
KITTY ALONE. *Fifth Edition.*
NOÉMI. Illustrated. *Fourth Edition.*
THE BROOM-SQUIRE. Illustrated. *Fourth Edition.*
DARTMOOR IDYLLS.

# FICTION

THE PENNYCOMEQUICKS. *Third Edition.*
GUAVAS THE TINNER. Illustrated. *Second Edition.*
BLADYS. Illustrated. *Second Edition.*
DOMITIA. Illustrated. *Second Edition.*
PABO THE PRIEST.

WINIFRED. Illustrated. *Second Edition.*
THE FROBISHERS.
ROYAL GEORGIE. Illustrated.
MISS QUILLET. Illustrated.
LITTLE TU'PENNY. *A New Edition. 6d.*
CHRIS OF ALL SORTS.
IN DEWISLAND.

## Robert Barr's Novels
*Crown 8vo. 6s. each.*

IN THE MIDST OF ALARMS. *Third Edition.*
'A book which has abundantly satisfied us by its capital humour.'—*Daily Chronicle.*
THE MUTABLE MANY. *Second Edition.*
'There is much insight in it, and much excellent humour.'—*Daily Chronicle.*

THE COUNTESS TEKLA. *Third Edition.*
'Of these mediæval romances, which are now gaining ground "The Countess Tekla" is the very best we have seen.'—*Pall Mall Gazette.*
THE LADY ELECTRA.

Albanesi (E. Maria). SUSANNAH AND ONE OTHER. *Fourth Edition.* Crown 8vo. 6s.
THE BLUNDER OF AN INNOCENT. *Crown 8vo. 6s.*
CAPRICIOUS CAROLINE. *Crown 8vo. 6s.*
LOVE AND LOUISA. *Crown 8vo. 6s.*
PETER, A PARASITE. *Crown 8vo. 6s.*
Anstey (F.), Author of 'Vice Versâ.' A BAYARD FROM BENGAL. Illustrated by BERNARD PARTRIDGE. *Third Edition. Crown 8vo. 3s. 6d.*
Bacheller (Irving), Author of 'Eben Holden.' DARREL OF THE BLESSED ISLES. *Third Edition. Crown 8vo. 6s.*
Bagot (Richard). A ROMAN MYSTERY. *Third Edition. Crown 8vo. 6s.*
Balfour (Andrew). VENGEANCE IS MINE. Illustrated. *Crown 8vo. 1s. net.*
Balfour (M. C.). THE FALL OF THE SPARROW. *Crown 8vo. 6s.*
Baring-Gould (S.). See page 34 and 1s. Novels.
Barlow (Jane). THE LAND OF THE SHAMROCK. *Crown 8vo. 6s.*
FROM THE EAST UNTO THE WEST. *Crown 8vo. 1s. net.*
Barr (Robert). See page 35 and 1s. Novels.
Begbie (Harold). THE ADVENTURES OF SIR JOHN SPARROW. *Crown 8vo. 6s.*
Belloc (Hilaire) MR. BURDEN, DEALER IN HARDWARE. With 36 Illustrations by G. K. CHESTERTON. *Crown 8vo. 6s.*
Benson (E. F.). DODO: A Detail of the Day. *Crown 8vo. 6s.*
THE CAPSINA. *Crown 8vo. 1s. net.*
Benson (Margaret). SUBJECT TO VANITY. *Crown 8vo. 3s. 6d.*
Besant (Sir Walter). A FIVE YEARS' TRYST, and Other Stories. *Crown 8vo. 1s. net.*

Bowles (C. Stewart). A STRETCH OFF THE LAND. *Crown 8vo. 6s.*
Bullock (Shan. F.). THE SQUIREEN. *Crown 8vo. 6s.*
THE RED LEAGUERS. *Crown 8vo. 6s.*
Burton (J, Bloundelle). THE YEAR ONE: A Page of the French Revolution. Illustrated. *Crown 8vo. 6s.*
DENOUNCED. *Crown 8vo. 6s.*
THE CLASH OF ARMS. *Crown 8vo. 6s.*
ACROSS THE SALT SEAS. *Crown 8vo. 1s. net.*
THE FATE OF VALSEC. *Cr. 8vo. 6s.*
A BRANDED NAME. *Crown 8vo. 6s.*
Capes (Bernard), Author of 'The Lake of Wine.' THE EXTRAORDINARY CONFESSIONS OF DIANA PLEASE. *Crown 8vo. 6s.*
Chesney (Weatherby). THE BAPTIST RING. *Crown 8vo. 6s.*
THE TRAGEDY OF THE GREAT EMERALD. *Crown 8vo. 6s.*
THE MYSTERY OF A BUNGALOW. *Crown 8vo. 6s.*
Clifford (Hugh). A FREE LANCE OF TO-DAY. *Crown 8vo. 6s.*
Cobb (Thomas). A CHANGE OF FACE. *Crown 8vo. 6s.*
Cobban (J. Maclaren). THE KING OF ANDAMAN: A Saviour of Society. *Crown 8vo. 6s.*
WILT THOU HAVE THIS WOMAN? *Crown 8vo. 6s.*
THE ANGEL OF THE COVENANT. *Crown 8vo. 6s.*
Corbett (Julian). A BUSINESS IN GREAT WATERS. *Crown 8vo. 6s.*
Corelli (Marie). See page 32.
Cotes (Mrs. Everard). See S. J. Duncan.
Crane (Stephen) and Barr (Robert). THE O'RUDDY. *Crown 8vo. 6s.*
Crockett (S. R.), Author of 'The Raiders,' etc. LOCHINVAR. Illustrated. *Second Edition. Crown 8vo. 6s.*
THE STANDARD BEARER. *Cr. 8vo. 6s.*

**Croker (B. M.).** ANGEL. *Third Edition.* *Crown 8vo.* 6s.
PEGGY OF THE BARTONS. *Fifth Edition. Crown 8vo.* 6s.
A STATE SECRET. *Third Edition. Crown 8vo.* 3s. 6d.
JOHANNA. *Second Edition. Cr. 8vo.* 6s.
THE HAPPY VALLEY. *Crown 8vo.* 6s.

**Doyle (A. Conan)**, Author of 'Sherlock Holmes,' 'The White Company,' etc. ROUND THE RED LAMP. *Ninth Edition. Crown 8vo.* 6s.

**Duncan (Sara Jeannette)** (Mrs. Everard Cotes), Author of 'A Voyage of Consolation.' THOSE DELIGHTFUL AMERICANS. Illustrated. *Third Edition. Crown 8vo.* 6s.
THE PATH OF A STAR. Illustrated. *Second Edition. Crown 8vo.* 6s.
THE POOL IN THE DESERT. *Crown 8vo.* 6s.
A VOYAGE OF CONSOLATION. *Cr. 8vo.* 3s. 6d.

**Fenn (G. Manville).** AN ELECTRIC SPARK. *Crown 8vo.* 6s.
A DOUBLE KNOT. *Crown 8vo.* 2s. 6d.

**Findlater (J. H.).** THE GREEN GRAVES OF BALGOWRIE. *Fourth Edition. Crown 8vo.* 6s.
A DAUGHTER OF STRIFE. *Crown 8vo.* 1s. net.

**Findlater (Mary).** OVER THE HILLS. *Second Edition. Crown 8vo.* 6s.
BETTY MUSGRAVE. *Second Edition. Crown 8vo.* 6s.
A NARROW WAY. *Third Edition. Crown 8vo.* 6s.
THE ROSE OF JOY. *Second Edition. Crown 8vo.* 6s.

**Fitzstephen (Gerald).** MORE KIN THAN KIND. *Crown 8vo.* 6s.

**Fletcher (J. S.).** THE BUILDERS. *Crown 8vo.* 6s.
LUCIAN THE DREAMER. *Crown 8vo.* 6s.
DAVID MARCH. *Crown 8vo.* 6s.

**Francis (M. E.).** MISS ERIN. *Second Edition. Crown 8vo.* 1s. net.

**Fraser (Mrs. Hugh)**, Author of 'The Stolen Emperor.' THE SLAKING OF THE SWORD. *Crown 8vo.* 6s.

**Gallon (Tom)**, Author of 'Kiddy.' RICKERBY'S FOLLY. *Crown 8vo.* 6s.

**Gaunt (Mary).** DEADMAN'S. *Crown 8vo.* 6s.
THE MOVING FINGER. *Crown 8vo.* 3s. 6d.

**Gerard (Dorothea)**, Author of 'Lady Baby.' THE CONQUEST OF LONDON. *Second Edition. Crown 8vo.* 6s.
HOLY MATRIMONY. *Second Edition. Crown 8vo.* 6s.
THINGS THAT HAVE HAPPENED. *Crown 8vo.* 6s.
MADE OF MONEY. *Crown 8vo.* 6s.
THE BRIDGE OF LIFE *Cr. 8vo.* 6s.

**Gerard (Emily).** THE HERONS' TOWER. *Crown 8vo.* 6s.

**Gilchrist (R. Murray).** WILLOWBRAKE. *Crown 8vo.* 6s.

**Gissing (George)**, Author of 'Demos,' 'In the Year of Jubilee,' etc. THE TOWN TRAVELLER. *Second Edition. Crown 8vo.* 6s.
THE CROWN OF LIFE. *Crown 8vo.* 6s.

**Glanville (Ernest).** THE DESPATCH RIDER. *Crown 8vo.* 3s. 6d.
THE INCA'S TREASURE. Illustrated. *Crown 8vo.* 3s. 6d.

**Gleig (Charles).** BUNTER'S CRUISE. Illustrated. *Crown 8vo.* 3s. 6d.

**Goss (C. F.).** THE REDEMPTION OF DAVID CORSON. *Third Edition. Crown 8vo.* 6s.

**Harrison (Mrs. Burton).** A PRINCESS OF THE HILLS. Illustrated. *Crown 8vo.* 6s.

**Herbertson (Agnes G.).** PATIENCE DEAN. *Crown 8vo.* 6s.

**Hichens (Robert)**, Author of 'Flames,' etc. THE PROPHET OF BERKELEY SQUARE. *Second Ed. Crown 8vo.* 6s.
TONGUES OF CONSCIENCE. *Second Edition. Crown 8vo.* 6s.
FELIX. *Fourth Edition. Crown 8vo.* 6s.
THE WOMAN WITH THE FAN. *Fifth Edition. Cr. 8vo.* 6s.
BYEWAYS. *Crown 8vo.* 3s. 6d.
THE GARDEN OF ALLAH. *Crown 8vo.* 6s.

**Hobbes (John Oliver)**, Author of 'Robert Orange.' THE SERIOUS WOOING. *Crown 8vo.* 6s.

**Hope (Anthony).** See page 32.

**Hough (Emerson).** THE MISSISSIPPI BUBBLE. Illustrated. *Crown 8vo.* 6s.

**Housman (Clemence).** SCENES FROM THE LIFE OF AGLOVALE. Illustrated. *Crown 8vo.* 3s. 6d.

**Hunt (Violet).** THE HUMAN INTEREST. *Crown 8vo.* 6s.

**Hyne (C. J. Cutcliffe)**, Author of 'Captain Kettle.' MR. HORROCKS, PURSER. *Third Edition. Crown 8vo.* 6s.

**Jacobs (W. W.).** See page 33.

**James (Henry)**, Author of 'What Maisie Knew.' THE SOFT SIDE. *Second Edition. Crown 8vo.* 6s.
THE BETTER SORT. *Crown 8vo.* 6s.
THE AMBASSADORS. *Second Edition. Crown 8vo.* 6s.
THE GOLDEN BOWL. *Crown 8vo.* 6s.

**Janson (Gustaf).** ABRAHAM'S SACRIFICE. *Crown 8vo.* 6s.

# FICTION 37

**Lawless (Hon. Emily).** TRAITS AND CONFIDENCES. *Crown 8vo. 6s.*
**MELCHO.** *Crown 8vo. 1s. net.*
**Lawson (Harry),** Author of 'When the Billy Boils.' CHILDREN OF THE BUSH. *Crown 8vo. 6s.*
**Linden (Annie).** A WOMAN OF SENTIMENT. *Crown 8vo. 6s.*
**Linton (E. Lynn).** THE TRUE HISTORY OF JOSHUA DAVIDSON, Christian and Communist. *Twelfth Edition. Medium 8vo. 6d.*
**Long (J. Luther),** Co-Author of 'The Darling of the Gods.' MADAME BUTTERFLY. *Crown 8vo. 6s.*
SIXTY JANE. *Crown 8vo. 6s.*
**Lorimer (Norma).** MIRRY ANN. *Crown 8vo. 6s.*
JOSIAH'S WIFE. *Crown 8vo. 6s.*
**Lyall (Edna).** DERRICK VAUGHAN, NOVELIST. *42nd Thousand. Crown 8vo. 3s. 6d.*
**M'Carthy (Justin H.),** Author of 'If I were King.' THE LADY OF LOYALTY HOUSE. *Crown 8vo. 6s.*
**Mackie (Pauline Bradford).** THE VOICE IN THE DESERT. *Crown 8vo. 6s.*
**Macnaughtan (S.).** THE FORTUNE OF CHRISTINA MACNAB. *Third Edition. Crown 8vo. 6s.*
**Malet (Lucas).** See page 33.
**Mann (Mrs. M. E.).** OLIVIA'S SUMMER. *Second Edition. Crown 8vo. 6s.*
A LOST ESTATE. *A New Edition. Crown 8vo. 6s.*
THE PARISH OF HILBY. *A New Edition. Crown 8vo. 6s.*
THE PARISH NURSE. *Crown 8vo. 6s.*
GRAN'MA'S JANE. *Crown 8vo. 6s.*
MRS. PETER HOWARD. *Cr. 8vo. 6s.*
A WINTER'S TALE. *Crown 8vo. 6s.*
THERE WAS ONCE A PRINCE. Illustrated. *Crown 8vo. 3s. 6d.*
WHEN ARNOLD COMES HOME. Illustrated. *Crown 8vo. 3s. 6d.*
**Marriott (Charles),** Author of 'The Column.' GENEVRA. *Crown 8vo. 6s.*
**Marsh (Richard).** MARVELS AND MYSTERIES. *Crown 8vo. 6s.*
THE TWICKENHAM PEERAGE. *Second Edition. Crown 8vo. 6s.*
A METAMORPHOSIS. *Crown 8vo. 6s.*
GARNERED. *Crown 8vo. 6s.*
A DUEL. *Crown 8vo. 6s.*
**Mason (A. E. W.),** Author of 'The Courtship of Morrice Buckler,' 'Miranda of the Balcony,' etc. CLEMENTINA. Illustrated. *Crown 8vo. Second Edition. 6s.*
**Mathers (Helen),** Author of 'Comin' thro' the Rye.' HONEY. *Fourth Edition. Crown 8vo. 6s.*
GRIFF OF GRIFFITHSCOURT. *Crown 8vo. 6s.*
THE FERRYMAN. *Crown 8vo. 6s.*

**Meade (L. T.).** DRIFT *Crown 8vo. 6s.*
RESURGAM. *Crown 8vo. 6s.*
'**Miss Molly**' (The Author of). THE GREAT RECONCILER. *Crown 8vo. 6s.*
**Mitford (Bertram).** THE SIGN OF THE SPIDER. Illustrated. *Sixth Edition. Crown 8vo. 3s. 6d.*
IN THE WHIRL OF THE RISING. *Second Edition. Crown 8vo. 6s.*
**Montresor (F. F.),** Author of 'Into the Highways and Hedges.' THE ALIEN. *Third Edition. Crown 8vo. 6s.*
**Morrison (Arthur).** See page 34.
**Nesbit (E.).** (Mrs. E. Bland). THE RED HOUSE. Illustrated. *Fourth Edition. Crown 8vo. 6s.*
THE LITERARY SENSE. *Cr. 8vo. 6s.*
**Norris (W. E.).** THE CREDIT OF THE COUNTY. Illustrated. *Second Edition. Crown 8vo. 6s.*
THE EMBARRASSING ORPHAN. *Crown 8vo. 6s.*
HIS GRACE. *Third Edition. Cr. 8vo. 6s.*
THE DESPOTIC LADY. *Crown 8vo. 6s.*
CLARISSA FURIOSA. *Crown 8vo. 6s.*
AN OCTAVE. *Second Edition. Crown 8vo. 6s.*
NIGEL'S VOCATION. *Crown 8vo. 6s.*
JACK'S FATHER. *Crown 8vo. 1s. 6d.*
LORD LEONARD THE LUCKLESS. *Crown 8vo. 1s. net.*
**Oliphant (Mrs.).** THE TWO MARYS. *Crown 8vo. 6s.*
THE LADY'S WALK. *Crown 8vo. 6s.*
THE PRODIGALS. *Crown 8vo. 1s. net.*
**Ollivant (Alfred).** OWD BOB, THE GREY DOG OF KENMUIR. *Sixth Edition. Crown 8vo. 6s.*
**Oppenheim (E. Phillips).** MASTER OF MEN. *Third Edition. Crown 8vo. 6s.*
**Oxenham (John),** Author of 'Barbe of Grand Bayou.' A WEAVER OF WEBS. *Crown 8vo. 6s.*
**Pain (Barry).** THREE FANTASIES. *Crown 8vo. 1s.*
LINDLEY KAYS. *Crown 8vo. 6s.*
**Parker (Gilbert).** See page 33.
**Pemberton (Max).** THE FOOTSTEPS OF A THRONE. Illustrated. *Second Edition. Crown 8vo. 6s.*
I CROWN THEE KING. With Illustrations by Frank Dadd and A. Forrestier. *Crown 8vo. 6s.*
**Penny (Mrs. F. E.).** A MIXED MARRIAGE. *Crown 8vo. 1s. net.*
**Phillpotts (Eden).** See page 34.
**Pickthall (Marmaduke).** SAID THE FISHERMAN. *Fourth Edition. Crown 8vo. 1 6s.*
**Pryce (Richard).** THE QUIET MRS. FLEMING. *Crown 8vo. 3s. 6d.*
'**Q.**' Author of 'Dead Man's Rock.' THE WHITE WOLF. *Second Edition. Crown 8vo. 6s.*

Queux (W. le). THE HUNCHBACK OF WESTMINSTER. *Second Edition.* *Crown 8vo.* *6s.*
THE CLOSED BOOK. *Crown 8vo. 6s.*
Rhys (Grace). THE WOOING OF SHEILA. *Second Edition. Crown 8vo. 6s.*
THE PRINCE OF LISNOVER. *Crown 8vo. 6s.*
Rhys (Grace) and Another. THE DIVERTED VILLAGE. With Illustrations by DOROTHY GWYN JEFFREYS. *Crown 8vo. 6s.*
Ridge (W. Pett). LOST PROPERTY. *Second Edition. Crown 8vo. 6s.*
SECRETARY TO BAYNE, M.P. *Crown 8vo. 6s.*
ERB. *Second Edition. Crown 8vo. 6s.*
A SON OF THE STATE. *Crown 8vo.* 3s. 6d.
A BREAKER OF LAWS. *Cr. 8vo.* 3s. 6d.
MRS. GALER'S BUSINESS. *Crown 8vo. 6s.*
Ritchie (Mrs. David G.). THE TRUTHFUL LIAR. *Crown 8vo. 6s.*
Roberts (C.G.D.). THE HEART OF THE ANCIENT WOOD. *Crown 8vo.* 3s. 6d.
Russell (W. Clark). MY DANISH SWEETHEART. Illustrated. *Fourth Edition. Crown 8vo. 6s.*
ABANDONED. *Second Edition. Crown 8vo. 6s.*
Sergeant (Adeline). Author of 'The Story of a Penitent Soul.' THE MASTER OF BEECHWOOD. *Crown 8vo. 6s.*
BARBARA'S MONEY. *Second Edition. Crown 8vo. 6s.*
ANTHEA'S WAY. *Crown 8vo. 6s.*
THE YELLOW DIAMOND. *Second Edition. Crown 8vo. 6s.*
UNDER SUSPICION. *Crown 8vo. 6s.*
THE LOVE THAT OVERCAME. *Crown 8vo. 6s.*
THE ENTHUSIAST. *Crown 8vo. 6s.*
ACCUSED AND ACCUSER. *Crown 8vo. 6s.*
THE PROGRESS OF RACHEL. *Cr. 8vo. 6s.*
Shannon (W. F.). THE MESS DECK. *Crown 8vo.* 3s. 6d.
JIM TWELVES. *Second Edition. Crown 8vo.* 3s. 6d.

Sonnichsen (Albert). 'DEEP SEA VAGABONDS. *Crown 8vo. 6s.*
Strain (E. H.). ELMSLIE'S DRAG-NET. *Crown 8vo. 6s.*
Stringer (Arthur). THE SILVER POPPY. *Crown 8vo. 6s.*
Sutherland (Duchess of). ONE HOUR AND THE NEXT. *Third Edition. Crown 8vo.* 1s. net.
Swan (Annie). LOVE GROWN COLD. *Second Edition. Crown 8vo.* 1s. net.
Swift (Benjamin). SIREN CITY. *Crown 8vo. 6s.*
Tanqueray (Mrs. B. M.). THE ROYAL QUAKER. *Crown 8vo. 6s.*
Thompson (Vance). SPINNERS OF LIFE. *Crown 8vo. 6s.*
Waineman (Paul). A HEROINE FROM FINLAND. *Crown 8vo.* 1s. net.
BY A FINNISH LAKE. *Crown 8vo. 6s.*
THE SONG OF THE FOREST. *Crown 8vo. 6s.*
Watson (H. B. Marriott). ALARUMS AND EXCURSIONS. *Cr. 8vo. 6s.*
CAPTAIN FORTUNE. *Cr. 8vo. 6s.*
Wells (H. G.) THE SEA LADY. *Crown 8vo. 6s.*
Weyman (Stanley), Author of 'A Gentleman of France.' UNDER THE RED ROBE. With Illustrations by R. C. WOODVILLE. *Eighteenth Edition. Crown 8vo. 6s.*
White (Stewart E.). Author of 'The Blazed Trail.' CONJUROR'S HOUSE. A Romance of the Free Trail. *Second Edition. Crown 8vo. 6s.*
Williamson (Mrs. C. N.), Author of 'The Barnstormers.' PAPA. *Second Edition. Crown 8vo. 6s.*
THE ADVENTURE OF PRINCESS SLYVIA. *Crown 8vo.* 3s. 6d.
THE WOMAN WHO DARED. *Crown 8vo. 6s.*
THE SEA COULD TELL. *Second Edition. Crown 8vo. 6s.*
Williamson (C. N. and A. M.). THE LIGHTNING CONDUCTOR: Being the Romance of a Motor Car. Illustrated. *Sixth Edition. Crown 8vo. 6s.*
THE PRINCESS PASSES. *Cr. 8vo. 6s.*
Yeats (S. Levett). ORRAIN. *Crown 8vo. 6s.*

## Boys and Girls, Books for

*Crown 8vo.* 3s. 6d.

THE ICELANDER'S SWORD. By S. Baring-Gould.
ONLY A GUARD-ROOM DOG. By Edith E. Cuthell-wood.
THE DOCTOR OF THE JULIET. By Harry Collingwood.
MASTER ROCKAFELLAR'S VOYAGE. By W. Clark Russell.
SYD BELTON: Or, the Boy who would not go to Sea. By G. Manville Fenn.
THE RED GRANGE. By Mrs. Molesworth.
A GIRL OF THE PEOPLE. By L. T. Meade.
HEPSY GIPSY. By L. T. Meade. 2s. 6d.
THE HONOURABLE MISS. By L. T. Meade.

# FICTION

## Dumas, The Novels of Alexandre

*Price 6d. Double Volume, 1s.*

THE THREE MUSKETEERS. With a long Introduction by Andrew Lang. Double volume.
THE PRINCE OF THIEVES. *Second Edition.*
ROBIN HOOD. A Sequel to the above.
THE CORSICAN BROTHERS.
GEORGES.
CROP-EARED JACQUOT.
TWENTY YEARS AFTER. Double volume.
AMAURY.
THE CASTLE OF EPPSTEIN.
THE SNOWBALL.
CECILE; OR, THE WEDDING GOWN.
ACTÉ.
THE BLACK TULIP.
THE VISCOMTE DE BRAGELONNE.
THE CONVICT'S SON.
THE WOLF-LEADER.
NANON; OR, THE WOMEN'S WAR.
PAULINE; MURAT; AND PASCAL BRUNO.
THE ADVENTURES OF CAPTAIN PAMPHILE.
FERNANDE.
GABRIEL LAMBERT.
THE REMINISCENCES OF ANTONY.
CATHERINE BLUM.
THE CHEVALIER D'HARMENTAL.

CONSCIENCE

*Illustrated Edition.*
THE THREE MUSKETEERS. Illustrated in Colour by Frank Adams.
THE PRINCE OF THIEVES. Illustrated in Colour by Frank Adams.
ROBIN HOOD THE OUTLAW. Illustrated in Colour by Frank Adams.
THE CORSICAN BROTHERS. Illustrated in Colour by A. M. M'Lellan.
FERNANDE. Illustrated in Colour by Munro Orr.
THE BLACK TULIP. Illustrated in Colour by A. Orr.
ACTÉ. Illustrated in Colour by Gordon Browne.
GEORGES. Illustrated in Colour by Munro Orr.
THE CASTLE OF EPPSTEIN. Illustrated in Colour by A. Orr.
TWENTY YEARS AFTER. Illustrated in Colour by Frank Adams.
THE SNOWBALL AND SULTANETTA. Illustrated in Colour by Frank Adams.
THE VICOMTE DE BRAGELONNE. Illustrated in Colour by Frank Adams.
AMAURY. Illustrated in Colour by Gordon Browne.
CROP-EARED JACQUOT. Illustrated in Colour by Gordon Browne.

## Methuen's Universal Library

EDITED BY SIDNEY LEE. *In Sixpenny Volumes.*

MESSRS. METHUEN are preparing a new series of reprints containing both books of classical repute, which are accessible in various forms, and also some rarer books, of which no satisfactory edition at a moderate price is in existence. It is their ambition to place the best books of all nations, and particularly of the Anglo-Saxon race, within the reach of every reader. All the great masters of Poetry, Drama, Fiction, History, Biography, and Philosophy will be represented. Mr. Sidney Lee will be the General Editor of the Library, and he will contribute a Note to each book.

The characteristics of METHUEN'S UNIVERSAL LIBRARY are five :—

1. SOUNDNESS OF TEXT. A pure and unabridged text is the primary object of the series, and the books will be carefully reprinted under the direction of competent scholars from the best editions. In a series intended for popular use not less than for students, adherence to the old spelling would in many cases leave the matter unintelligible to ordinary readers, and, as the appeal of a classic is universal, the spelling has in general been modernised.

2. COMPLETENESS. Where it seems advisable, the complete works of such masters as Milton, Bacon, Ben Jonson and Sir Thomas Browne will be given. These will be issued in separate volumes, so that the reader who does not desire all the works of an author will have the opportunity of acquiring a single masterpiece.

3. CHEAPNESS. The books will be well printed on good paper at a price which on the whole is without parallel in the history of publishing. Each volume will contain from 100 to 350 pages, and will be issued in paper covers, Crown 8vo, at Sixpence net.

4. CLEARNESS OF TYPE. The type will be a very legible one.

5. SIMPLICITY. There will be no editorial matter except a short biographical and bibliographical note by Mr. Sidney Lee at the beginning of each volume.

Where it is possible, each separate book will be issued in one volume, but the longer ones must be divided into several volumes. The volumes may also be obtained in cloth at One Shilling net, and where a single book is issued in several Sixpenny volumes it may be obtained in cloth in a double or treble volume. Thus GIL BLAS may be bought in two Sixpenny volumes, or in one cloth volume at 1s. 6d. net, and SHAKESPEARE will be given in ten Sixpenny volumes, or in five cloth volumes at 4s. 6d. each.

The Library will be issued at regular intervals after the publication of the first six books, all of which will be published together. Due notice will be given of succeeding issues. The order of publication will be arranged to give as much variety of subject as possible, and the volumes composing the complete works of an author will be issued at convenient intervals.

The early Books are in the Press.

## Novelist, The

MESSRS. METHUEN are issuing under the above general title a Monthly Series of Novels by popular authors at the price of Sixpence. Each number is as long as the average Six Shilling Novel. The first numbers of 'THE NOVELIST' are as follows:—

1. DEAD MEN TELL NO TALES. By E. W. Hornung.
2. JENNIE BAXTER, JOURNALIST. By Robert Barr.
3. THE INCA'S TREASURE. By Ernest Glanville.
4. A SON OF THE STATE. By W. Pett Ridge.
5. FURZE BLOOM. By S. Baring-Gould.
6. BUNTER'S CRUISE. By C. Gleig.
7. THE GAY DECEIVERS. By Arthur Moore.
8. PRISONERS OF WAR. By A. Boyson Weekes.
9. A FLASH OF SUMMER. By Mrs. W. K. Clifford.
10. VELDT AND LAAGER : Tales of the Transvaal. By E. S. Valentine.
11. THE NIGGER KNIGHTS. By F. Norreys Connel.
12. A MARRIAGE AT SEA. By W. Clark Russell.
13. THE POMP OF THE LAVILETTES. By Gilbert Parker.
14. A MAN OF MARK. By Anthony Hope.
15. THE CARISSIMA. By Lucas Malet.
16. THE LADY'S WALK. By Mrs. Oliphant.
17. DERRICK VAUGHAN. By Edna Lyall.
18. IN THE MIDST OF ALARMS. By Robert Barr.
19. HIS GRACE. By W. E. Norris.
20. DODO. By E. F. Benson.
21. CHEAP JACK ZITA. By S. Baring-Gould.
22. WHEN VALMOND CAME TO PONTIAC. By Gilbert Parker.
23. THE HUMAN BOY. By Eden Phillpotts.
24. THE CHRONICLES OF COUNT ANTONIO. By Anthony Hope.
25. BY STROKE OF SWORD. By Andrew Balfour.
26. KITTY ALONE. By S. Baring-Gould.
27. GILES INGILBY. By W. E. Norris.
28. URITH. By S. Baring-Gould.
29. THE TOWN TRAVELLER. By George Gissing.
30. MR. SMITH. By Mrs. Walford.
31. A CHANGE OF AIR. By Anthony Hope.
32. THE KLOOF BRIDE. By Ernest Glanville.
33. ANGEL. By B. M. Croker.
34. A COUNSEL OF PERFECTION. By Lucas Malet.
35. THE BABY'S GRANDMOTHER. By Mrs. Walford.
36. THE COUNTESS TEKLA. By Robert Barr.
37. DRIFT. BY L. T. Meade.
38. THE MASTER OF BEECHWOOD. By Adeline Sergeant.
39. CLEMENTINA. By A. E. W. Mason.
40. THE ALIEN. By F. F. Montresor.
41. THE BROOM SQUIRE. By S. Baring-Gould.
42. HONEY. By Helen Mathers.
43. THE FOOTSTEPS OF A THRONE. By Max Pemberton.
44. ROUND THE RED LAMP. By A. Conan Doyle.
45. LOST PROPERTY. By W. Pett Ridge.
46. THE TWICKENHAM PEERAGE. By Richard Marsh.
47. HOLY MATRIMONY. By Dorothea Gerard.
48. THE SIGN OF THE SPIDER. By Bertram Mitford.
49. THE RED HOUSE. By E. Nesbit.
50. A HOLE IN THE WALL. By A. Morrison.
51. A ROMAN MYSTERY. By Richard Bagot.
52. THE CREDIT OF THE COUNTY. By W. E. Norris.
53. A MOMENT'S ERROR. By A. W. Marchant.
54. PHROSO. By Anthony Hope.
55. I CROWN THEE KING. By Max Pemberton.
56. JOHANNA. By B. M. Croker.
57. BARBARA'S MONEY. By Adeline Sergeant.
58. A NEWSPAPER GIRL. By Mrs. C. N. Williamson.
59. THE GODDESS. By Richard Marsh.
60. MRS. PETER HOWARD. By M. E. Mann.

## Sixpenny Library

THE MATABELE CAMPAIGN. By Major-General Baden-Powell.
THE DOWNFALL OF PREMPEH. By Major-General Baden-Powell.
MY DANISH SWEETHEART. By W. Clark Russell.
IN THE ROAR OF THE SEA. By S. Baring-Gould.
PEGGY OF THE BARTONS. By B. M. Croker.
THE GREEN GRAVES OF BALGOWRIE. By Jane H. Findlater.
THE STOLEN BACILLUS. By H. G. Wells.
MATTHEW AUSTIN. By W. E. Norris.
THE CONQUEST OF LONDON. By Dorothea Gerard.
A VOYAGE OF CONSOLATION. By Sara J. Duncan.
THE MUTABLE MANY. By Robert Barr.
BEN HUR. By General Lew Wallace.
SIR ROBERT'S FORTUNE. By Mrs. Oliphant.
THE FAIR GOD. By General Lew Wallace.
CLARISSA FURIOSA. By W. E. Norris.
CRANFORD. By Mrs. Gaskell.
NOEMI. By S. Baring-Gould.
THE THRONE OF DAVID. By J. H. Ingraham.
ACROSS THE SALT SEAS. By J. Bloundelle Burton.
THE MILL ON THE FLOSS. By George Eliot.
PETER SIMPLE. By Captain Marryat.
MARY BARTON. By Mrs. Gaskell.
PRIDE AND PREJUDICE. By Jane Austen.
NORTH AND SOUTH. By Mrs. Gaskell.
JACOB FAITHFUL. By Captain Marryat.
SHIRLEY. By Charlotte Brontë.
FAIRY TALES RE-TOLD. By S. Baring Gould.
THE TRUE HISTORY OF JOSHUA DAVIDSON. By Mrs. Lynn Linton.
A STATE SECRET. By B. M Croker.
SAM'S SWEETHEART. By Helen Mathers.
HANDLEY CROSS. By R. S. Surtees.
ANNE MAULEVERER. By Mrs. Caffyn.
THE ADVENTURERS. By H. B. Marriott Watson.
DANTE'S DIVINE COMEDY. Translated by H. F. Cary.
THE CEDAR STAR. By M. E. Mann.
MASTER OF MEN. By E. P. Oppenheim.
THE TRAIL OF THE SWORD. By Gilbert Parker.
THOSE DELIGHTFUL AMERICANS. By Mrs. Cotes.
MR. SPONGE'S SPORTING TOUR. By R. S. Surtees.
ASK MAMMA. By R. S. Surtees.
GRIMM'S FAIRY STORIES. Illustrated by George Cruikshank.
GEORGE AND THE GENERAL. By W. Pett Ridge.
THE JOSS. By Richard Marsh.
MISER HOADLEY'S SECRET. By A. W. Marchmont.

www.ingramcontent.com/pod-product-compliance
Lightning Source LLC
Chambersburg PA
CBHW031942230426
43672CB00010B/2019